SEALs Mission 5: "Firefight"

After moving about 200 meters, the unit turned to 36 degrees, rough north-northeast, for another leg, this one about 125 meters long. The zigzag pattern was intended to patrol the ground well between the insertion point and ambush site. The different lengths of march line would make it harder for any enemy observers to estimate where the platoon would be going in case they wanted to set up an ambush.

But it was an ambush the platoon walked into. On the next change of direction in the line of march, the platoon turned 90 degrees due east, and the point man changed over from Scott to Antone. The patrol had barely turned and moved out when the Viet Cong opened fire.

It was 1715 hours on 23 December and Bravo platoon had just walked into a VC regimental headquarters . . .

Other Titles by
Kevin Dockery

POINT MAN
(with James Watson)

SEALs IN ACTION

THE TEAMS

THE UNITED STATES NAVY SEALs WORKOUT GUIDE
(with Dennis Chalker)

WALKING POINT

FREE FIRE ZONES

THE TRUE STORY
OF U.S. NAVY
SEAL COMBAT
IN VIETNAM

KEVIN DOCKERY

HarperTorch
An Imprint of HarperCollinsPublishers

HARPERTORCH
An Imprint of HarperCollins*Publishers*
10 East 53rd Street
New York, New York 10022-5299

Copyright © 2000 by Bill Fawcett & Associates
ISBN: 0-380-80826-9

First HarperTorch paperback printing: October 2000

HarperCollins®, HarperTorch™, and ✦™ are trademarks of Harper-Collins Publishers Inc.

Printed in the United States of America

Visit HarperTorch on the World Wide Web at www.harpercollins.com

OPM 10 9 8 7 6 5 4 3 2 1

A Note on Maps

Good maps of an area of military operations can literally be worth a man's life. Accurate representations of the surrounding area, a target area, and any safe havens that might exist allow a combat unit to move, attack, and withdraw from areas of the world they have never seen before. Despite the fact that they depict millennia-old civilizations, accurate maps of Southeast Asia and the Mekong Delta in particular were very difficult to come by in the early 1960s. The ebb and flow of rivers and tides in the Mekong Delta could change the landscape, move streams and canals, and flood or expose land within a period of months, if not days, during the monsoon season.

With the increase of U.S. involvement by the mid- to late 1960s, the U.S. Army Corps of Engineer's Army Map Service combined earlier maps, aerial photography, and on-site examination, along with modern topographical systems, to produce a wide variety of detailed maps of Southeast Asia.

Maps used at the lower unit levels were usually 1/25,000 or 1/50,000 in scale. In these scales, one unit of measurement on the map, such as 1 inch, is equal to 25,000 or 50,000 units of measurement on the land. Using a standardized grid coordinate system, it was not difficult to locate an area only a few meters in size and describe the location exactly to a supporting unit.

In spite of their detail, these same maps would not show native buildings (hooches) or other hastily erected structures. The SEALs would use what maps were available and combine them with an aerial overview of an area when planning a mission. Other maps were available in the form of "pictomaps," which were quickly produced from high altitude and general aerial photography.

Today, the small-scale maps used by military units in Vietnam are hard to come by. Universities and library collections supply the bulk of what is available for examination. The maps used in this book are from those collections. The large-scale maps of whole provinces and Corps areas were taken from the Central Intelligence Agency's Directorate of Intelligence, Office of Basic and Geographical Intelligence publications. The South Vietnam provincial maps were produced in February 1973 and represent one of the last detailed descriptions of the land and area prior to the Communist takeover in 1975.

SOUTH
VIETNAM

THE MEKONG DELTA

The Mekong River is one of the primary rivers of Southeast Asia, flowing from the mountains of eastern Tibet to the South China Sea. In South Vietnam, the Mekong splits into four major rivers before reaching the sea. The Bassac River, to the south, is the largest, having split off from the Mekong up in Cambodia. At roughly Vinh Long, north of the Bassac, the Mekong separates into the Co Chien River to the south, the My Tho River to the north, and the Ham Luong River between the two.

Mud and silt washed down the Mekong during its 2,600-mile trip is deposited between and around these rivers, making the Mekong Delta some of the most fertile land in Asia.

The geographical area of the Mekong Delta was unique and difficult for the U.S. forces to operate in. Not since some of the worst of the island-hopping campaign against the Japanese in World War II did U.S. servicemen have to fight and survive in such wide areas of swamp, marsh, canals, rivers, and streams. Just moving through the dense plant growth could sap a unit of strength, slowing their progress to a bare crawl. Even the SEALs found the Mekong Delta a harsh and difficult area, in spite of their extensive training in wet environments.

Whole maps of an area in the Mekong would list their highest elevations as only a few feet above sea level. Incoming tides could cover thousands of square meters of land. When outgoing, those same tides would uncover acres of thick silt that would clutch and draw back on every step taken through it. The phrase *mud suck* came to mean any form of enveloping trap or situation to the men of the Teams.

In spite of the difficulties of operating in such terrain, the SEALs moved in on areas where regular U.S. and South Vietnamese forces couldn't exist. Quickly learning the specifics of operating in such an environment, the Teams took the war to the enemy's doorstep. They soon became better at operating in the wetlands of the Mekong Delta than most of the Viet Cong volunteers who had been born and raised there.

Vietnam:
The History, the Enemy, and the Task

Prior to World War II, the French held control of Indochina, that part of the world now known as Southeast Asia. The occupation of the area by the Japanese Imperial Army in World War II threw an already restless area into open combat. When the Japanese surrendered in 1945, the area returned to French rule—but not for long. The Viet Minh, a local guerrilla force led by staunch Communist Ho Chi Minh, were established in late 1945. Soon open warfare broke out between the Communist Viet Minh and the French, culminating in an armistice signed in July 1954.

The armistice of 1954 led to the establishment of the Communist Democratic Republic of Vietnam, known to the rest of the world as North Vietnam. South of the dividing line at roughly the 17th parallel was the Republic of Vietnam, known more simply as South Vietnam.

In violation of the armistice agreement, the Workers Party of [North] Vietnam left intact in the South a network of guerrilla fighters who had gained experience while fighting the French. This guerrilla network continued to grow in South Vietnam through the latter half of the 1950s and into the 1960s. Under the name Viet Cong (VC), the

Communist guerrillas moved more and more toward a philosophy of using violence to overthrow Diem's regime in the South, eventually moving away from political actions altogether.

The United States recognized that guerrilla warfare was becoming the mode of operation for the Soviet Union as the Cold War progressed into the 1960s. The threat of nuclear retaliation prevented an all-out war, but the Soviet Union, supported by Red China, openly stated that it would support "just wars of liberation and revolution." To combat this growing menace, the new administration of President John F. Kennedy directed the United States military to increase its counter-guerrilla capability, establishing entire new units to fight the hot portions of the Cold War.

The U.S. Army had the Special Forces, the Navy had the UDTs. From the UDTs came a new unit, able to fight from the sea, in the air, and on the land. Effective January 1, 1962, SEAL Team One was commissioned on the West Coast at Coronado, California, and SEAL Team Two in Little Creek, Virginia. The Navy now had a counter-guerrilla force ready and able to fight at a moment's notice anywhere in the world.

Within weeks of their commissioning, men from the SEAL Teams were in South Vietnam to help train and advise the U.S. allies fighting the Communist insurgency. Men from the teams were constantly in South Vietnam under various advisory and study roles, learning in detail how the Communist guerrillas operated.

With the increase in the U.S. commitment to help defend our allies in South Vietnam, the U.S. military presence in the area became larger and more active. Political developments and actions by the North Vietnamese led the United States to commit active troops to land operations by 1965. By 1966, it was time for the U.S. Navy SEALs to begin operations against the Viet Cong and North Vietnamese guerrillas in the swamps and waterways of South Vietnam.

The Delta and the Rung Sat:
The SEAL Cauldron

The entire east coast of South Vietnam borders the South China Sea. The thousand miles of coastline are rippled with rivers, small streams, canals, bays, and harbors opening onto the sea. With much of Vietnam's population dependent on the sea for its protein supply, fishing craft of all sizes, from small sampans to large trawlers, ply the waters of the South China Sea. Fish, as well as other commodities, were brought into the many ports and villages along the shore. To supply the Communist Viet Cong forces in the South, the government of North Vietnam smuggled tons of weapons and supplies in fishing trawlers and other such craft during the first half of the 1960s.

To combat the infiltration of supplies and equipment from the Communist North to South Vietnam by sea, the U.S. Navy Seventh Fleet and the South Vietnamese Navy established the Coastal Surveillance Force, Task Force 115, as the operational arm of Operation MARKET TIME on 24 March 1965. Inside of a month, seventeen 82-foot U.S. Coast Guard cutters were ordered to Vietnam to operate with and augment the Market Time forces. The operation patrolled the coastline of South Vietnam, from the Demilitarized Zone

(DMZ) at the north border to the southernmost tip of the Ca Mau Peninsula.

The Market Time forces severely hampered the North Vietnamese ability to supply the Viet Cong by sea. The dense jungle and swamp areas of the Mekong Delta and the Rung Sat region, however, were still largely controlled by Viet Cong forces. In 1965, up to 75 percent of the Vietnamese population of the Mekong Delta was considered to be under the control of the Viet Cong.

On 18 December 1965, the River Patrol Force, as Task Force 116, was established as the operational arm of OPERATION GAME WARDEN to end the movement of the Viet Cong, their logistical bases, and routes of supply in both the Mekong Delta and Rung Sat Special Zone. Task Force 116.1 was assigned to operations in the Mekong Delta while Task Force 116.2, about half the size of 116.1, was assigned to operate in the Rung Sat Special Zone. With the forces of Operation Market Time blocking the seaborne routes into South Vietnam, Game Warden forces would go into the rivers, streams, and canals to rout the enemy in his own backyard.

Because only one major hard-surface road, Route 4, ran through the area, the primary means of movement through much of the Delta had to be by water. Even this movement wasn't easy. Many of the canals had a depth of less than six feet, preventing a number of the U.S. and South Vietnam Navy craft from traveling along them.

New watercraft—especially the thirty-one-foot Patrol Boat, River (PBR), and the fifty-foot Patrol Craft, Fast (PCF), commonly called the Swift boats—were developed to navigate the waters of the Mekong Delta and the Rung Sat. To operate in both the Mekong Delta and the Rung Sat, the operational assets of Game Warden were divided into two task forces.

To the southeast of Saigon, between the city and the South China Sea, is an area of mangrove swamps that was known to the U.S. military as the Rung Sat Special Zone (RSSZ) or simply the Rung Sat, which is Vietnamese for "dense jungle."

The area was of strategic importance to Saigon as it covered all of the major water approaches to the city. Any ship trying to reach Saigon would have to navigate through forty-six miles of bending river before reaching the city.

Almost four hundred square miles of delta area between two rivers, the Rung Sat has rich soil that encourages heavy plant growth. The vegetation, streams, and mud combine to make the Rung Sat some of the most impenetrable terrain in Southeast Asia. The twisted roots of mangrove mix with tight packs of nipa palm to create a barrier at the water's edge. The almost four-foot tide that affects much of the Rung Sat leaves a heavy, slimy mud of river silt behind it when the tide is out. The mud often proved to be hip-deep or deeper, even on a tall man. Inland from the waterways, on some of the drier land, a double canopy of trees hides much of the ground from aerial view.

Native Vietnamese called the Rung Sat the Forest of Assassins. For hundreds of years, the area had been a relatively safe haven for pirates, smugglers, and bandits who plied both the rivers and the South China Sea. For the Viet Cong, the Rung Sat proved just as hospitable and useful a sanctuary as it had to others over the centuries.

The population of the Rung Sat had changed gradually during the 1960s. In 1966, there were about 16,000 civilians in and around the Rung Sat, most of them living in the nine major villages and twenty or so smaller hamlets. The agricultural economy of the area had most of the civilians earning their living by fishing, rice farming, or woodcutting. Living conditions were poor and, even by Vietnamese standards, the area was impoverished.

The poor civilian forces in the Rung Sat area were no match for the aggressive VC and what little resistance they could raise was quickly and harshly put down. Viet Cong forces in the Rung Sat grew tremendously during the mid-1960s. In 1964, an estimated two hundred VC were hidden in the Rung Sat. By 1966, this number had increased to regiment-sized units. VC units in the Rung Sat included support facilities, jungle hospitals, and even munition factories.

The Viet Cong quickly learned their new operational area. Every inch of the Rung Sat, each navigable waterway, and every bend in the river become an important piece of intelligence to the VC guerrillas. A large number of the Viet Cong had previously been hunters and fishermen, which helped them take advantage of the natural conditions.

The ships and watercraft of Market Time and Game Warden had done a great deal to take back some control of the major waterways of South Vietnam. But regular South Vietnamese military forces could not operate effectively in either the Mekong Delta regions or the Rung Sat. Even with the increase of U.S. ground forces in 1965 and 1966, conventional units simply found the going too rough for quick movement in the marshes and swamps of South Vietnam. By the time an Army or Marine unit was able to move in on a suspected Viet Cong stronghold, facility, or area, the VC would have had ample warning to leave or engage the forces in an area of their choosing. This was soon going to end as the Game Warden forces received their own special ground forces in the form of U.S. Navy SEAL detachments.

SEAL Team One:
The First Combat Deployments

The Navy SEALs had been involved in Vietnam since shortly after their commissioning in 1962. SEAL advisors and instructors had been working with special units of the South Vietnamese military and navy from mid-1962 to 1966. But the SEALs had been operating in an advisory mode only. What little combat action the SEALs had seen was not considered "official," and the men from the Teams were not supposed to directly engage the enemy.

In early 1966, this situation changed and the first direct action SEAL detachment was deployed to South Vietnam to take up a direct combat role. Three officers and fifteen enlisted men, a reinforced platoon, from SEAL Team One arrived in country in February 1966. Put under the command of the Commander, U.S. Naval Forces, Vietnam (COMUS-NAVFORV), the group was initially identified as Detachment Delta.

Already recognized by some in the command structure was the ability of the SEALs to stage an operation very quickly. This allowed the SEALs to react to timely information about a situation that would change long before a conventional unit could arrive on the scene. In addition, the

SEALs were very flexible and could quickly react to a new situation even during an operation.

The SEAL detachment was directed against the Viet Cong operating in the Rung Sat. Stationed at the naval base at Nha Be, the SEALs were at the northwest corner of the Rung Sat and were easily able to reach any major portion of the area by water. The main mission of the SEALs, however, remained vague, and they were given little in the way of specific direction. This lack of specific orders and targets gave the SEALs a great deal of flexibility in how they conducted their operations.

Very few of the SEALs had direct combat experience prior to that first tour. Many of their operational techniques were far from being fully developed. But the men were very well trained, intelligent, and creative. This combination proved to be a very bad one for the Viet Cong.

Generally limited to intelligence gathering and reconnaissance patrols, the SEALs spent much of their first weeks determining Areas of Operations (AOs), setting up Standard Operating Procedures (SOPs), and figuring out what size SEAL element worked best for each situation.

The general type of operations conducted by the SEALs that first year included general harassment of the enemy, hit-and-run raids, reconnaissance patrols, intelligence collection, and blocking guerrilla movements with ambush and counterambush tactics. The most common SEAL operation conducted in the Rung Sat was the ambush and listening post. The ambushes did not result in a high body count, but the results were greater than the numbers indicated.

For the first time in the war, the VC were not able to move at will in the Rung Sat. Previously, the VC had traveled along canals and streams at night wherever they wished. Now their situation was very different. Instead of being safe in their almost impenetrable jungle and swamps, the VC were being ambushed in areas even they had a hard time moving in. The fear of combat in their own backyard cut back on all VC movement in the Rung Sat.

Limited firsthand knowledge and up-to-date intelligence

on the Rung Sat and its environs prevented the SEALs from being as effective as they could have been during some early operations. This situation quickly changed as the SEALs gathered intelligence on how the Viet Cong moved and operated. As this information grew, the SEALs became more and more efficient at taking the war to the Viet Cong.

By July 1966, the first detachment from SEAL Team One had proven itself, and the number of men committed to the action increased. The manpower allowance for the detachment was increased to five officers and twenty enlisted men, two full platoons of 2:10. The extra officer was the SEAL command element in charge of what was now renamed Detachment Golf.

Techniques were still being refined and patrols continued to be difficult, but the SEALs were rapidly moving up the learning curve. The worst areas of the Rung Sat were the first to be examined and patrolled by the SEALs. It was these almost impassible regions that surrounded the drier and more hospitable areas where the VC had built many of their facilities. SEAL squads would often find themselves waiting for long hours in the leech-infested waters, often within a few dozen yards of a VC outpost. If the group of VC proved too large for the SEALs to ambush, they would call in fire from artillery fire support, helicopter gunships, or waiting support boats.

The SEALs had learned early on that their operations were constantly under observation by Viet Cong sympathizers. When a SEAL element left Nha Be for an operation, they did so in small craft that could be easily seen by the local population. The Viet Cong quickly received word when a SEAL operation was under way, and VC activity in the area quickly halted. Thus a lot of early ambushes that looked promising turned into dry holes with no enemy contact.

Gearing up the boats in Nha Be but putting the SEALs on board in a second location proved to be one way to beat VC intelligence agents. When this was first done in the middle of April, the SEALs were successful on the initial mission and later ambushed a sampan with three VC on board. SEAL Team One was now successfully running operations from two platoons based out of Nha Be, but intelligence sources and cooperation between elements of the U.S. military, intelligence agencies, and the South Vietnamese military were still a long way from being fully developed.

Mission One, 18 August 1966:
"The First Loss"

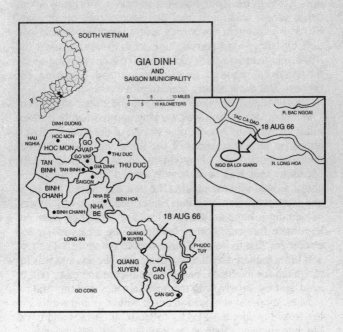

By August 1966, one of the two platoons was having trouble getting any enemy contact during their night ambushes in the Rung Sat. Daylight operations presented another problem. Daylight allowed men to closely examine sites, but SEALs tended not to be very comfortable about the duty. The same light that allowed the SEALs to see further and locate the enemy exposed them as well.

   Patrols extended deep into the Rung Sat, and the discoveries they made and the intelligence they gathered were valuable. An operation could easily extend for forty-eight or even seventy-two hours, allowing the SEALs to immediately act on discoveries or contacts made during the operation. Areas of the Rung Sat were so heavily overgrown with dense jungle and thick mud that even a well-conditioned SEAL squad might cover only a few hundred yards in one day. On some long patrols, support craft would insert the SEAL element and later pick them back up, moving along the water to another insertion point and repeating the process. But these actions were to prove costly.

   On 18 August, an eight-man patrol under the command of Lieutenant (jg) Truxell was working approximately thirteen miles southeast of Nha Be on a section of the Dinh Ba River, almost in the exact center of the Rung Sat. Inserting from their support boat, a modified LCM (Landing Craft, Medium) that had been heavily armed and armored, the patrol moved into the jungle. The unit discovered two large and well-concealed buildings, described as silos by others, containing a huge amount of rice. The buildings were not legitimate farmer's storage buildings: the area was far too remote for that to be even a reasonable possibility. The rice was taxes gathered by the Viet Cong, and the amount was far too much for the SEAL patrol to confiscate and carry out, or even destroy or burn with the materials they had on hand.

   Marking the exact location of the buildings and withdrawing from the site, the SEALs called in air strikes and naval bombardment to destroy the estimated 306,000 pounds of rice. Targets of this nature would prove a constant problem for the SEALs during their actions in Vietnam. Rice caches wouldn't burn well, even when ignited with thermate or special napalm grenades. Explosives would scatter the rice, but not actually destroy it. And making a majority of the rice unfit for use by poison or other means was out of the question.

   The eight-man SEAL patrol concluded that calling in heavy fire was the best option for the 153 tons of rice they had uncovered. The loss even of half of such a large cache of food was certain to affect Viet Cong operations in the Rung Sat area for some time. The SEALs continued with their patrol into the next day.

During the daylight hours of 19 August, a helicopter pilot reported seeing two hidden sampans (small boats) and a hut near the area where the SEALs were operating. The two U.S. helicopters remained on station while the SEAL patrol moved toward the location.

Petty Officer Billy W. Machen was the point man on the patrol that day. The point man in the patrol moved ahead of the main body of men, keeping within sight of the unit but able to examine the area the patrol would move into. The point man would have to stay alert for any signs of enemy activity as well as booby traps, mines, impassable areas, or anything that looked or sounded bad.

It was the point man's job to warn the patrol following him before they could get into trouble. It was a nerve-wracking position to operate from, but the men who were good at the job wanted no other. Billy Machen was just such a man.

Machen discovered a set of fresh tracks that led the patrol to bunkers and fighting positions along the river. One SEAL later remarked that the bunkers weren't like any he'd ever seen before. He described the bunkers as looking "like huge beehives." The unusual configuration of the bunkers was probably dictated by the mud and plants used to build them. Checking the area carefully, the SEALs determined that the bunkers and positions were empty.

The patrol was now within about five hundred meters of the reported position of the sampans and hut. The two helicopters that had been orbiting the area had run low on fuel and had been forced to return to their base. The SEALs were now very much on their own with no immediate fire support to call on if they got into more trouble than they could handle.

Firepower in the SEAL squad was greater than that found in a normal military unit of the same size. But the time the SEALs could pour out a heavy curtain of fire was limited by the amount of ammunition they had on hand. In 1966, the weapons used by a SEAL squad were mostly standard issue; special hardware for the Teams was still being examined and evaluated while requirements were still being discovered. M16 rifles with ammunition loads of several hundred rounds per man, M79 40mm grenade launchers, twelve-gauge pump-action shotguns, and M60 light machine guns were the primary arms of the SEAL squad.

It was this firepower in the hands of his Teammates that Billy Machen had behind him as he approached a clearing in the jungle growth. Machen moved slowly and carefully into the clearing to make sure the way was open. When he was almost across the clearing, the balance of the patrol started to move into the open area, following their point man.

Machen had located a Viet Cong camp consisting of several bunkers and a tower. As the rest of the patrol moved in, Machen suddenly spotted a group of Viet Cong waiting in ambush for his patrol to move into the killing zone, the clearing Machen was standing in. Rather than try to make it to cover or retrace his steps—which would have cost time and endangered his entire team—Machen forced the enemy to initiate the ambush prematurely.

Falling to the ground, Billy Machen opened fire from inside the killing zone to warn and cover his Teammates. The rest of the SEALs immediately opened fire on the now exposed enemy positions, fanning out to limit their exposure to enemy fire and concentrating their fire to the front. All the firepower they had available was poured into the Viet Cong positions.

Machen was struck in the neck while he was down in the prone position. The bullet passed down through his neck and into his abdomen. Another round struck the AR-15 Machen was holding, shattering the projectile and parts of the rifle and spraying his face with fragments. Mortally wounded, Machen managed to make his way back to his squad while they poured in fire on the VC. The squad corpsman started working on Machen immediately but there was little he could do. Within a minute of getting back to his squad, Machen died.

An estimated twenty to thirty Viet Cong faced the eight SEALs, but strong leadership by the lieutenant and his leading petty officer, as well as the SEAL squad's skills and bravery, suppressed the enemy's fire and prevented further SEAL casualties.

Petty Officer Moscone, the squad's assistant fire team leader and leading petty officer, volunteered to carry Machen's body back out with the patrol. The squad began to fall back through five hundred meters of swampland. The situation was a very serious one for the small unit of SEALs, and it wasn't until helicopter support arrived on the scene that they were able to extract and take Machen's body along with them.

The air support suppressed the Viet Cong pursuit of the SEAL squad long enough for the men to reach the river and the LCM that had come to pick them up. SEALs commented later that this was the first time they had seen .50-caliber machine guns fired so hard that the barrels turned white-hot.

SEALs never left anyone behind, living or dead, during the Vietnam War. Just how far the members of the Teams would go to fulfill that promise they had made to each other was proven by the men's actions during that first loss. A SEAL had given his life to protect his Teammates; the Vietnam War had taken on a new dimension. For the first time, a SEAL had been killed in combat. For his sacrifice, Machen was posthumously awarded the Silver Star, the nation's third-highest award for valor.

Mission Two, 7 October 1966:
"Ambushed"

Modified landing craft were used by the SEALs a great deal during that first year in country to move units in and out of operational areas. To support the SEAL element while they were operating, the modifications to the landing craft included mounting a number of .50-caliber and 7.62mm machine guns as well as 40mm grenade launchers and even a 60mm M2 mortar set in a box of sand. The smaller of the two landing craft models used could transport a SEAL squad with all of its equipment. The larger "Mike" boats could move an entire SEAL platoon and still have room to allow enough crew to man at least some of the weapons lining the sides of the craft.

The landing craft were constantly being changed, upgraded, and further modified as new materials came to hand or experience dictated. Some of the modifications came after very hard experience in the field.

Through the early fall of 1966, SEAL Team One continued its operations in the Rung Sat with increasing success. Platoons were rotating back to the United States and new platoons were coming in to relieve them. Charlie platoon had recently arrived in country on October 7 and was taken out for a "break-in" op by the departing platoon. This procedure, which was new at the time, would soon become standard practice. The system would allow the new SEALs to gain experience and knowledge about the local conditions and procedures without having to learn them all from scratch.

Nineteen men—more than a full platoon—were on board the LCM boat as it moved out on a night ambush operation. The majority of the men were SEALs, the balance being the crew from Boat Support Unit One, who operated the craft. Moving along the Long Tau River in the Rung Sat, the LCM turned into a small tributary of the main river to approach their combat area.

The tributary narrowed to where the shores were only about ten feet from either side of the boat. The LCM had moved about fifty yards up the waterway when it suddenly started taking fire from both sides of the river.

Whatever the Viet Cong had been expecting, the armed LCM with SEALs on board proved to be a very difficult target. Every available weapon on board the LCM immediately began firing out at the enemy on all sides. If they didn't have a mounted weapon, the SEALs fired their personal weapons at the Viet Cong. Within seconds of the ambush being initiated, the Viet Cong struck with one of their best shots of the war against the Teams.

Bob Henry was up on the open deck manning the M2 60mm mortar in its sandbox when the attack began. Henry quickly realized that the enemy were too close for the mortar to do much good. As he loaded his second round and was preparing to fire, a VC mortar round scored a direct hit on the LCM. Of the nineteen men on board the boat, sixteen were immediately wounded, some very seriously.

Henry was blown almost completely off the LCM, landing on the sandbag armor secured to the side of the boat. Pulling himself back on board, Henry discovered that the blast had paralyzed his legs. Someone on board the boat pulled Henry to the deck as the ambush continued to rage around them.

SEAL Chief Churchill had not fared much better. He had been manning one of the mounted .30-caliber machine guns when the ambush began. The gun had almost immediately jammed, however, and as Churchill tried to clear it the mortar round struck not six feet away.

The blast knocked Churchill down and he was and badly wounded by fragmentation. Struggling to retain consciousness, his mind focused on the smoke rising from a stack of wooden boxes. A hot mortar fragment was starting to set fire to the wooden ammunition boxes holding the LCM's highly explosive 60mm mortar rounds. Ignoring the pain as it burned into his hands, Churchill picked up the searing piece of metal and threw it overboard.

Meanwhile, the SEALs were doing everything they could to hold the enemy at bay. This was not the time for firing in controlled bursts, which are intended to conserve ammunition and wear on the weapons. Instead, those men still able fired their weapons in long, sustained bursts. At one of the .50-caliber guns, Petty Officer Pearson ignored the heavy incoming artillery barrage and fired all out into the enemy position, despite serious fragmentation wounds in the hand and the head. Petty Officer Shenners, also manning a .30 caliber, poured deadly fire into the VC positions firing down on the boat. When his machine gun jammed from overheating, he switched to a grenade launcher and continued his accurate fire. Lieutenant (jg) Truxell was nearby, firing his personal weapon into enemy positions, passing ammunition to the mounted weapons, and caring for the wounded men.

One of those wounded men was SEAL Seaman Penn. When the mortar round struck just aft of his position, Penn was returning accurate fire from his heavy machine gun. Severely wounded in the back and head from fragmentation, Penn continued to fire his weapon until his wounds proved too much and he slumped to the deck unconscious. Chief Churchill—who had attempted to operate a .50-caliber machine gun after throwing the shrapnel overboard but was too severely wounded to be effective—risked himself to care for Penn and the other wounded SEALs on deck, despite heavy incoming fire.

In less than two minutes, the situation had become dire. Almost all of the men on board were wounded, the incoming fire was relentless, and the guns were beginning to overheat. The men who could kept up a steady barrage of return fire. The others passed ammunition to the gunners and helped the more seriously hurt. The firepower was blistering, but there was only one real hope: to get out of the killing zone. The tributary, though, was too narrow to turn the boat around. Leon Rausch, the acting coxswain of the LCM, had been wounded almost immediately in the ambush, but that didn't keep him from understanding the situation. Thinking fast, Rauch steered the boat *up* the tributary and out the other end of the ambush.

Now it was only a matter of making it back to the main river. While the SEAL corpsman treated the severely wounded, the LCM cautiously approached a group of Vietnamese junks. Although the SEALs were ready to open fire despite their weapons smoking and crackling from the heat of the fight, they passed the junks without incident and were soon back on the Long Tau River. The Vietnamese Regional Forces camp from which the mission began was not too far away, and soon the three most seriously wounded SEALs were being medevaced to a field hospital for treatment.

The actual ambush was over in minutes, but they were

some of the longest minutes of the SEALs' lives. Examinations after the incident indicated that the LCM had come across a large-scale Viet Cong water crossing. The heavy fire the VC were able to bring down indicated they had prepared their ambush well ahead of time and were waiting for any river traffic to enter their killing zone. The LCM must have looked like a slow-moving and relatively easy target, but the reality proved more along the lines of kicking over a hornet's nest.

It was estimated that several hundred VC were involved in the ambush, with minimum estimates ranking the VC at battalion strength. Later, it was reported that the LCM had broken up a concealed night movement by a large VC Rung Sat force. And yet, even at such a numerical and tactical disadvantage, the SEALs' sustained return fire had caused the Viet Cong to break and run. Once the SEALs were out of danger, heavy artillery and air strikes were called in to further devastate the area. The effect of the failed ambush was a cutback on all VC movement in the Rung Sat for about two weeks.

The ambush was almost a successful one for the Viet Cong, though they would never know it. Of the SEALs wounded on board the LCM, three of the men, Lieutenant (jg) William Pechacek, Petty Officer First Class Robert Henry, and Petty Officer Third Class Penn, had to retire from the service due to their extensive injuries.

Recognition of the outstanding actions of the men on board the LCM did not take long to arrive. The decorations awarded to the SEALs from that single action included a Silver Star for Chief Churchill and Bronze Stars for Lieutenant (jg) Truxell, Seaman Penn, Petty Officer Shenners, and Petty Officer Pearson.

In the eleven months of 1966 that SEAL direct action platoons from just Team One were in action in Vietnam, the men had conducted 153 operations in the Rung Sat, resulting in:

86	VC killed in action (confirmed)
15	VC killed in action (estimated)
21	sampans destroyed
2	junks destroyed
33	huts-bunkers destroyed
521,600	pounds of rice captured or destroyed

Additionally, a number of arms caches were captured, as well as a large number of enemy documents, papers, and diaries. Included in the captured papers were maps showing Viet Cong defensive positions and mine locations in the Long Than Peninsula where the Rung Sat meets the South China Sea. All this came at a cost to SEAL Team One of one man killed and over a dozen wounded, three severely.

SEAL Team One had more than proven that the SEALs were able to operate effectively against the Viet Cong in areas where conventional operations proved impossible. In October, the commitment of men from SEAL Team One to Vietnam was increased to seven officers and thirty men. Three full direct-action platoons were operating at one time against the Viet Cong in the Rung Sat. To meet their greater commitment to the Vietnam War, the manpower allowance of SEAL Team One was again increased to twenty-one officers and 105 enlisted men. The increase was projected into the 1967 fiscal year but the great need for the men pushed the increase in Team size ahead of schedule.

SEAL Support:
Boats and the Brown Water Navy

During their operations in Vietnam, the SEALs received support from a number of sources. Several of these organizations and units developed strong reputations from the results of their own operations. One of these such units were the sailors and boats of the Brown Water Navy.

"Brown water" refers to the riverine environment that these units operated in rather than the "blue water" deep ocean Navy. The riverine area includes both the coastline and inland waterways of a given area such as the Mekong Delta. All of the rivers, streams, lakes, canals, marshes, and wetlands would be part of the riverine environment as well as the ocean shoreline and the shallows. In Vietnam, the riverine environment covered most of the Mekong Delta and IV Corps in South Vietnam.

To fight and operate in these waterways, the Navy needed new small craft, lightweight so that they had a shallow draft and could work in the streams and canals. The boats would also have to be well armed in order to be effective in a fight. The Navy used a wide variety of small craft to meet these demands. Most of these craft were based on modifications of various marks of landing craft that were available cheaply and in good numbers. The establishment of Operation Market Time and then Operation Game Warden also created a new boat that would gain as great a reputation as the SEALs themselves: the Patrol Boat, River (PBR).

The first Mark I PBRs began arriving in Vietnam in March 1965. The thirty-one-foot craft had a fiberglass hull based on commercial designs that was lightweight and had a shallow draft. A water-jet propulsion system allowed the PBR to ply waters too shallow for propellers or rudders. In a marvelous adaptation of design, a water pump from a Jacuzzi hot tub was fitted to a tunnel system to direct the water jets. With no propeller to strike the bottom, the PBR could operate in any body of water deep enough to let it float.

To give the PBR speed and maneuverability, two 440-horsepower GM diesel engines powered the water pump. This system, called a hydrojet propulsion system, could drive the PBR to speeds of 25 knots (29 mph) and more when new. The water jet system also gave the PBR amazing maneuverability. The boat could turn in its own length as much as 180 degrees while moving at top speed. The movement caused the bow of the boat to dip very sharply forward and kick up a large wave, giving the bow gunner quite a bath. When moving forward at top speed, the PBR could "crash" stop, also driving the bow down, but coming to a halt within its own length.

The ability to fight had also been designed into the PBR. In the bow of the boat was a sunken gun tub that usually mounted two M2 .50-caliber machine guns with a large supply of ammunition. The two guns were fired by a sailor sitting behind and between them in the sunken tub. The bow guns had a good field of fire and they could sweep from side to side, crossing at the bow, and angling back partly toward the stern. Amidships were two gun stations with some armor shielding in front of them. The two stations usually mounted an M60 machine gun on one side and a Mark 18, rapid-fire 40mm grenade launcher on the other side. Both weapons could be quickly dismounted and switched from side to side as the situation warranted. The Mark 18 was an unusual design that fired the same ammunition as the M79 grenade launcher but used 24- and 48-round ammunition belts. To fire the Mark 18, a manually operated side crank was turned by the gunner, much like an old Gatling gun.

At the stern of the PBR was a Mark 16 stand that usually had a .50-caliber machine gun mounted on it with an armor shield that followed the movement of the gun. To operate all of these weapons as well as drive the boat was a crew of four sailors, a boat captain, coxswain, and two gunners. All crewmen were volunteers from the fleet for the Brown Water Navy.

The sailors of the Brown Water Navy took great pride in the job they did and showed it in the actions they performed and the missions they accomplished. Though they were not supposed to operate on land, the men of the Brown Water Navy often traveled canals so narrow you could reach out from either side of the boat and touch the bank. To augment their firepower, the men of the PBRs carried small arms that included pistols, M79 grenade launchers, M16A1s, and any weapon they felt would give them an edge in a firefight. Rocket launchers, recoilless rifles, Miniguns, 20mm cannon, sniper rifles, even flamethrowers were used at one time or another. Though they would wear steel helmets and body armor on a mission, the sailors of the Brown Water Navy liked to sport black berets at other times to indicate just who they were and what they did. The distinctive headgear earned the men the nickname the Black Berets.

One hundred sixty of the Mark I PBRs were built and in use in Vietnam by the end of 1966. Though an excellent design overall, the Mark I PBR did have some problems, most of these centering on the fiberglass hull and the water jet propulsion system. The fiberglass hull of the Mark I was very susceptible to damage. Though it was relatively easy to repair, the boats wore out their hulls fast in the inland waters. The inlets for the water pumps also became clogged in the dirty water and wore out quickly. With plugged water pumps and worn internal parts, the PBR was losing one of its best defenses, its speed.

An improved Mark II PBR was designed and became

available in December 1966 for operations in Vietnam. Mounting the same weapons complement that the earlier PBR had, the Mark II had an improved propulsion system that was still based on the water jet. In addition, the Mark II PBR had a stronger hull with aluminum reinforcing. The top speed of the improved design was now 29 knots (33 mph).

The PBRs soon became the workhorses of the Game Warden forces as part of the River Patrol Force. Operating in two-boat patrols, the PBRs were assigned to ten-boat sections up and down the major rivers. PBR bases and sections were at Can Tho/Binh Thuy as River Division (RIVDIV) 51, My Tho as RIVDIV 53, Sa Dec (later Vinh Long) as RIVDIV 52, Nha Be as RIVDIV 54, and Da Nang as RIVDIV 55 by 31 August 1968. As the war progressed, more PBRs came on line for operations and some River Patrol Group sections were based from modified LSTs (Landing Ships, Tank) anchored at river mouths.

PBRs were assigned to the Game Warden task forces and the River Patrol Force that had been established in December 1965. They became a very common sight moving up and down the waterways of the Delta and Rung Sat. Rather than use more specialized craft that would stand out in the area, the SEALs operated from PBRs for a great majority of their operations. Inserting off a PBR, the SEALs would gather on the bow of the craft and jump off as it slowed near shore. An even more difficult to detect insertion technique involved the SEALs rolling off the rear of the PBR as it passed near shore. When men used that method, the engine noise of the PBR would barely change as it moved along and therefore would not attract any extra attention at all.

The PBRs did have the problem of not being the quietest boats on the river. On a quiet night, the Mark I PBR could be heard two miles away, especially as wear loosened the hull and fittings. Even the quieter Mark II PBR could be heard over a mile away.

To increase their firepower and for illumination at night, a lot of PBRs carried an Army 60mm mortar that they would fire off the engine hatch cover. The mortar could put an illumination round up that would light up an area, or drop an HE round behind a wall or bunker. But the recoil of the weapon shook the hatch covers loose. Silencing material would work loose and then could clog the engine air intakes. At the first sight of the material getting loose, the PBR crews peeled it off the hatch covers. Better a little noise than a stalled engine.

The PBRs operated in the shallows and the narrow inland waterways. For the deeper rivers and inshore waters of Operation Market Time, the Navy adopted another new model of small craft, the Patrol Craft, Fast, commonly called the Swift boat. Like the PBRs, the Swifts were modifications of civilian craft. This made the adoption and availability of the boats much faster than if they had been designed from scratch.

Using a supply boat designed to transport workers and supplies to the off-shore oil rigs in the Gulf of Mexico, the Navy added weapons mounts, eliminated the passenger seating, and reinforcing the hull and superstructure. The aluminum-hulled Swifts were 50 feet in length, 13.5 feet wide, drew 4 feet, 10 inches of water, and displaced 22 tons. Two 475-horsepower diesel engines drove the boat at 25 knots in good seas. For mounted weapons, the Swifts had a twin .50-caliber machine gun tub on top of the superstructure. On the rear deck, the Swift carried an unusual over/under 81mm Mark 2 mortar with a .50-caliber machine gun mounted on top of it. The rear deck gunner could fire the mortar like a cannon, directly at targets, go for extreme range firing the Mark 2 in a high arc like a normal mortar, or switch to the .50-caliber machine gun.

Swift boats were commanded by a single officer, usually a lieutenant, junior grade (jg), and carried a crew of five enlisted men. Crew accommodations were sparse and the Swifts were usually limited to twenty-four-hour cruises. Acting as interceptors, the Swifts could move in the relatively shallow off-shore and river waters, stopping junks and large sampans that could not be reached by the larger Navy ships further out to sea.

The SEALs operated off of Swift boats when the circumstances allowed. The deeper water the Swifts needed to operate limited the areas the boats could cover, but the 81mm mortar on the Swifts was a welcome piece of fire support during more than one SEAL operation. The Swifts sometimes worked so close to shore in support operations that the ammunition to their main gun, the 81mm mortar, didn't have time to arm before hitting the target. For these close encounters, the Navy designed a flechette round for the Mark 2 mortar that turned it into a giant shotgun. When caught in an ambush from the shore, the Swift's mortar gunner could swing the 81mm around, aim it like a cannon, and pull the trigger on the pistol grip. With a Mark 120 flechette round loaded, the mortar would launch 1,300 finned steel flechettes in a widening cloud. The needlelike flechettes would shred any soft targets in their path out to several hundred yards.

MOBILE SUPPORT UNIT

The SEALs also had their own direct support units in the way of specialized craft designed for SEAL operations. Some of these craft had been developed within the SEAL Teams themselves: others were field modifications of existing craft to meet a need that was discovered during combat operations. To maintain and operate these craft was Boat Support Unit One (BSU-1) and their forward area component, the Mobile Support Teams (MST).

Established in February 1964, BSU-1 operated out of Coronado, California, under the same command as SEAL Team One. The unit worked on two major assignments:

1. To develop, test, and evaluate procedures, techniques, and equipment and to improve and document tactics in river and restricted water craft.
2. To man, maintain, and operate assigned craft in support of naval special operations.

To carry out these assignments in Vietnam, Mobile Support Team One was stationed in Da Nang. Regular naval personnel filled the ranks of the MST, pulling six-month tours of duty in country. When the first platoon from SEAL Team One arrived in Vietnam for combat duty, MSU-1 was ready to assist them. Two Landing Craft, Medium, Mark Six's (LCM [6]), commonly called the Mike boat, and four Landing Craft, Personnel, Large Mark IVs (LCPL Mk IV) were converted for SEAL use in less than two weeks under Project Zulu. All of these craft were in Vietnam operating in support of the SEALs very soon after conversion.

The LCPLs and the LCMs were changed respectively into medium and heavy SEAL Support Craft (MSSC and HSSC). The specialized craft were to act as communications bases to maintain contact with SEAL units in the field and to relay messages from the SEALs to other units if necessary. The boats also acted as close-in fire support and transportation over long distances. The Mike boat and the LCPLs could also act as insertion or extraction craft, but that was a secondary mission.

The two Mike boats conversions were so extensive they were only just recognizable as the original craft. The sides and front bow were cut down to improve visibility. Heavy armor was placed all around the Mike boat, making it able to stop even a .50-caliber armor-piercing round fired from within one hundred meters. Bar armor and steel plates stepped out from the hull and body gave resistance to recoilless rifle and light antitank weapons. The after two thirds of the central well deck was covered with a layer of plating resistant to fragmentation and supported on pipe stanchions. Two 225-horsepower diesel engines were silenced and given underwater exhausts. The Mike boats were so quiet they couldn't be heard fifteen yards away. One drawback to all of this heavy armor and engine silencing was that the Mikes' were slow, with a top speed of between 5 and 7 knots depending on conditions.

But while the Mike boats were slow, they were very much able to put up a fight. Mounted weapons varied from year to year, but the standard heavy weapons included a 106mm M40 recoilless rifle secured on the overhead cover of the well deck. There was also a mounted 81mm Mk 2 direct-fire mortar in the front of the well deck. Along the sides of the Mike boat were mounting sockets that would accept most machine gun pintles. Initial machine guns included four or five .50-caliber M2 machine guns and one or two M21 machine guns that were Navy conversions of the Browning M1919A4 to allow it to fire the same 7.62mm ammunition belts as the M60 machine gun. Later weapons included Mk 18 40mm rapid-fire grenade launchers in place of some of the machine guns. At least one Mike boat received a gun tub in 1967 that carried a M134 Minigun and 4,000 rounds of ready ammunition in its magazine.

Electronics on board the Mike boat included a radar set that could help direct SEAL insertion boats to their targets. The Mike crew would watch the radar and direct the SEALs to their target over the radio. The communications system on board the Mike was very complete and the craft were even used as Command and Control boats for some operations with the Brown Water forces. For creature comforts, the Mikes had a small refrigerator and hot plate to feed the crew on the long, slow trips.

The heavily armed and armored Mike boat could pull a SEAL unit out of trouble even in a hot engagement. For most insertions, the Mike boat drew too much water and wasn't configured so that a SEAL unit could slip on or off easily. Instead, a smaller craft was usually tied to the side of the Mike boat and towed to the target area. For the mission, the SEALs would get into the smaller craft and the Mike boat would stand off where it could put its firepower to the best use.

Able to transport an entire fourteen-man SEAL platoon, the Mike boats had one problem that couldn't be changed— the craft stood out, even among the different Navy craft up and down the rivers on the Mekong Delta. Since they were the primary users of the Mike boats, some SEALs thought the craft drew too much enemy attention. If a VC agent was watching one of the bases the SEALs operated from and saw the Mike boat pulling away, he could be fairly certain a SEAL op was coming up. But the Viet Cong didn't like ambushing the Mike boat after their first few tries. The heavy armor allowed the boat to absorb a lot of punishment. And once the Mike boat crew could see where the ambush forces were firing from, the return fire from the boat's guns could rip up a large portion of the surrounding real estate.

The Medium SEAL Support Craft converted from the Mk IV LCPL was a smaller version of the heavier Mike boat. Limitations due to the size of the craft and its single-engine propulsion system made the changes in armor and armament less than the larger boats, but it was still an impressive package. The sides and bow were cut down and armor plate installed wherever possible; the stand-off plates and bar armor could not be mounted on the LCPLs and the overhead cover was not fragment resistant. Instead of the plating above the well deck, plywood covered with sandbags served as the most successful installation on an LCPL. A tightly stretched tarp over the sandbags helped ensure that a tossed hand grenade would roll off into the water.

Difficulties in the engine arrangements on the LCPL made silencing the system a more complex job than on the Mike boat. But when finally completed and in good running order, the LCPL was even quieter than the Mike boat, even when moving at top speed. Being lighter, the LCPL was much faster than the Mike boat. A top speed of fifteen knots could be reached without straining the engine, even faster if the boat was going downstream.

The LCPL was more lightly armed than the larger craft, but it could defend itself and well support a SEAL unit in trouble. Initially, the LCPLs were armed with three .50-caliber machine guns, one on each side and one at the stern. A forward gun tub carried a pair of 7.62mm Mark 21 machine guns and a large supply of ammunition for them. In the well deck was a sandbox that carried an Army M19 60mm mortar for both night illumination and fire support with high explosive rounds. The mortar and sandbox was later replaced with a 60mm Mark 4 direct-fire mortar, essentially a smaller version of the M2 81mm mortar found on the Mike and Swift boats. Other heavy weapons such as 57mm M18 and 75mm M20 recoilless rifles were tried from the overhead cover, in a miniature version of the 106mm RR on the Mike boats. But the backblast of these weapons was too much of a danger to the occupants of the LCPL and tended to rip off chunks of the overhead.

The smaller LCPL could carry a full SEAL squad and a crew from MST-2 to operate the craft. Heavy operational demands on the four converted LCPLs wore the boats out fast. By 1969, a purpose-built Medium SEAL Support Craft had been designed and produced, using experience developed from the earlier boats. Ten of the Mark II MSSCs were delivered in 1969 and saw heavy duty in Vietnam. The weapons stations had been changed to include a 7.62mm Minigun installation as primary firepower. An assortment of other weapons, including several .50-caliber machine guns, made sure that the new MSSC could live up to the reputation earned by the earlier LCPL.

The new boats had a range of 150 miles, being driven by a pair of Mercruiser engines. With its twin engines, the new craft could hit a top speed of 25 knots. The MSSCs operated along with the last operational LCPLs until the end of the Vietnam war.

SEALs also operated two other small craft as well. The first were the SEAL Team Assault Boats (STABs). The original three STABs were converted by SEAL Team Two from standard commercial hulls for the twenty-four-foot Power Cat Trimeran. The fiberglass hulls of the Trimerans were reinforced with armor sufficient to withstand small arms fire up to .30 caliber. Reinforcing was placed at strategic areas on the hull to support the ten weapons stations around the boat. A central post station could be added or removed for space and pintle sockets around the gunwales to accept machine guns. Fifty-caliber machine guns, M60s, and 40mm Mark 18 grenade launchers could be installed as the mission required.

To drive the STAB, two 100-horsepower Mercury outboards were mounted on the stern. The tops of the engines were covered with armored boxes to give them additional protection. With the powerful engines, the STAB could reach speeds of 30 knots, even when fully loaded. This speed is not unusual considering the original civilian boat had been popular with waterskiers.

The coxswain's position was moved to the center of the bow. A circular casing protected the seat and a domelike fiberglass cover could be pulled over the top of the coxswain's head to protect him from hit brass being ejected from the boat's guns.

Four of the new STABs had been built at Little Creek, Virginia, under the direction of men from SEAL Team Two. One of the boats was destroyed in an accident; the remainder were sent off to Vietnam with the first deploying platoons from Team Two. The small boats were popular due to their speed and maneuverability. The original armament of two .50-caliber machine guns on swivel mounts on either side of the STABs were removed. The bulky ammunition cans of the .50s took up too much space for the number of rounds that could be carried. In the same space the SEALs could carry four 200-round M60 ammunition cans. A pair of M60 machine guns replaced the .50s and remained the standard armament of the first STABs.

With a full six-man squad, the STAB could still carry a good load of ammunition and three men to operate the boat. In spite of its excellent service to the SEALs, the STABs had some serious drawbacks. The fiberglass hulls could not stand up to the rough handling demanded by some SEAL missions. In addition, the rivers and streams of the Delta were full of debris, logs, and materials floating down from the jungle. Hitting this debris at speed damaged the STAB hulls badly over time.

A replacement for the Mark I STAB was designed by the Navy as a purpose-built craft for the SEALs. Designated the Light SEAL Support Craft (LSSC), the new boats became available in 1969. Several modifications were determined from operational experience with the new LSSCs and demands for a light boat from the Game Warden forces. The modified LSSC became the Mark II STAB, only this time the designation stood for Strike Team Assault Boat since

both the SEALs and the Game Warden forces were using the
same craft.

The STAB Mk II was twenty-two feet long and armored
with ceramics and ballistic nylon blankets. Any fragmentation from the ceramic armor was prevented from entering
the boat by the nylon blankets. The hull of the Mk II STAB
was made of styrofoam-filled aluminum, giving it great
strength and resistance to impact that made the boat effectively unsinkable. Powered by two 350-horsepower Ford
Mercruiser III engines, the STAB used a water-jet propulsion system that gave it a very shallow draft and a top speed
of forty to forty-five knots. And the STAB could reach its
top speed in fifteen seconds. Two 150-gallon gasoline tanks,
self-sealing and explosion proof, gave the STAB a maximum range of 190 nautical miles.

Heavy soundproofing and careful design made the STAB
the quietest of the SEALs small craft. Waves slapping
against the hull of the boat could be heard over the slight
engine sounds. Armament included five pintel sockets that
could accept 7.62mm machine guns or 40mm grenade
launchers. STABs used for patrols by the Game Warden
forces mounted as many as four M60 machine guns and an
additional 40mm Mark 20 grenade machine gun. The
SEALs liked these new STABs and used them whenever
available. The STAB could move a full SEAL squad of
seven and a crew of three for insertions or extractions.

In addition to their special craft, the SEALs used a number of small boats in Vietnam. These boats included the IBS,
or Inflatable Boat, Small, eighteen-foot commercial Boston
whalers mounting an outboard motor and a single M60
machine gun, or any of the many different types of boats
found in Southeast Asia. Sampans, junks, and even submarines were all used by the Teams in Vietnam at one time
or another.

SEAL Team Two:
The First Combat Deployments, 1967

By September 1966, it was known on the East Coast at Little Creek that SEAL Team Two would be joining SEAL Team One in conducting combat operations in Vietnam. The initial commitment for SEAL Team Two was for five officers and twenty enlisted men, two platoons of 2:10 with an officer to command the new detachment, "Det Alfa."

Up until this time, SEAL Team Two was organized into assault groups. Within a short time of receiving the commitment to Vietnam, SEAL Team Two reorganized to ten platoons of two officers and twelve men each. New men started arriving at SEAL Team Two from the UDTs in Little Creek to meet the Teams' new manpower requirements.

The two new platoons who would first deploy to Vietnam followed a heavy training schedule to prepare for the combat deployment. Facilities at Camp LeJeune, Camp Picket, and Dam Neck, Virginia, were all utilized to develop the new predeployment training program. The platoons from SEAL Team Two were able to build their program from some of the lessons learned by the SEAL Team One platoons that had been in combat in the Rung Sat for the better part of 1966.

By December 1966, it was already apparent that the

SEAL Team Two commitment to Vietnam and Det Alfa would probably increase to seven officers and thirty-six enlisted men, three full platoons of 2:12 in early 1967. A rotational plan was put into place that would increase the platoon deployment after the first two platoons had returned from Vietnam. The plan would put a new platoon in country every six months, relieving a previously deployed platoon. The heavy stress and physical demands of their method of operating and the tropical environment made a six-month tour of duty the maximum a SEAL could run while maintaining peak efficiency.

Both Second and Third platoons of SEAL Team Two left for deployment in Vietnam on 12 January 1967. Both platoons had a short stopover in Coronado, California, to meet with elements from SEAL Team One and discuss actions, standard operations procedures (SOPs), and areas of responsibility/operations (AOs) once in country. The SEAL Team Two platoons had been training for months to prepare for their deployment in combat as direct action platoons.

The two SEAL Team Two platoons arrived in Vietnam on January 29, 1967. Their primary area of operation was to be the Mekong Delta, where they would be attached to the Game Warden Task Force as Det Alfa. The platoons would be originally stationed in Binh Thui on the shores of the Bassac River near the center of its course through South Vietnam.

Mission Three, 18 May 1967:
"Attack on Illo Illo"

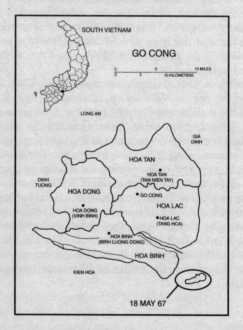

At the mouth of the My Tho river, where it empties into the South China Sea, is a small island named Illo Illo. The island is only about one and a half miles long and a quarter mile wide on an east-west axis at low tide and is so low to the water that it doesn't even appear on some maps of the area. A slightly rectangular shape, Illo Illo has a single large canal that runs twisting and turning from its western (upriver)

end to roughly the center of the island. Covered in thick underbrush and trees, the island is impassible in many areas.

As early as January 1964, Illo Illo had been a target for the South Vietnamese military. To eliminate the Viet Cong threat on the island, the South Vietnamese Army and Navy staged a joint operation against the island in early January 1964. Operation SEA DOG began on 6 January 1964. A full ARVN (Army of the Republic of Viet Nam) battalion was landed on Illo Illo from an LST. The unit was to conduct a full sweep of the tiny island while the Navy conducted operations offshore.

During six days of operations, the ARVNs destroyed a VC medical training center and two munitions factories. The South Vietnamese Navy supported the onshore operations with naval gunfire support, blockaded the island, and destroyed six VC junks. An estimated thirty VC were thought to be on the island at the beginning of the operation. One VC was killed and another wounded by the ARVN forces. The rest of the VC escaped.

The civilian population of Illo Illo was relocated to the mainland as part of Operation Sea Dog. Fifty-one men, women, and children were moved. On January 11 the operation was over and the Army and Navy forces withdrew. By 1967, Illo Illo had been declared a free-fire zone. Any personnel found on the island would immediately be suspected Viet Cong.

Second Platoon of SEAL Team Two was in My Tho by the middle of April 1967. Second's Alfa squad had been operating in Tre Noc while Bravo worked out of My Tho. The environment was "target rich" enough at My Tho to give the full Second Platoon enough operations for both squads. By May, the Second Platoon was coming to the end of their first tour. Det Alfa had proven itself a successful idea and the number of Team Two men assigned to it would soon be increasing.

As a final major operation for his squad in Vietnam, the squad office of Bravo squad, Ensign Richard Marcinko, wanted a large target whose destruction would hurt the VC noticeably. He looked to Illo Illo Island as that possible target.

Official intelligence channels had not listed any enemy activity on Illo Illo. The NILO (Naval Intelligence Liaison Officer) didn't even know it existed. But the SEALs were gradually developing their own intelligence net to give them the kind of small-unit movement information they could act on quickly. Along the My Tho river, locals would speak of Illo Illo, captured VC would bring up its name. Chieu Hoi (VC deserters) would mention the island. But no one could give up any hard intel on what might be on Illo Illo other than VC. The best intel "rumor" said that a VC medical training center might be on the island again, as it had been back in early 1964.

A plan was suggested and approved for a daylight operation on Illo Illo. The SEALs would insert just a dawn and patrol the entire island. Arrangements were made with support. The Seawolf detachment at Vung Tau was down for maintenance and repair and wouldn't be available for gunship support. Illo Illo was some forty miles downriver, far out of the range of the STABs the SEALs wanted to use as an insertion boat. A heavily armed and armored Mike boat would be used to move the SEALs close to Illo Illo; then they would insert using a STAB towed by the Mike boat.

It seemed the operation might never come off in spite of careful planning. First, the Seawolves were still not ready to support the SEALs for their planned operation on May 17. At 0001 hours on Wednesday the 17th, the squad gathered along with Lieutenant Fred Kochey, the second Platoon leader, who joined the operation and decided to go without the Seawolves. Despite the senior platoon officer's presence on the operation, the overall command still went to Ensign Marcinko, who had planned the op for his squad.

No amount of planning, however, could have foreseen the Mike boat's port engine not starting. The Mike boat made only about eight knots (a little over nine mph) moving downriver with both engines. With only one engine, it wouldn't be able to get back or even move if there were any problems. The operation was postponed and a request sent up to command for a twenty-four-hour extension on the operational plan. The request was granted and the op planned for the next day, May 18. The Seawolves were notified of the change in hopes of their being able to provide air support the next day.

At 0001 hours on the morning of 18 May, the SEALs again gathered up their gear and prepared for the mission. The Seawolves still would not be available, so the SEALs could only depend on themselves and the Mike boat if they got in trouble. They secured STAB to the Mike boat and both engines started. It was a slow four-hour trip downriver to Illo Illo.

At the mouth of the My Tho River, near Illo Illo, another problem showed up. The Mike boat almost ran aground and stuck on the many sandbars and built-up silt beds at the mouth of the river. The Mike boat managed to stay free of the mud on the upriver side of the island. Moving to their STAB, the SEALs cast off and moved to the eastern (downriver) end of the island in hopes of missing the worst of the mud banks.

Instead of a clear trip in to the shore of Illo Illo, the relatively shallow-draft STAB also ran aground in the mud. At 0500 hours, the SEALs left the STAB and slipped into the water, intending to walk in and insert on the island. The mud at Illo Illo was built up over centuries from the silt and topsoil that had washed down the length of the Mekong River. The SEALs found themselves on a mud flat hundreds of feet wide, and the flat was made up of a thin, gooey mud that let you sink into it and pulled back on you when you tried to pull out.

The mud flats every SEAL experienced during Hell Week were back in each man's memory as the squad struggled through the grasping, liquid earth. As the men continued on their exhausting way, the sun came up behind them. Now the situation was very serious as the SEALs were still some distance from the shore, wallowing through the mud in the plain sight of any VC on the island who cared to look.

Finally, at 0600 hours, after more than an hour of struggle, the SEALs reached the shore of Illo Illo.

The island was not much drier than the mud of the river had been, but at least it was firm enough to stand up and walk on. Normal SOP called for the squad to wait at the insertion point, listening and watching to see if their actions had drawn any attention. The problem with the SOP this time was that the SEALs and their weapons were too mud-coated for them to be able to fight back well if anyone had seen them insert.

As they waited, the squad wiped off their weapons as best they could. Moving inland a short distance, the squad stopped at a canal, where they quickly established a perimeter and then stripped and cleaned their weapons. Even the magazines had to be emptied, opened up, and washed out. As some of the men cleaned their gear, others kept watch; then they exchanged positions. The temperature rose as did the sun; the day was going to be a hot and humid one, easily 100 degrees and almost 100 percent humidity.

The operation was going to be far from easy, but the SEALs had already come in by the most difficult approach to the island. The patrol lined up and moved out behind the point man. The SEALs traveled the width of Illo Illo, moving back and fourth in a tight S-shaped search pattern. The point man was some short distance ahead of the squad, staying alert for any warning signs that he could see of VC, their movement, or their booby traps. For this mission, the point man was carrying a CAR-15, the short version of the M16 rifle. At the head of the squad, but well behind the point man, was the automatic weapons man. Armed with a Stoner light machine gun, he could put out a heavy curtain of fire to try and protect the point man if he tripped an ambush or uncovered some VC. The squad leader was behind the automatic weapons man, with the radio man close in behind the squad leader. The rest of the men followed, spaced out and moving silently. The last man in the patrol, the rear guard, kept watch behind the squad to see if any VC were following their line of march.

The men didn't speak; they communicated only by hand signals. These SEALs had been operating together for months and knew almost instinctively what each Teammate would do in almost any situation. The long hot day continued as the SEALs moved deeper into Illo Illo. The point man was relieved by the squad's alternate point man at regular intervals. The constant stress and strain of being on point, every nerve and sense almost tingling to detect the slightest sign in the environment, sapped even the SEALs' strength.

Slowly, the morning burned into the afternoon. The SEALs had been crisscrossing Illo Illo for hours and had found little for their efforts. They had found some well-worn foot paths near the southwestern side of the island; the eastern side seemed completely deserted. A quick rain broke out near two o'clock, cooling the squad off a little. But the break was soon over and the oppressive heat and humidity returned, pressing the men down and fraying tempers short.

Finally, one of the point men called a halt and told the squad officer that there was little to be seen on the island. The statement was made hardly above a whisper, but spoke volumes of the frustration of the SEALs. After a short break, the point man switched places and the patrol continued. The SEALs hadn't moved ten feet when the point man put up his hand, fist clenched, signaling the squad to halt immediately. Turning back to the squad, the point man first pointed to his eyes and then spread his hand in front of his face indicated that he had seen something and it was danger.

The point man who had just moved back to the squad was astonished. The squad officer moved up to where the point man knelt and looked to where he pointed. The men were on the banks of a canal, perhaps ten feet wide. Behind the other bank was a small structure, and a Viet Cong camp.

The structure was a small, open bamboo hooch, called a bohio by some of the men after the sleeping platforms they had learned to build at the Army Jungle School in Panama. Packages and other supplies were scattered underneath the structure. Bringing the rest of the squad up, the SEALs formed a skirmish line, stretched out in a line 90 degrees to the target, so they could bring maximum firepower to bear if something happened.

Silently slipping over the canal bank, the squad swam across the water and crept up the four-foot-high bank on the opposite side. The side of the canal protected the bulk of the squad from the site as the squad officer signaled two men to slip over the bank and investigate the area. After a quick moment, the two men returned with the information that the site was empty but hadn't been for long. The ashes of a cooking fire had been laid in a grate and were still warm to the touch.

The squad officer silently signaled his SEALs to move over the bank and establish a perimeter. With the area reasonably secured, a detailed search could be made of the bamboo platform and the packages. A variety of medical supplies, documents, and books were found and confiscated. The confiscated materials included:

27	tubes of penicillin ointment
8	10cc syringes
250	grams of benzoic acid
100	vitamins
100	cc of sulfuric acid (destroyed on site)
	medical textbooks
	medical notes
	personal documents

It was about 1600 hours when the squad found the Aid station at location XS 941 287, west of the center of the island. The confiscated materials were gathered and stuffed into two empty rucksacks brought along for just such a purpose. Contact was made with the Mike boat maintaining its station offshore and the crew notified about what had been found and that VC activity was definitely on the island.

Now the squad moved back into the canal and used it as a pathway through the remainder of the island. It was obvious that the VC were using the canal for passage and the SEALs were most likely to find the VC along its banks. Besides, slipping through the water came naturally to the SEALs and was far easier than trying to move through the thorns and brush. The squad still moved cautiously in its normal silent manner, with the point man forward and the rear guard keeping watch behind.

It wasn't more than a few minutes later, the squad only having moved a hundred feet, that the point man suddenly stopped and gave the rest of the squad the spread-fingers danger signal. The point man indicated that he heard something (pointed to his ear) and smelled something (pointed to his nose). The second point man moved up alongside the first to back him up. Both men smelled wood smoke drifting back from out of sight beyond the bank of the canal.

The word was passed quickly and quietly through the squad. A close whisper would be made into one man's ear and then he would turn and tell the man behind him as necessary. Slipping up silently and carefully along the two-foot high mud bank, the SEALs looked over the edge.

Not twenty feet in front of their location on the canal, six Viet Cong were settling in for a meal. A fire was going in the center of the roughly twenty by twenty-five-meter clearing and the VC were relaxing, some smoking, none apparently on guard. The Viet Cong had been in control of Illo Illo Island for some years and were confident in the impossibility of anyone slipping up on them.

The two SEAL officers with the squad were weighed down with rucksacks they had filled with the materials taken from the aid station. The officers remained on rear guard as the squad's chief petty officer moved the men up to the bank of the canal for a hasty ambush. The course of the canal took a bend around the location of the clearing, making for a natural and efficient killing zone since the men could bring their fire in from almost three sides. The side of the canal screened the SEALs as they moved into position for the ambush. Though the term was a hasty ambush, the SEALs were anything but sloppy. They had practiced this maneuver over and over again during training until the actions were second nature to them. The details of the ambush might be different, but the actions were essentially the same.

On signal, the SEALs raised up over the bank and opened fire. Six M16 and CAR-15 rifles poured in fire on the target area, saturating the clearing. The squad's automatic weapons man included his Stoner machine gun in the fire base. Almost two hundred 5.56.mm projectiles swept the clearing in under thirty seconds.

Following their standard procedures, the SEALs near the middle would fire two magazines, the Stoner man one belt, and then reload. The men on either end flank would each fire one magazine and then throw a fragmentation grenade. Looking to each other, the flanking SEALs pitched their M26A1 fragmentation grenades into the clearing at the same time.

Murphy's Law—"Anything that can go wrong, will go wrong"—seems to come into play more often in the military than any other place. One of the grenades thrown by the two flanking SEALs struck an overhanging branch in the clearing and came bouncing back behind the canal bank. The one-pound steel egg was filled with over a quarter pound of Composition B high explosive. The notched wire coil that made up the interior of the grenade body would blast apart into hundreds of fragments, most moving several thousand meters per second from the point of the blast. As they watched their own grenade come back at them, the SEALs dove for cover, burying their faces into the mud of the canal bank.

The errant hand grenade sailed over the heads of the squad and exploded harmlessly behind them, the muddy waters of the canal absorbing the deadly fragmentation. Looking back over the bank after the blast, the SEALs could see five bodies in the clearing and a sixth VC running through the trees on the far side. The squad opened fire on the fleeing VC, but it wasn't his day to die.

It was the last day for the remainder of the VC. While maintaining a watch on the surrounding area, the SEALs quickly moved over the mud bank and searched the area. Two mud bunkers were spotted. Fragmentation grenades insured that there were no active VC inside the structures before the SEALs went in and searched. In the clearing they found three small hooches, which they quickly searched.

Several of the dead VC had been armed with AK-47s. At that point in the war (1967) it was not common to see the AK-47 in VC hands. What was much more common were a couple of bolt-action rifles that were found along with the AKs. Since the AK-47 was in relatively short supply with the Viet Cong at the time, they were only issued to important people, couriers and high-level bodyguards. This had been a good hit and that was obvious to the SEALs.

Along with the rifles, the SEALs found a number of documents, two small sampans, cooking equipment, and 20 kilos of rice. The documents and the weapons were taken, the cooking gear and rice destroyed. The most unusual items discovered were several pairs of bamboo frames with mats and foot straps made of canvas and rubber (old tires). With some puzzlement the SEALs examined the very odd footwear until the reason for them suddenly dawned on the men. They were mud "snowshoes" that allowed the much more lightly built VC to move over the mud flats that surrounded Illo Illo at low tide. Instead of sinking in as the SEALs had done, the VC would be able to walk across the mud like insects.

Feeling that they were pushing their luck, and that the surviving VC may have reached help nearby, the squad went back to the canal for a fast route out. Calling to the Mike boat, the squad officer told the crew the situation concisely and had the STAB prepared for their extraction from the canal mouth. It was getting late in the afternoon when the SEALs moved through the canal once more. One of the sampans was being used to float along their captured materials, the craft being far too small to bear large-bodied Americans. It was on the patrol off the island that the squad found that what they had thought was a bitch on their insertion turned out to be a blessing.

The tide had been out when the squad had first arrived at

Illo Illo twelve hours earlier. The low water had uncovered
mud flats on the west side of the island, preventing them
from inserting up the canal as had been originally planned.
Instead, they had had to go on the east side of the island and
their miserable crawl through the thin, stinking mud.

What the squad found now were booby traps hanging in
the trees over the canal. Explosive charges and fragmentation grenades were festooned around the trees over the canal
like some deadly fruit. Spun between these fruit like mad
spider webs were the strands of wires. The booby traps were
rigged to be command-detonated. Someone, maybe even the
VC they had ambushed, would have spotted the SEALs
coming in the canal and detonated the bombs, possibly wip-
ing out the squad in a moment.

The squad took down and destroyed the booby traps.
Soon, they heard gunfire behind them as the Viet Cong
started searching for the SEALs. Time for the mission was
up and the squad began moving more rapidly down the
canal. As the SEALs came close to the mouth of the canal,
the Mike boat radioed to ask if they wanted covering fire on
the island. Once the SEALs broke out into the open at the
mouth of the canal, their location was known and the Mike
boat could start dropping 81mm mortar rounds in the jungle
behind them from its 81mm Mk 2 mortar.

And the SEALs needed the cover since they weren't
going to be leaving in as big a hurry as they would have
liked. The day had passed and the tide was out again. Mud
flats stretched out in front of the squad as they had on their
insertion, and the Mike boat could be seen off the flats, firing
in behind the SEALs. The STAB had moved in as close as it
could without running aground, but the SEALs again had to
crawl through the mud to reach safety.

The squad made it to the STAB, but not without one more
incident to punctuate the mission. As the SEALs struggled
through the mud, their sampan in tow, the direct fire mortar
on the Mike boat (which can be aimed like a cannon) fired
one round that was a little too close for comfort. A nine-
pound 81mm mortar round, with its over two pounds of

Composition B high explosive filler, came skipping along the mud through and past the group of SEALs like a flat stone skipping on the water. The mortar round didn't detonate until it hit the island behind the SEALs, but it did make for an interesting moment as it went by.

Returning to the STAB and then finally the Mike boat, the squad looked back at a job well done. It had been a long day, but it had netted excellent results. The intelligence they had found in the documents and records would tell about the size and the composition of VC units that used the island. The medical record could even tell analysts how effective some of their operations had been by the number and type of casualties that had been treated after the date of a given operation.

The huts, bohio, and clearing could not have been seen from the air. The command-detonated booby traps would have made it very expensive for any unit coming in the "easy" way via the canal. It was the SEALs and their ability to come in by the back door that had made the operation possible and successful. Indications pointed to the possibility of a large VC complex on the western side of Illo Illo. Further operations could net good results. Second Platoon was only a short time from the end of their tour of duty. Their last combat operation would be on May 20, only two days later. It was a good ending for the first tour of a SEAL Team Two direct action platoon.

```
PLATOON LOG    116.1.9.2    DET. ALFA
2ND PLATOON-MY THO (30 MAR 67-18 May 67 (Thurs)
Quarters, 0001H Underway for op-area. Insert on
Illo Illo 0500H. STAB ran aground-inserted NE end
of island 0600H. Patrolled from 0600-1500 width
and length of island. Found well traveled foot
paths on South Western tip of island. Found aid
station at canal. Destroyed station, confiscated
medical supplies + documents. Went SW on canal.
Found 6 VC, 3 huts, 2 bunkers, 2 sampans, 5 VC
KIA, 1 VC WIA, 20 kilo rice destroyed, booby-
straps destroyed. Captured 4 Chicom rifles + doc-
```

uments. Extracted by STAB 1730H. Returned My Tho 2130H. R. A., Brumuller, Fox cleaned, inventoried, & stowed equipment in Quonset hut. Mail from Skipper. Hoa Binh sub sector compromised SEAL Ops again in clear.

20 May 1967
From: Second Platoon, Seal Team #2, Detachment Alfa
To: Commanding Officer, Seal Team #2, USNAB, Little Creek, Virginia
Subj: SITREP; period of 8-20 May 1967
1. A chronological SITREP of 8-20 May is hearby submitted:
18 May 1967 (Thurs)
Underway 0001H for OPARRA. Insert 0600H. Extract 1730H. Combat patrol whole island, all mangrove found VC aid station, destroyed same, confiscated medical supplies and documents. Found 3 huts, 2 bunkers, 6 VC in command. 4 CHICOM rifles, boobytraps captured. 2B plus Mr. Kochey. 2A at My Tho cleaning and inventorying gear. Hoa Binh Sub Sector compromised, Seal ops again in clear.

Very Respectfully,

RICHARD MARCINKO
ENS, USN

The Tools of War:
Uniforms, Gear, Weapons, and Ammunition

UNIFORMS AND GEAR

Preparation for deployment to Vietnam included additional training for the environment in Southeast Asia, and the kind of combat fought there. Predeployment training included a wide variety of skills and was constantly updated with feedback from returning platoons from Vietnam—in general, training included patrolling, night operations, ambushes, and a great deal of live firing. Specific instruction was given on all of the small arms the SEALs were using in Vietnam, and the men were given the opportunity to fire them all and see which suited them best. Initial quick-reaction live firing took place on short-distance ranges where on operator would walk down a lane through bush, trees, and other terrain, firing at targets as they appeared. From the experiences of SEAL Team One in the Rung Sat, the average range of engagement on the ranges was twenty-five meters.

It was at this point in their training that the men developed the same general basic equipment for all of the operators. Each man carried his primary weapon along with ammunition pouches, a flashlight with both red and green lenses, medical kit, M26 fragmentation grenades, a knife, often a Navy Mark II (K-Bar), two canteens, and a small combat field pack (butt pack). The equipment was secured to an equipment belt (pistol belt) that was also attached to a set of field pack suspenders (H-harness).

In general, every SEAL wore his equipment in the same location. In the dark or during an emergency, each man would then be able to quickly find needed gear on any rig. The ammunition pouches held four 20-round M16 magazines or three rounds of 40mm ammunition. Men armed with the M60 machine gun or M79 grenade launcher carried their ammunition load differently than those SEALs carrying M16s, but otherwise the men began their tour with the same equipment layout. Additional weapons or equipment for an operation would be determined by the squad or platoon leader with the weight of such gear spread out among the men.

A lot of latitude was given to the SEALs on the whole as to what kind of uniform they wanted to wear on operations. Initially, the standard uniform was the same as the Army model, the tropical-weight uniform jacket and trousers. These uniforms were reasonably light, especially for wearing around the base so that the SEALs didn't stand out from the other Navy personnel.

But the light uniform just didn't stand up to the amount of wear the SEALs would subject it to in an average operation.

The SEALs spent a great deal of time in the water and the mud, and when they weren't in the wet, they were moving or crawling through the bush. The jungle was full of thorns and tough plants that would rip a uniform to shreds after just a few operations. What the SEALs found worked very well in the jungle was a pair of civilian Levi's jeans. The tough cloth of the Levi's could stand up to the rigors of the jungle much better than the standard uniform. It wasn't uncommon to see an entire squad going out on an op, each man wearing Levi's in different shades of faded blue. The color wasn't considered a problem as the blue cloth was quickly covered with mud and soaked with water, darkening it and blending it into the shadows.

Locally produced tiger-stripe uniforms also became very popular with the SEALs. Often a returned platoon had most or all of its members wearing new tiger stripes, showing that they had "been there and done that." Later rip-stop uniforms were available in camouflage from the military and these too became popular with the Teams in the later years of the war.

Headgear was also left up to the individual operator. The only thing that wasn't worn commonly was the M1 steel helmet. Occasionally, a SEAL would put on a helmet and flak (armor) vest while traveling on board one of the riverine craft. But such heavy materials were never taken on patrol. The GI helmet would block hearing and weighed as much as several loaded M16 magazines.

Berets became popular with the Teams for wearing both on and off operations. Teams chose black berets the first year or so because they were also worn by the Brown Water Navy, which the Teams worked with very closely. But later the SEALs adopted a more distinctive, camouflage beret both for its looks and because no one else was wearing one. Berets were seen occasionally in the field, but the lack of a brim to shade the eyes and protect the face and neck made the beret impractical. Originally the Marine Corps Utility Hat or "cover" was by far the most common headgear in the Teams. The cover was worn by most of the Navy and therefore blended in with other personnel on base.

The floppy "boonie" hat became very common in the deployed platoons as it became available in numbers. The wide brim of the hat protected the skin and eyes and the loose, crushed look of the hat did not stand out in silhouette. The boonie hat became available in tiger-stripe camouflage, locally produced in Southeast Asia. Some SEALs took to wearing not much more than a sweatband in the form of a forty-inch triangular bandage rolled up and wrapped around the head. Other SEALs would wrap the olive-drab bandage around their heads, tying the corners together at the back of the neck. The triangular bandage kept the sweat out of a man's eyes, was easy to replace if lost, and could be used as a tie or even a medical bandage if needed.

Footwear was also a matter of personal taste to the SEALs. Some SEALs even took to walking barefoot on patrol, the lack of footwear giving the point men greater sensitivity to boobytraps, tripwires, and the like. But this practice didn't protect the feet from the rigors of jungle travel and wasn't a very popular style in most platoons. As a kind of trade-off, some SEALs would wear locally produced sandals that protected the soles of their feet but left the toes and top skin fairly open. The sandals were made by native cobblers who cut the soles from the treads of old tires.

The standard, canvas-sided, leather jungle boot developed for Vietnam was very popular with a lot of SEALs. The boot drained water well due to its design, and the sole would give a lot of protection against the sharpened bamboo punji stakes that were a common hazard in some areas. Though they didn't give any protection to the foot from stakes, the coral shoe, issued in the Teams since World War II, was the most common lightweight footwear for the SEALs and the UDTs. The coral shoe was similar to a low-sided tennis shoe made of canvas with a rubber sole. The coral shoes were developed to protect the bottom of the foot from the sharp edges of marine coral during water operations, so they were more than sufficient for the average thorn, rock, and stick walked over in the jungle.

WEAPONS

To fight in Vietnam, the SEALs had some of the most modern weapons issued to the U.S. forces. The Teams tried experimental weapons available in very small numbers if they thought the design would give them an edge in firepower or some other advantage. For example, the SEALs received the first AR-15 rifles used in the Navy, within a few months of their being commissioned in 1962.

The small-caliber, high-velocity round of the AR-15 had terrific terminal effects on soft targets at any reasonable range the SEALs were expecting to fight at. In addition, the AR-15 was a very lightweight rifle—more like a regular carbine in length and weight—could fire fully automatically, and carried twenty rounds in its lightweight aluminum magazines. Not being available through regular supply channels, the first AR-15s in SEAL hands were 136 weapons purchased on the open market with funds available to the Teams for their outfitting. The officer who made the purchase wanted only the best equipment he could get for his men, but he faced court-martial charges for going around normal supply and procurement channels. When a sitting U.S. president got directly involved, those charges quietly went away.

The AR-15 was adopted by the U.S. military as the M16, later M16A1, rifle by the mid-1960s. The M16A1 rifle with a sling weighs 7.61 pounds loaded with a twenty-round magazine. A twenty-round magazine weighed less than three quarters of a pound, though many SEALs would only load the magazine with eighteen rounds to insure the best feeding. A thirty-round magazine was available in very small numbers in the mid 1960s, becoming more plentiful by 1969. The M16A1 fires at a rate of 700 to 800 rounds per minute, emptying a twenty-round magazine in under two seconds. With standardization of the M16A1, the SEALs had a much easier time obtaining magazines, ammunition, and repair parts through normal channels. But they always remembered that theirs had been the first ones.

An even lighter, more compact version of the M16A1 became available to the SEALs just as they were deploying platoons to Vietnam. Long known by its first commercial name of CAR-15, the shortened M16A1 had only a ten-inch barrel, later lengthened to 11.5 inches. A sliding stock made the weapon even more compact. The CAR-15 became a very favored weapon with some point men who liked the fast handling characteristics of the little weapon. Firing at the same rate and using the same magazines and ammunition as the M16A1, the Teams wanted all of the CAR-15s they could get.

One thing that the SEALs were constantly trying to

achieve was overwhelming firepower, even for a short time. In the kind of small-unit operations the SEALs conducted in Southeast Asia, it was very easy for a SEAL unit to find themselves facing a much larger enemy force. In these sudden encounters, it was the ability of the SEALs to put out a heavy volume of fire in only a few seconds' time that sometimes completely broke a VC ambush. The VC would have a hard time maintaining discipline among their troops when a six-man unit of SEALs were returning fire with a higher rate than an entire VC platoon. The ability to overwhelm an enemy with a high volume of fire is called a force multiplier in the modern military. The term refers to a small force having the power to fight like a much larger force, even for only a short time.

A simple class of weapon that was very popular with the SEALs and acted like a force multiplier was the combat shotgun. A standard 12-gauge shotgun firing 00 buckshot would put out nine .33-caliber projectiles with every round fired. That was close to the amount of fire put out from a submachine gun in a single burst. When fired with number 4 buckshot, twenty-seven 0.24-caliber projectiles went downrange with every shot. Though the shotgun did not have the range of a submachine gun, and a much shorter range than a CAR-15 or M16, in the twenty-five-meter-range fights the SEALs often found themselves in, it was one of the most devastating shoulder weapons a man could carry.

Almost all of the shotguns used by the SEALs in Vietnam were variations of the Ithaca Model 37, an all-steel 12-gauge, manually operated, pump-action weapon. The Ithaca was very rugged and mechanically simple. Even when coated with mud after a long crawl through the muck, the Ithaca would operate. Simply swishing it around in a stream or canal would often remove most of the fowling and the shotgun would operate.

SEAL point men, who were often the first to see a VC on a patrol—and then suddenly and up close—liked the shotgun for its simplicity and firepower. To make the Ithaca a more efficient jungle weapon, special Navy facilities made modifications to the SEALs weapons. The normal five-shot fixed magazine capacity of the Ithaca was extended to eight shots with a longer magazine tube. A special duck-bill muzzle diverter was issued to the SEALs on their modified Ithacas. The duck-bill changed the normally round pattern of shot fired from the weapon to an oval, four times wider than it was tall. This oval pattern made it even easier to hit a running target with only a single round from a SEAL shotgun.

Some SEALs modified their shotguns to make them easier to handle when on point or in other tight situations. One SEAL cut off the stock of his modified Ithaca, leaving only a pistol grip for him to hold. Another SEAL cut off the barrel of a standard five-shot Ithaca to just in front of the barrel, making it a classic "sawed-off" shotgun.

For ammunition, some SEALs liked the old combat buckshot load. The 00, pronounced "double-ought," load had heavier projectiles that carried further and had more penetration on a target. For the normally slightly built Asian, most SEALs found the XM257 round with its twenty-seven pellets of number 4 buckshot preferable. Number 4 buckshot isn't as heavy or large as the older 00, but the much greater number of shot in the round allowed for more projectiles to hit on the target, making up for the lack in power by an increase in hit probability. Other more exotic loads of shotgun ammunition, including tear gas, flares, and flechettes— which are small finned needles, about the size of finishing nails—were produced for and used in the field by the SEALs in Vietnam. But it was the standard buckshot load that was the most popular ammunition for SEALs with a taste for the shotgun.

Another family of weapons used by the Teams was the 40mm grenade launcher. The 40mm launcher fired a small, high-explosive shell out to a maximum distance of 400 meters. The 40mm grenade would explode into hundreds of fragments on impact, striking VC standing five meters from where the projectile struck. The first 40mm grenade launcher used in the Teams was the M79, a short, stubby-barreled, single-shot weapon that looked like a fat version of a hunting shotgun. The M79 would put its 40mm grenades into a five-gallon bucket at 150 meters and further in the hands of a competent shot. And the SEALs who carried the M79 practiced with it until they were very competent.

The usefulness of the M79 was increased by the wide variety of ammunition available for it as the war continued. Originally, the SEALs only had the high-explosive fragmentation round, known as the golden bullet because of its identifying color. Soon additional rounds including a wide variety of flares and signal rounds, buckshot loads, and CS tear gas were in use by the Teams. The real limiting factor of the M79 was the way it operated and the basic design of the weapon. The M79 was single shot; once it was fired, the operator had to open the action, remove the fired casing, and load another round before he could fire again. Between shots, the grenadier armed with the M79 was standing with an empty weapon in his hands. In addition, the M79 was referred to as a "dedicated weapon"—if the range was too great, or too short, the man who was carrying it couldn't add his firepower to that of the squad without having another weapon such as a CAR-15.

To increase the firepower of a man armed with a 40mm grenade launcher, a model was designed that would fit underneath the barrel of one of the M16 family of weapons. The original design, called the XM148, was a single-shot weapon with a forward-sliding barrel. The barrel would be slid forward to load or eject a fired casing, a fresh round inserted, and the barrel pulled back to lock into place.

A flimsy folding trigger extended along the right side of the rifle carrying the launcher so that the operator could fire either weapon with his normal trigger finger. Often carried mounted on one of the short CAR-15 models, the XM148 gave the firer a choice of an area-effect 40mm grenade or a point target rifle all in the same package.

For real close-in firepower, the XM148 could be loaded with one of the XM576 buckshot rounds developed for point-blank antipersonnel use from the M79. Carrying the XM148 on a CAR-15 would give a SEAL the effectiveness of a shotgun and the range of a submachine gun in a weapon weighing just slightly over ten pounds. In a firefight, a SEAL could initiate firing with his XM148, and by just moving his trigger finger, immediately follow up with the fire from his CAR-15.

The XM148 was an experimental weapon, testing out the idea of an over/under rifle–grenade launcher. The mechanism was not sealed against the jungle mud and dirt and could be jammed fairly easily. In addition, the exposed trigger could hang up on brush, possibly firing the weapon accidentally. The delicate nature of the XM148 caused it to be removed from field use in the other services. The SEAL continued to use the weapon until the end of the Vietnam War.

The replacement for the fragile XM148 was the M203 40mm grenade launcher beginning in 1969. The barrel of the M203 slides forward for loading by thumbing in the release latch just above the barrel on the left side of the weapon. Mounted underneath one of he M16 family of weapons, the trigger of the M203 is protected by a separate trigger guard and is just in front of the magazine well of the parent weapon. To fire the M203, the operator holds on to the magazine of the parent weapon with his firing hand and uses either the simple folding-leaf sight on top of the barrel of the more complex quadrant sight on the left side of the carrying handle of the parent weapon.

Constant practice and experience with all of the 40mm grenade launchers made some SEALs expert shots without ever using the sights. Even with the XM148 and M203 grenade launchers being available, some SEALs preferred the M79 for its simplicity, accuracy, and higher rate of fire. To increase the grenadiers rate of fire even higher, the SEALs had a limited number of pump-action 40mm grenade launchers that looked like giant shotguns. The pump-action grenade launcher could put out four 40mm high explosive grenades within a few seconds, but it also weighed over ten pounds fully loaded and was somewhat fragile due to the materials it was made of to help keep down the weight.

The 40mm grenade launcher—like the M79, the XM148,

and the M203—was very popular with the Teams throughout the Vietnam War. Even after the XM148 had been replaced with the more rugged and simpler M203 40mm grenade launcher in 1969, Some SEALs still preferred the earlier weapon.

But the real force multiplier the SEALs had available was the machine gun. The belt-fed M60 machine gun was one of the weapons on which the SEALs built their philosophy of overwhelming firepower. The belt-fed machine gun can fire hundreds of rounds of ammunition in well under a minute, adding a constant stream of projectiles to the volume of fire that can be put out by a SEAL squad or fire team for a short period of time.

In the mid-1960s, when the SEALs knew they were going to be going into combat in Vietnam within a short time, the M60 was the machine gun they were issued. Instead of being loaded with magazines, the M60 would carry its ammunition in long, linked belts. As the rounds were fired, expending links would be ejected from the weapon along with the fired casings, keeping a long empty belt from dragging on the ground.

The M60 was designed to meet an Army requirement for a new machine gun light enough to be operated by one man. The M60 weighs over 31 pounds, loaded with a 100-round belt in an attached bandoleer. A strong man can easily fire the M60 from the shoulder like a rifle, and the Teams are full of strong men. An attached bipod allows the weapon to be fired from the ground accurately. The 7.62mm ammunition fired in the M60 was much more powerful than the 5.56mm projectile launched from the M16A1. The M60 could quickly cut down trees, blast through walls, and shred a bamboo hooch. SEAL automatic weapons men who liked the M60 liked it a lot. It was dependable, powerful, and put out a stream of projectiles for as long as you kept it loaded. But the weapon was heavy, heavier than it had to be, in the SEALs' opinion.

SEAL armorers modified their M60s to better fit the mission profile of the Teams in Vietnam. The barrels were cut back, removing the bipod and the front sight in the process. The end of the barrel was threaded and the flash hider reinstalled. Since the front sight was missing, the back sight could also be removed. Even the buttstock was sometimes taken off and replaced with a simple rubber boot. The result was a lighter—only twenty-seven pounds loaded—shorter, and handier weapon that one SEAL could easily carry and operate.

But the M60 was not the only light machine gun used by the SEALs in Vietnam. A much smaller and lighter weapon was used by the SEALs to such an extent that it almost become a symbol of the Teams. The Stoner 63 was a very new idea from the designer of the AR-15/M16, Eugene Stoner. Using a basic receiver and a set of parts, any of six different types of weapons—from a carbine to a fixed machine gun—could be assembled for use.

In early 1967, the SEALs received the first of their new Stoners, in the belt-fed, light machine-gun version. The belt-fed weapon was the only version of the Stoner to see wide use in the Teams. After some minor problems had been worked out of the Stoner 63, a modified version, the Stoner 63A, started arriving at SEAL Teams One and Two. The Stoner 63A could carry a 150-round belt of ammunition in a reloadable drum mounted underneath the weapon. With a fully loaded drum, the Stoner 63A only weighed a little over seventeen pounds, and it could empty its drum in eleven seconds.

At its normal rate of fire of eight hundred rounds per minute, the Stoner put out thirteen 5.56mm projectiles every second. Since it fired the same ammunition as the M16A1, ammunition supply wasn't a problem, though in the early years of the Stoner the SEALs sometimes had a link up their own belts of ammunition. A final version of the Stoner weapon, officially designated the Mark 23 machine gun, had a short barrel, an improved cocking system, faster system for reloading, and other improvements over the original design. Now known as the Stoner 63A1, the weapon was used everywhere the SEALs operated. The firepower of the

Stoner was so great that it stood out even in the Teams. When a small unit of SEALs went out on a mission, it was almost certain that one of them would be carrying a Stoner.

Other weapons the SEALs used ranged from the simple to the exotic. Every SEAL carried at least one knife on an operation. Some operators purchased civilian knives worth hundreds of dollars and used them exclusively. For most SEALs, the Navy Mark II, called the K-Bar after its largest manufacturer, was the knife of choice. The hard plastic scabbard of the Mark II often had a mark 13 pyrotechnic flare taped to it. The carrying of the signaling device that way was a habit developed in the UDTs.

Pistols were also issued to the SEALs in larger numbers than other units. When a SEAL went into town off duty, he was usually armed with either a Smith and Wesson .38 caliber Combat Master piece revolver or a 9mm Smith and Wesson Model 39 automatic under his shirt or on his belt. Modified to accept a sound suppressor and specially waterproofed, the Model 39 became the Mark 22 Hush Puppy, a "silenced" pistol used to take out sentry dogs and other targets without making a loud gunshot.

Hand grenades of all types were carried by the SEALs. The "pocket artillery" of the Army infantryman, the fragmentation grenade could be used to attack a target behind a wall, a hill, or in a bunker without exposing the operator to return fire. Other grenades, such as the Mark 3A2 Offensive, were simple pack ages of explosives that would usually stun a VC rather than kill him. Smoke grenades of all colors were used for signaling and other specialized types, such as AN-M14 TH3 Incendiary, were used for burning targets. The M34 White Phosphorus would also be used to set fire to targets, and it would create large clouds of dense white smoke for signaling or screening.

AMMUNITION

All of the weapons carried by the SEALs had one limiting factor: the amount of ammunition that could be carried with them. The tremendous firepower that could be put out from a SEAL squad could usually only be maintained for about 90 seconds. Usually, a unit would fire heavily for less than 30 seconds to break contact with an enemy force. An even shorter period of fire would be used on the average ambush.

Armed with an M16A1 or CAR-15, an average SEAL would carry ten to fourteen twenty-round magazines, loaded with only eighteen rounds for the best functioning. That load would give the average SEAL rifleman 180 to 252 rounds of ammunition.

A SEAL armed with an M79 grenade launcher usually carried around thirty high-explosive grenades. The number of high-explosive (HE) rounds ranged from twenty-four to fifty-four, depending on the type of operation he was going out on. In addition to the high-explosive rounds, an average of ten antipersonnel buckshot rounds would be included. A CS gas round or several pyrotechnic signaling rounds, such as white parachute flares, would round out the M79 grenadier's load.

A grenadier armed with an XM148 or M203 would have to carry ammunition for both his grenade launcher and rifle. Twenty rounds of 40mm high explosive would be carried along with eight rounds of buckshot for the grenade launcher. For the CAR-15 or M16A1, nine or ten twenty-round magazines would give the operator an additional 162 to 180 rounds of fire.

The amount of ammunition carried by an automatic weapons man armed with an M60 depended in part on the size and strength of the operator. Two hundred rounds would be carried for the M60 on even a light mission. For a big SEAL, 1,200 rounds was an average load. Going in on a hot operation, a large SEAL with an M60 might carry as much as 3,000 rounds of ammunition. But he would be carrying that and little else.

The light weight of the Stoner and its ammunition is part of what gave the weapon such appeal to the SEALs. On an average operation, a Stone man carried 500 to 600 rounds of ammunition. Depending on how he set up his weapon to be fed, either from a drum or boxes, the Stoner man might drape the extra ammunition across his shoulders and chest. For a hot operation, 1,200 rounds and up was a common load.

Hand grenades were carried by all members of the squad. Usually, each man would have two M26A1 fragmentation grenades on his web gear. On operations where they expected to run into a lot of bunkers or other emplacements, the number of fragmentation grenades carried might be as high as ten per man. Each SEAL also carried colored smoke grenade, most commonly green although red and yellow were used in smaller numbers. A tear gas grenade, incendiary grenades, or white phosphorus might be carried, depending on the tastes of the individual and especially what kind of operation they were going out on.

A Claymore mine or M72A2 LAW rocket (Light Antitank Weapon) might be carried on a patrol, several of the weapons being spread out among the members of the squad. Each SEAL would have one or more Mark 13 flares on his rig. The flares were not only useful for signaling: they were lighter than incendiary grenades and could be used to start fires. Other pyrotechnics, such as hand-launcher rocket (pop) flares or miniature pencil (pen gun) flares would be carried for illumination or emergency signals.

For SEALs assigned to handle and control prisoners, handcuffs were sometimes carried. The handcuffs were the same style and type as used by the police. To handle larger numbers of prisoners, and to save weight, plastic "riot" handcuffs were later used. The one-use plastic handcuffs were simply very strong plastic ties that once secured had to be cut off the prisoner. To make captured VC easier to handle extra morphine syrettes were occasionally carried. The little syrettes were a single injection of morphine that would relieve pain, or make a man quiet.

By the middle of the Vietnam War, SEAL squads had developed a fairly standard load of weapon and ammunition. For every three men, one would be carrying a belt-fed automatic weapon, usually a Stoner. Another SEAL would have a 40mm grenade launcher, the XM148 being the most common. And the third SEAL would have an M16A1 or a shot-gun. A SEAL squad had at least two automatic weapons men, often three. Several SEALs would have a grenade launcher; the radio man usually carried a CAR-15 or M16A1, and the point man used the weapon of his choice, a shotgun or CAR-15. The patrol leader carried a Hush Puppy when it was available in addition to his shoulder weapon, probably a CAR-15.

Mission Four, 26 April 1967:
"Snatch"

The third Platoon from SEAL Team Two had established a good reputation for success in their operations against the Viet Cong as part of Detachment Golf in early 1967. The key was not only great training and execution, but also good intelligence data. An op could be put together quickly by well-informed SEALs much faster than many of the regular military units, both Army and Marine. And the SEALs were still the only U.S. forces able to operate successfully in the more impassable areas of the Mekong Delta.

Information for one Third Platoon operation in late April

1967 had come from a number of sources. A strong guide-
line in the planning of SEAL operations was to confirm
information for an operation from at least two sources whenever possible. Though this may have prevented the SEALs
from going on some operations where the intel couldn't be
reinforced, it also kept them out of traps and ambushes. The
Viet Cong had almost immediately realized the value of the
SEALs, and they had become a very popular target.

For this particular operation, the intelligence had been
compared and developed through a number of sources. The
Can Tho post for the National Police of South Vietnam had
interrogated a local farmer who had reported that a meeting
of several high-level Viet Cong cadre would be happening
very shortly. The meeting would take place in a small village
on the shores of the Bassac River, well within the operating
area of Third Platoon.

The National Police were not known for the quality of the
information they developed. Harsh interrogations, corruption,
and simple misinformation often tainted any reports coming
from their offices. But several sources reinforced the VC cadre
report. The watch commander of the Game Warden Tactical
Operations Center (TOC) for the area reported that a sampan
occupant who had been stopped by a river patrol the evening
before had also said something was going to take place the
next day. The fairly vague information from the sampan occupant indicated the action was going to take place in the same
general location indicated by the National Police report.

Additional information came from the Naval Intelligence
Liaison Officer (NILO) for the IV Corps area, which took in
most of the Mekong Delta. NILOs would gather intelligence
from different sources and see to it that it arrived in the
hands of people who could best act on it. The intelligence
reported by the NILO also came from the National Police
but involved different information. A group of eight to ten
VC guerrillas, including the local VC district chief, would
be at a meeting in the area.

Some information may also have come from a Hoi Chanh
who lived in the area of the suspected meeting. If so, the

information was delivered to a higher source and handed down to the SEALs. Hoi Chanhs were a result of the Chieu Hoi ("Open Arms") program, where Viet Cong could surrender and be absorbed back into the South Vietnamese community, often by working as scouts for the U.S. forces. The U.S.-backed program offered amnesty for surrendering VC and a reward for them if they also brought in their weapons or told of weapons cache locations. Intelligence from a Hoi Chanh could be very accurate regarding their local area.

The intelligence indicated a village would be used as the meeting site. Further investigation found that the "village" wasn't much more than a loose line of buildings on the South shore of the Bassac in two different locations. The decision was made to attack both locations simultaneously by splitting Third Platoon into two squads.

The plan as finalized by the platoon officers called for a simple daylight abduction raid targeting the key VC personnel mentioned in the intelligence reports. Insertion would be from standard PBRs, which would be conducting what appeared to be a standard river patrol. Such PBR patrols took place often enough that the SEALs operation would appear to be nothing out of the ordinary. In addition, the PBRs would be able to provide strong close-in fire support if something went wrong and the plan "went south."

Any available additional support units, such as Seawolf helicopter gunship support, was arranged for through the TOC at CTF-116. This was also the point at which the specific PBRs for the operations were assigned. The PBR crews were briefed for the operation and then the SEAL squads were each briefed by the officer.

The fact that the operation was going to take place in daylight held no problems for the SEALs. The Team had been operating together for several months and the men knew their individual responsibilities completely. In addition, the SEALs knew almost instinctively how each member of their squad would act in any given situation and had complete confidence in each other.

Briefings had become quick and concise as the men

gained experience. In general, the men all knew what was expected of them, what to take with them, and how they would operate together. The squad was given the mission specifics and details about insertion and extraction, other support, radio call signs, and who would be going with them.

Lieutenant Jake Rhinebolt the officer in charge of Detachment Alfa, would be accompanying Squad 3B on the operation. This was not an unusual situation as Lieutenant Rhinebolt had a reputation as an operator who didn't like spending too much time behind a desk. In spite of Rhinebolt's greater rank, assistant Third Platoon Leader Lieutenant (jg) Robert Gormly would lead the squad as usual.

The SEALs gathered on board their respective PBRs and left for the target area early in the afternoon of 26 April. It was noted that the Bassac was particularly calm that day. Arriving at the target, Squad 3A inserted first, moving off the bow of their PBR rapidly as it ran up to the shore and quickly reversed engines. Squad 3B moved further downriver to their insertion point, about 1,700 meters (a little over one mile) away.

There was no sign of VC sentries or any other enemy activity on shore. This made the leader of Squad 3B a bit concerned that the meeting was at a different time, and that they had missed it, or were too early, or that the whole situation was a setup and the SEALs were moving into an ambush.

Squad 3A inserted without incident. The area was wooded and there were gardens of banana trees. Inland from the river, past the trees, the area was largely rice paddies, little more than low open fields in the dry season. Moving up to the two target houses, several SEALs quickly searched the bamboo hooches. No VC were found, but the area was not uninhabited.

One VC scrambled out of a house and ran just ahead of the SEAL search party. Quickly, several members of the squad took chase after the fleeing man who was moving inland across the rice paddies and fields. Chasing the VC around the edge of a field, the SEALs saw five to seven more men running across the open field some distance away.

Even though the area was an open field, the fleeing VC were over 800 yards away, far out of normal effective range for the weapons the SEALs had with them. The squad opened fire anyway. Each time the SEALs fired, the fleeing men dropped to the ground. When the firing stopped, the VC again got up and started running. Though the VC were out of the range of the SEALs' weapons, they were not out of range for the SEALs' radio.

Calling up support, the SEALs had Seawolf helicopter gunships on the way. As the squad fired and the VC stopped to take cover, their time ran out. The Seawolf gunships arrived on the scene and first tried to make the VC stop and hold position. The VC continued to get up and run as soon as the firing stopped. Finally tired of issuing warning shots that were being ignored, the Seawolves strafed the VCs' position.

In spite of a literal rain of 7.62mm projectiles all around him, one young VC was only struck in the hand. The SEALs watched from a distance as the VC just stood there, the mud and dirt kicking up in spurts all around him. The VC held up his hands, holding the wounded hand with the other, and stared down the multiple gun barrels and rockets of the circling helicopters. Finally, one Seawolf landed and took the wounded VC prisoner.

One man evaded both the helicopter and the SEALs. With his much better knowledge of the immediate area, the one fleeing VC disappeared and escaped. Five VC were later confirmed killed by body count. The prisoner was later turned over to the IV Corps Riverine Intelligence Advisor for interrogation and further disposition.

Moving back to the river and their PBR for extraction, the SEALs passed out Chieu Hoi leaflets to the wives and children of known VC as well as to residents of another two hooches in the immediate area.

Squad 3B, meanwhile, scanned the shore from their position on a PBR downriver. The lack of enemy movement of any kind made the patrol leader a bit concerned, so he had the support PBR move to the right flank, where he would be better able to cover the target area with his guns. The squad's PBR moved in quickly and reversed its engines just short of the shoreline. The SEALs had been crouched on either side of the forward gun tub and quickly jumped from the boat as the craft decelerated and hit the shore. The PBR then moved off fast to cover the SEALs on their left flank in case of trouble.

The PBR made relatively little noise bringing the SEALs in, but the squad established a fast perimeter and held their position for a short time as per the unit's SOP. With no warning sights or sounds, the SEALs quickly moved to two houses that had been previously targeted as probable meeting sites.

The squad officer and one of his men who spoke a little Vietnamese entered the hooch that was the primary target. A quick search of the building found little more than two rooms separated by a bamboo wall, an old woman, and a young woman and a small child. No men or other obvious sign of additional people could be found. But the women had been laying out a meal on the floor mat, with places for five people.

The two SEALs entering the building suddenly with no warning, heavily armed, with their bodies covered with equipment and their faces painted in camouflage, had startled the woman badly. Grabbing up the young woman, the SEAL who could speak some Vietnamese asked her when the VC would be there. Apparently so frightened she couldn't think, the woman said that the VC would be there in a few minutes.

The frightened woman spoke quickly and was being drowned out by the shouts of the old woman, which made it very hard for the SEAL to understand what was being said. In the few minutes that it took to interrogate the woman and understand the answer, actions were taking place outside the hooch with the remainder of the SEAL squad that eliminated most questions.

The squad officer inside the hooch heard a burst of gunfire from his automatic weapons man's Stoner. It is impossible to mistake that sound for any other weapon, and the two SEALs ran from the hooch to see what was happening to the rest of the squad.

Four armed Viet Cong had been walking next to the tree line nearby, paralleling the river. The squad's Stoner man had opened fire on the VC, hitting at least one of them. Now three armed Viet Cong were running from the village and the SEALs, moving through the tree line toward the rice paddies away from the river. The heavy foliage covered the fleeing VC well, making it very difficult for the SEALs to open fire and stop them.

The squad officer directed Lieutenant Rhinebolt and the Stoner man to take a position at the edge of the rice field and cover the rest of the squad. With that, the other five SEALs took off in pursuit of the fleeing VC. One VC was spotted and taken under fire. Badly hit, the VC fell to the ground as the rest of the SEALs rushed past. The squad officer told the corpsman to stop and tend to the wounded VC.

The remainder of the squad reached the end of the trees and were on the edge of the rice paddies. The VC were running into a second tree line some fifty meters away and to the side. Forming into a quick skirmish line, the SEALs moved out across the field and continued their chase of the Viet Cong. Keeping up the chase forced the Viet Cong to flee instead of turning and quickly ambushing the SEALs as they continued forward. These constant, aggressive tactics, combined with the experience of when and when not to use them, gave the SEALs an additional edge when working against the Viet Cong. As the SEALs reached the second tree line, they spotted another group of hooches just ten meters away.

As one of the SEALs cried out in warning, the squad dove for cover. Directly in front of the SEALs was a VC bunker, the firing opening facing directly at them. If the running Viet Cong had taken cover in the bunker, they could open fire on the SEALs at any moment. Long moments passed for the squad as they stared through the jungle brush. No fire came from the bunker or any of the other hooches. There was no sign of life at all in the group of buildings except for some livestock wandering between the hooches.

As the squad leader began to move forward, one of the more experienced SEALs in the squad pointed out the poor position the unit was in. The SEALs had run out of range of their PBR support and were no longer in sight of their own automatic weapons man back at the edge of the rice paddies. That thought, and the fact that the village was deep in Viet

Cong territory, convinced the squad officer that pulling back was the best option. Any locals hiding in the bunkers would probably be VC themselves, and the three armed VC they had been chasing could already be under cover and keeping the SEALs in their sights.

The squad moved back to where they left their corpsman in a normal squad order. The point man was up front leading the way. The rear guard was walking backward much of the way, keeping a close eye on the area that the squad had just left. Returning to the corpsman, the squad officer found the man still working on the VC shot earlier. The officer was convinced that he wouldn't be able to interrogate the shot VC, as his brains had been mostly blown out of his head. Gathering up the dead VC's weapon, the squad moved back to where their Teammates were covering them, taking their very unhappy corpsman along with them.

The entire chase had only taken about fifteen minutes to run its course. The squad returned to the hooch to interrogate the women about who the running men had been. Convincing the frightened women that the SEALs were not going to kill them out of hand took another few minutes. Further questioning convinced the squad that they had broken up a VC meeting. The younger woman's husband had been in the group of VC that had approached the hooch for the meeting before being surprised by the SEALs.

Seeing that there was little more that could be done in the area, the squad officer called in the PBRs for extraction. No further action took place and the SEALs returned to their Binh Thuy base. Later intelligence reports from the National Police indicated that the SEALs had broken up at least a local VC cadre meeting. The husband of the older woman in the hooch had been the local Viet Cong leader. He had kept out of sight in the tree line when the SEALs gave chase to the fleeing Viet Cong.

BARNDANCE #25A   COORD: XR025942
DATES: 26 April   TIMES: 1300-1345
  1. UNITS INVOLVED: 3A

2. TASK: Secure known VC area & abduct selected cadre from houses

3. METHOD OF INSERTION: PBR EXTRACTION: PBR

4. TERRAIN: Wooded, Banana gardens, Rice fields

5. TIDE: Low WEATHER: Clear

6. MOON:-

7. ENEMY ENCOUNTERED: One VC escaped due to lack of knowledge of area. 5-7 VC observed fleeing across field. 1 captive

8. CASUALTIES: No friendly, Possible 5 KIA VC

9. NAMES OF SEALS INVOLVED: Bailey, Waugh, Estok, Goines, Detmer, Tahn, Tohieen, That

10. RESULTS: Helo's fired on running VC, killing 5 and captured one. One VC successfully evaded

11. REMARKS/RECOMMENDATIONS:-
INCLUDE INTELLIGENCE INFORMATION GATHERED, MATE-RIAL FOUND, DESTROYED, CAPTURED, ETC.

BARNDANCE #25B   COORD: XR 037 930
DATES: 26 April [1967]   TIMES: 1300-1345

1. UNITS INVOLVED: 3B

2. TASK: Moved into VC houses and snatch known local VC leaders. Info supplied by Chieu Hoi from area

3. METHOD OF INSERTION: PBR EXTRACTION: PBR

4. TERRAIN: High ground, Tree line 100 meters, deep opening up to fields

5. TIDE: Low WEATHER: Clear

6. MOON:-

7. ENEMY ENCOUNTERED: 4 Armed VC, one killed by M16, one other possible kill by M16

8. CASUALTIES: No friendly

9. NAMES OF SEALS INVOLVED: Lt Gormly, Tolison, Garnett, McCarty, Birtz, Lt Rhinebolt, (One interpreter from RAG base)

10. RESULTS:-

11. REMARKS/RECOMMENDATIONS:
INCLUDE INTELLIGENCE INFORMATION GATHERED, MATE-RIAL FOUND, DESTROYED, CAPTURED, ETC.

Orders and Briefings:
The Warning Order and Patrol Leader Order

Prior to any operation going forward, the Teams followed a set of guidelines in preparing everyone involved for the mission. The constant training done by the platoons in the Teams is what gave the SEALs such a good basis for their operational success in Vietnam. Predeployment training, given the few months before a platoon left for a tour in Vietnam, gave the men a chance to learn more about how that specific platoon worked together. Because platoons were built up prior to their scheduled deployment, and SEALs could rotate from platoon to platoon within the Team, each deployment was effectively for a new group of men. A platoon would be made up of SEALs who had been with each other for some time, new men fresh in the Teams, and SEALs who volunteered in as the opportunity to go back to Vietnam came up. Predeployment training gave these men time to learn about each other and to learn the newest "lessons learned" from Vietnam.

The experiences of previous platoons were brought back to the SEAL Teams and spread to the new platoon going over. In this way, the experience level of the Teams as a whole kept growing as the SEALs continued operating in Southeast Asia.

Some SEALs became fairly fluent in Vietnamese, not from attending any of the military language schools, but just from having spent so many months operating in country.

This experience increased the Teams success rate on operations in Vietnam as the years progressed. During the first tours, orders for operations were issued with a great deal more care than was necessary in the later years. Individual platoons might begin a deployment receiving fully detailed briefings on an upcoming op. After months of operating together, the length of the briefings usually became much shorter. "We're going to go here and do this," was about all a very experienced platoon needed to know. Each man knew his position in the squad for a patrol. Reactions to a given situation were rapid and automatic. Men knew from experience what they needed and what they carried.

But the Teams were also a very professional military organization. The men followed set procedures in preparation for an operation. Experience might have shortened the steps, but the men followed each step regardless. Whenever possible, the SEAL unit would receive a Patrol Warning Order (PWO) prior to going out on an op. The warning order was intended to give the men a very general outline of what actions were coming up so that they could prepare ahead of time. Even experienced SEAL leaders used the outline of the warning order to prepare for a mission. This prevented missed objectives from screwing up what would have otherwise been a successful operation.

PATROL WARNING ORDER

A normal Patrol Warning Order consisted of the following:

I. **A brief statement of the situation, both enemy and friendly.** The SEALs were told what was going on in the area, who else was holding operations, or what may have led to the upcoming op.

II. **The mission of the patrol.** The who, what, where, when, and why of the op. This was primarily what the operation was going to be—a body snatch, patrol and ambush, raid, or whatever—who or what the target was, how long the mission would take, and when the op was coming down.

III. **General Instructions**

    A. *General and specific organization.* This was a summary of what each part of the platoon or squad was going to do in support of the mission. Individual duties were specified here and assignments such as point man, automatic weapons man, and radio man were given out. Men assigned to special teams were told what they would be doing, such as prisoner handling, etc. The order would also outline the equipment: what it was, how much would be needed, how much was expected to be used on the mission, and who would prepare it.

    B. *Uniform and equipment common to all.* What the unit would be wearing in terms of uniform, web gear, number of canteens, life vest, etc. Escape and evasion gear was listed, as well as any required civilian, camouflage, or deceptive clothing listed.

    C. *Weapons, ammunition, and equipment.* This order included information on what each man would carry in terms of ordnance; how they would be armed; how much ammunition they would carry, including extra ammunition for special weapons or demolitions; how many rations; grenades, including smoke grenades, how many and what colors; and any specialized equipment such as demolition gear, Claymore mines, radios, etc. Mission-critical items, such as special detonators, signaling gear, or munitions would be doubled. This was also when the men would be told where to go to draw rations, water, weapons, ammunition, and other equipment.

    D. *Chain of command.* Men were told who would take over an operation if the platoon or squad leader and their assistants were hit.

    E. *A time schedule.* A general timetable of the opera-
    tion, especially when the unit was to be ready, when
    transportation would arrive or be prepared to leave,
    and when any special issue was going to be made.
    Times for mustering up, test-firing weapons, and
    any further or specialized briefings would be given.
    F. *Time, place, uniform, and equipment for receiving
    the Patrol Leader's Order.* In other words, when and
    where the men would receive the full details of the
    operation.
    G. *Times and places for inspections and rehearsals.*

IV. Specific instructions.
    A. *To subordinate leaders.* How the squad or fire team
    leaders would prepare their men or equipment if
    anything out of the ordinary were required.
    B. *To special purpose teams or key individuals.* How
    the radio man might have to prepare special encryp-
    tion equipment or how a prisoner-handling group
    may have to secure more than one individual if mul-
    tiple targets were expected on a snatch.

Prior to issuing the warning order, the individual who was
putting together the mission, whether he was a SEAL Officer, platoon chief, leading petty officer, or PRU advisor, had
several steps he had to examine to plan the details of the
operation. Sometimes, the plan would be a very simple one,
using techniques that the SEALs had experience with and
only the specifics about the target really had to be considered. Other plans had to deal with larger teams on complex
operations that either had to be coordinated with other units
or higher-level support than was normally used by the unit.

The SEAL making the final decisions on the nuts and
bolts of an operation usually went by the KISS rule: Keep It
Simple, Stupid. Depending on how the emphasis was put on
certain words, KISS was either a principle or a personal
warning not to go overboard. The input of other experienced
members of the SEAL unit would be sought out. It was not
unusual in a SEAL operation not to have the highest ranking

man leading the op. A higher ranking officer or petty officer might be along, but if he was not the individual who planned or developed the operation, he was not the leader of it.

A list of patrol steps was taught to all SEAL leaders. They were to consider all of the steps in planning and operation. The steps they considered important or practical for a specific operation would be accomplished. Other steps could be disposed after they were considered. There was no particular order to the patrol steps.

PATROL STEPS
1. Study the mission.
2. Plan the use of time.
3. Study the terrain and the situation.
4. Organize the patrol.
5. Select the men, weapons, and equipment.
6. Issue the Warning Order.
7. Coordinate with other organizations.
8. Make reconnaissance of the target area.
9. Complete detailed plans.
10. Issue Patrol Leader's Order.
11. Supervise, inspect, and rehearse.
12. Execute the mission.

The final briefing would usually be given as part of the Patrol Leader's Order (PLO). This was the final set of instructions the SEALs would receive for an operation. During the PLO, the intelligence that led up to an operation would be described in at least a brief form. What the exact plan was, who and where the support would come from, and all other details for the op were all part of the PLO. It was very important that each member of a unit knew what the plan was; what the intent of the operation was: how, when, and where they were to carry out their specific orders; and what part they were going to play in the overall operation.

Items in the PLO that were the same as those specifics given in the earlier Warning Order were covered by stating "same as warning order" or "no change from warning order." It was probably the PLO, given as the final briefing, that changed the most as a platoon gathered experience in the field. In Vietnam, the SEALs might operate every other day, either as a platoon, squad, or fire team. The fine details of a formal briefing or PLO were often unnecessary. For the big ops, the "long version" of a PLO was usually followed.

PATROL LEADER'S ORDER

I. SITUATION (as it affects the patrol)
   A. *Enemy forces:* Weather, terrain, identification, location, activity, strength
   B. *Friendly forces:* Mission of next higher unit, location and planned actions of units on right and left, fire support available for patrol, missions and routes of other patrols
   C. *Attachments and detachments*

II. MISSION: What the patrol is going to accomplish and the location or area in which it is going to be done

III. EXECUTION
   A. Concept of operation: The overall plan, and the missions of elements, teams, and individuals in the objective area
   B. Other missions, not in the objective area, for elements, teams, and individuals; included would be tasks such as navigation, security during movement, and security at halts
   C. Coordinating instructions
      (1) Time of departure and return
      (2) Primary and alternate routes
      (3) Departure and re-entry of friendly forces
      (4) Organization for movement
      (5) Actions at danger areas
      (6) Actions on enemy contact
      (7) Rallying points and actions
      (8) Actions in objective area
      (9) Debriefing

      (10) Other actions
      (11) Rehearsals and inspections
IV. **ADMINISTRATION AND LOGISTICS**
   A. Rations
   B. Arms and ammunition
   C. Uniforms and equipment (state which members will
      carry and use which items)
   D. Method of handling wounded and prisoners
V. **COMMAND AND SIGNAL**
   A. Signal
      (1) Signals to be used within the patrol
      (2) Communication with higher headquarters—
         radio call signs, primary and alternate frequen-
         cies, times to report and special code to be used
      (3) Challenge and password
   B. Command
      (1) Chain of command
      (2) Location of leaders during movement, at danger
         areas, at the objective

Many of the details on the formal Patrol Leader's Order format were accomplished long before the SEAL platoon arrived in Vietnam. Drills for actions on enemy contact, ambush, and danger were conducted constantly during patrols in predeployment training. Training and experience under fire would burn these lessons home until they would be done by a SEAL even if he was half-comatose. Items such as signals within a patrol would remain unchanged from mission to mission and often from deployment to deployment. These would have been practiced so long and were so familiar that a SEAL unit could hold small conversations in the field without a single word being spoken.

Other details in the PLO format would always be issued, such as call signs and frequencies for support. Items like this would change from mission to mission, and the lives of a SEAL unit could easily depend on their being known. The experience of a SEAL radio man or operator might also give

him standard frequencies for additional units or support that
may not have been officially on call for the operation. These
bits of knowledge pulled more than one SEAL unit out of
the fire while in enemy territory. Challenges and passwords
might remain the same within a unit during an entire tour,
such as the question and answer being two numbers that add
up to ten. Code words for reporting extraction, insertion, or
arrival on the target site would change regularly.

The detailed, formal following of a Warning Order or
Patrol Leader's Order format was usually dispensed with
quickly on arrival in Vietnam, if they hadn't already been
dropped during predeployment training back in the states.
Briefings for men in a unit could be a sudden and short as
"Get your Stoner, we have an op." It was the trust the SEALs
had in each other and their leadership within the Teams that
allowed such brevity to be used in a combat zone. It wasn't
that the SEALs didn't know and understand the formal procedures thoroughly and completely—they were profession-
als in a job where death was waiting for any mistakes—it
was just that they often chose not to use them.

Mission Five, 23 December 1967:
"Firefight"

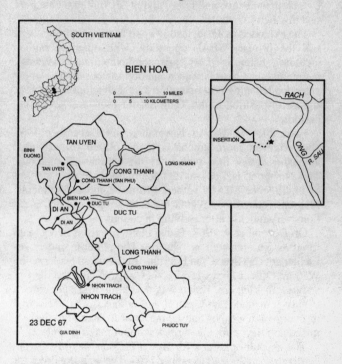

SEAL Team One had expanded in size over 1967 to meet the heavy commitment the Team had to Southeast Asia. The manpower authorization for the Team reached thirty-two officers and 132 enlisted men. This gave SEAL Team One eleven operational platoons of two officers and twelve enlisted men each, identified Alfa to Lima (India omitted). Five platoons were deployed to Vietnam at any one time from SEAL Team One. Three platoons went to Detachment Golf, their primary operational area remaining the Rung Sat Special Zone. One further platoon each was assigned to Detachments Bravo and Echo, giving SEAL Team One over seventy men in country.

The extended ambush, lasting up to forty-eight hours, was still the primary SEAL operation, with other operations including listening posts, prisoner abductions (snatches), reconnaissance patrols, and some diving operations. A new extended listening post operation had been adopted that kept squads in position in the Rung Sat for four- and seven-day periods.

Favorable weather in November and December 1967 allowed even more emphasis to be placed on extended ambushes rather than patrols by the operational platoons. This change in tactics was dictated by the extensive amount of intelligence SEALs gathered from captured documents. Platoons rotated on a regular basis and going out on operations very quickly after arriving in country.

On December 9, 1967, Bravo Platoon arrived in Vietnam for its six-month tour at Nha Be. The platoon leader was Lieutenant (jg) Bruce Van Heertum, his assistant leader being Warrant Officer First Class David Casey. Within ten days of arriving in Vietnam, Bravo was out on its first operation, a twenty-four-hour recon patrol and ambush. The accidental discharge of a weapon caused the ambush site to be compromised and the platoon withdrew without making contact.

The second operation for Bravo Platoon was just before Christmas, on 23–24 December 1967. The warning order for the operation was issued the day before. The SEALs knew what the general mission would be, what they were expected to carry, and a time schedule for the day of the operation and the operation itself. With this information, the men would be able to prepare for the operation. The briefing just prior to the op would give them the additional specific operational details.

Intelligence for the operation was limited. The platoon

was going to patrol through an area known as T-10 in the northern end of the Rung Sat. The T-10 area was a known VC rest area and staging area for troop movements. Surrounded by swamps, the T-10 area was relatively high ground as compared to the rest of the Rung Sat, and this gave it large dry areas. The number of streams and canals surrounding the T-10 area, combined with the dense jungle growth, made patrolling it difficult, even for the SEALs. But the large number of Viet Cong that were suspected of being in the area made it a good target.

The operation itself was to be a simple one, though the T-10 area wasn't normally assigned to a platoon newly in country. The platoon would be moving through an area where no specific VC forces were known to exist. Once the patrol was completed, the SEALs would set up an ambush overlooking part of the Rach Ong Keo, a tributary of the Song Dong Tranh River. The operation was to follow a predawn helicopter insertion.

The Army insertion helicopters did not show up at the planned time, 0645 hours. Instead, the platoon had to wait until well after noon for the needed air assets to show up. The helicopters were UH-1Bs set up for troop transport. Armed with only one flexible M60 machine gun on each side for protection, the birds were known as "slicks" because their sides were clear of weapons mounts. The short, roughly twelve-kilometer flight was over quickly and the SEALs inserted by 1420 hours.

The platoon had about an 800-meter march due east of their insertion point to reach their planned ambush site. Not ordered to move in a straight line from the landing zone, however, the platoon moved out on a heading of 112 degrees, roughly east-southeast. The order of march was:

  point man
  LDNN scout
  patrol leader
  radio man
  automatic weapons man

rifleman/alternate point man
grenadier
automatic weapons man
LDNN scout
assistant patrol leader
radio man
automatic weapons man
grenadier
rear security

The automatic weapons men were in a position to protect the radio men, who stayed next in position to the two platoon officers. Since the full platoon was involved in the operation, along with two Vietnamese scouts, the patrol group was a long one and the men were stretched out along the line of march. After moving about 200 meters, the unit turned to 36 degrees, roughly north-northeast, for another leg, this one about 125 meters long. The zigzag pattern of the march was intended to patrol the ground well between the insertion point and the ambush site. The different lengths of march line would make it harder for any enemy observers to estimate where the platoon was going in case they wanted to set up an ambush.

But it was an ambush the platoon walked into. On the next change of direction in the line of march, the platoon turned to 90 degrees, due east, and the point men rotated from Scott to Antone. The patrol had barely turned and moved out when the Viet Cong opened fire.

It was 1715 hours on 23 December, and Bravo platoon had walked into a VC regimental headquarters without noticing it. The dense jungle had screened the Viet Cong positions from the SEALs. The platoon was almost surrounded by VC, who began firing into the SEALs from all sides. Frank Antone was struck and killed instantly in the first volley. Immediately behind Antone was PO3 Nhoi, a South Vietnamese LDNN (VN SEAL), who was also hit in the first volley of fire from the VC. Severely wounded, Nhoi died within ten minutes of being hit.

The platoon was under the fire of at least four VC automatic weapons. In the volley that killed Antone, the platoon leader, Van Heertum, and Scott, the alternate point man, were both hit. Two rounds struck Van Heertum in the jaw. Scott had quickly dropped to the prone position, but may not have been as flat to the ground as he would have wished. In the initial fire, he was struck in the buttocks by a projectile that was later thought to have ricocheted off something and spent much of its energy before striking.

In spite of his wounds, Van Heertum pulled the SEALs together and they established a perimeter, returning fire at the surrounding enemy. The enemy's fire came in waves, the first of which did the most damage. One of the radio men was struck in the back as he dove for cover. Lying on the ground, the SEAL felt warm liquid flowing down from his scalp and into his eyes. He figured he had been hit badly— the bullets having knocked him down—but what he had heard about a bad head wound was true: it didn't hurt. The reason the SEAL felt no pain, however, was that the enemy rounds had struck the two-quart collapsible bladder canteen he had secured above his radio. The radio man was fine, though his AN/PRC 25 radio and canteen had taken several rounds and neither one was working.

The other radio man in the platoon had not been hit, and his radio was operational. An emergency scramble call for help went out from the platoon to their arranged air support.

A Seawolf helicopter unit was on call for the SEALs, operating out of Nha Be. The helicopters were in the air and on their way to the stricken SEALs as soon as they received the radio call. Having only a relatively short distance for the Seawolf gunships to fly, they were on the scene over Bravo platoon within minutes.

But any time the SEALs spent on the ground was too much. In the third volley of incoming fire, one of the automatic weapons men, Payne, was hit in the leg and right shoulder. The SEALs were in the process of pulling back from the thicket where they had been hit to a nearby clearing where a landing zone (LZ) for the helicopters could be set up. An estimated thirty or forty VC were giving chase, firing on them almost constantly. In the first six major volleys the VC fired into the SEAL platoon, one third of the platoon had become operational casualties.

When the Seawolves arrived, they identified the SEALs on the ground and began putting their own perimeter of fire around the platoon. Rockets and 30-caliber machine-gun fire rained down on the Viet Cong all around the SEALs. The SEALs arranged their wounded and dead in the center, then established a perimeter and secured a landing zone as best they could.

Each man in the platoon was carrying a Swiss seat—a length of rope and carabiner (snap link)—as part of his basic equipment. For the first time under fire from the enemy, the SEALs put the Swiss seats on their wounded men, the least wounded handling their dead Teammates. The Army slicks came in and the first one dropped a McGuire rig to pull the casualties out quickly.

A McGuire rig involves a helicopter dropping a length of line, often with a sandbag attached to get through any trees to the ground. Loops are tied into the long rope, then put around the shoulders and under the arms of the men going into it. A Swiss seat, also used for rappeling, is placed around the thighs of the riders and the carabiner is snapped into place on a smaller loop tied into the lifting rope. The helicopter can then rise straight up, pulling the riders off the ground and out of the area without ever having to land. This system can work very fast, and it allows helicopters to be used for extractions in clearings too small for the aircraft to set down in.

In spite of the heavy enemy fire, the platoon was able to successfully lift out its casualties by McGuire rig with no further losses. Now the main body of the platoon had to get out. The landing zone was a hot one, and the SEALs couldn't stop the incoming enemy fire. The Seawolves were doing their best to keep the Viet Cong away from the beleaguered platoon, but even the accuracy of the helicopter gunships wasn't enough to risk firing too close to the platoon in the clearing.

With fire from both sides exploding around them, two Army slicks came in to the hot LZ and put down. With enemy fire still coming in on all sides, the SEALs piled on board the helicopters, the last men standing on the skids to save time. Pulling out, the birds took heavy fire. The SEALs could see all kinds of red warning lights on the instrument panel, flashing that a system had taken damage. Miraculously, The Army pilots were able to nurse their stricken craft the twelve kilometers to Nha Be, pulling Bravo platoon out of the fire.

Frank Antone had been killed in the ambush. So had one of the South Vietnamese LDNN scouts. The other SEALs recovered from their wounds. The two Army helicopters that extracted the SEALs were too shot up to repair. In spite of the enemy's overwhelming firepower and tactical advantage, the SEALs had been able to beat back an enemy force at least two or three times their number.

```
BARNDANCE # 371          COORD: YS 0285 7840
DATES: 23 DEC 67 TIMES: 1400-1800
 1. UNITS INVOLVED: BRAVO Platoon/MST-3/Seawolf/
2 slicks.
 2. TASK: 36 hour recon patrol/ambush.
 3. METHOD OF INSERTION: Helo EXTRACTION: Helo
 4. TERRAIN: Dense vegetation, some nipa/mangrove.
 5. TIDE: low at 1334H, 3.3 WEATHER: Hot/humid
 6. MOON: None
 7. ENEMY ENCOUNTERED: Base camp with 3 A/W min-
imum
 8. CASUALTIES: 1 KIA (US), 1 KIA (VN), 3 WIA
(US), VC unknown
 9. NAMES OF SEALS INVOLVED: LT (jg) Van Heertum,
WO1 Casey, CS3 Scott, RMSN McHugh, GMG3 Jewett,
SA Keith, AN Klann, ETNSN Luksik, TM1 Payne, SN
Antone, EM2 DiCroce, FN Hyatt, PO3 Nhoi (LDNN),
PO3 Hyugen (LDNN)
10.RESULTS: Patrolled 112 degrees from insertion
point for 200 meters. Turned to 036 degrees for
```

125 meters. Turned to 090 degrees and was immediately taken under fire (A/W) from front (multiple positions). Point man (Antone) and LDNN scout (Nhoi) KIA. Went into defensive perimeter, returned fire. Seawolf Army LHFT overhead within five minutes. Sustained 3 WIA (US) in subsequent A/W bursts while extracting. Six persons (KIA/WIA taken out first). Extracted by McGuire rig. Eight remaining taken out by Army slick. No weapons lost/captured.

11. REMARKS/RECOMMENDATIONS: Believe VC were defending base camp with supplies to be taken out during Christmas truce.

INCLUDE INTELLIGENCE INFORMATION GATHERED, MATERIAL FOUND, DESTROYED, CAPTURED, ETC.

Air Support:
The Seawolves, the Black Ponies, and the Huey

SEAWOLVES

Within a few months of the Brown Water Navy initiating operations in the Mekong Delta, it became obvious that the Navy required its own air support that could work with the small boats. The PBRs and Swift boats could deal with the small arms fire of VC engagement. But a dug-in VC force using heavy weapons such as B-40 antitank weapons and recoilless rifles were another matter. The new helicopter gunships the Army used would be a satisfactory answer to this problem. The gunship carried heavy weapons in the form of rockets and was not affected by the twisting, turning waterways of the delta. But the Navy had no such armed helicopters in the mid-1960s.

Army helicopter assets operated with the Navy's forces in the delta as much as they could. But the Army's resources were also committed to the vast land operations being conducted in South Vietnam at the time. Thus Army helicopters were not always being available when the Navy needed them. The Navy needed to develop a helicopter squadron of its own that could operate in the gunship role.

Navy helicopters were primarily designed for anti-submarine warfare or search-and-rescue type operations. The birds the Navy used were large and could carry out extended flights, but they did not have great maneuverability, nor could they mount the proper weapons to act in the gunship role. The Army had the Utility Helicopter, Model 1B (UH-1B "Huey") outfitted for the gunship role in Vietnam. The UH-1B had proven the effectiveness of the helicopter as both a transport and an offensive weapon. Seeing Navy's needs, the Army loaned them twenty-two UH-1B birds, each outfitted with an M16 weapons system.

A very common sight in Vietnam throughout the war, the UH-1B "Huey" was the workhorse helicopter for almost every role. Powered by a single turbine engine turning a forty-four-foot twin-blade rotor, the UH-1B had a total length of fifty-three feet. The Huey could carry a crew of four and four thousand pounds of cargo at speeds of up to 120 knots (138 mph). At a more reasonable cruising speed of 90 knots (about 104 mph), the UH-1B could carry its load for 253 miles and still have fuel reserves.

The UH-1B was crewed by four men; a pilot who flew in the left-hand seat, the copilot, a crew chief, and a gunner. In the troop-carrier version of the UH-1B, called a slick due to its smooth sides, the bird could carry eight passengers without much trouble. Even the slick version was armed with two M60 machine guns, one on each side of the bird. The crew chief and the gunner manned these weapons as the door gunners during operations.

The M16 weapons package was the first such system to see wide use in Vietnam. The M16 gun mounts were on either side of the helicopter, back at the rear section of the fuselage. The outboard mounts carried two M60C machine guns on its far end, triggered electrically and capable of being aimed by the pilot or copilot. Each M60C had room for fifteen hundred rounds of ammunition in feed trays within the helicopter; the weapons could be fired at a cyclic rate of six hundred rounds per minute per gun.

The M60Cs could be tracked inboard 11 degrees or outboard

70 degrees, an automatic safety system cutting out the guns if they pointed near the aircraft. Elevation could also be remotely adjusted from plus 11 or minus 63 degrees. A gunsight inside the pilot's cabin allowed the guns to be finely aimed, the rough aiming being taken care of by pointing the aircraft.

The big punch for the gunship came in the form of two M158C rocket pods, one on each side of the bird and hanging from the M16 gun mounts. Each rocket pod could carry seven electrically fired 2.75-inch rockets. Each rocket had folding fins that deployed when fired to give it stability and could carry a variety of warheads. The most common warheads carried on the Navy's gunships were seven- or ten-pound high explosive ones.

The rockets had an effective range of about three thousand yards, though accuracy suffered at the longer ranges. Each rocket pod would launch one rocket at a time, both pods synchronized together to maintain balance. Rockets could be fired in pairs or ripples of multiple rounds. The pilots handled firing the rockets, which required aiming the aircraft. The copilot operated the outboard machine guns aiming with the sight system. Additional weapons included M16A1s and an M79 grenade launcher. An assortment of different-colored smoke grenades were carried to mark targets on the ground.

The gunships were unlike any helicopters the Navy pilots had flown before. Eight pilots and eight crewmen volunteered from the Navy's Helicopter Combat Support Squadron One (HC-1) to man the new gunships. The new detachment arrived in Vietnam in July 1966 and began training with the 197th Army Aviation Helicopter Company. After weeks of instruction in tactics, operation, maintenance, and practice missions, the new Navy unit, HC-1 Detachment Vung Tau (for their base station), was ready for operations.

Operating with the Game Warden forces by 19 September 1966, the Navy helicopter gunships, nicknamed Rowell's Rats, worked in pairs. The helicopters proved a very valuable asset to the Game Warden forces. The Navy pilots were able to communicate well with the Brown Water forces and cooperated closely with the PBRs on several major operations. As more UH-1B gunships became available from the Army, additional HC-1 detachments were assigned to different areas of the Delta.

In the spring of 1967, the various HC-1 detachments were consolidated into a new Navy squadron. Helicopter Attack Squadron, Light Three (HAL-3) was commissioned on 1 April 1967 at its headquarters base at Vung Tau. As the first Navy squadron to be activated in a combat zone, HAL-3 was in operations within hours of its official creation.

Making the original helicopter detachments a squadron gave the unit additional men, materials, and mission responsibility. The original four detachments were increased to seven "dets" of two birds each. Two gunships made a single Light Helicopter Fire Team (LHFT), the most common formation used by HAL-3. Air crews were volunteers from the Navy fleet and squadrons and served a twelve-month tour of duty. Crews operated on a twenty-four-hour rotation. Going from noon to noon the next day, an aircrew would remain ready for immediate action if a "scramble" call came in. Crews often slept in their uniforms and gear to speed up the reaction to a mission call.

During their first Army training in August 1966, the Army helicopter instructors took to calling the Navy men Seawolves. The different detachments of HC-1 used Seawolves as their radio callsigns. With the creation of the new squadron, Seawolves was taken as their official name. The Seawolf crews soon racked up an impressive accounting for themselves. As a member of the Seawolves, a crewman could expect to fly an average of six hundred missions during his 365-day tour. That number of missions averaged out 3,500 hours in the air a year.

By the end of their first year, the Seawolves had twenty-two helicopters operational, manning seven dets throughout the Mekong Delta. Two helicopters were assigned to each det. The extra eight birds remained in reserve, rotating among the various dets as other helicopters had to be pulled off for maintenance or repair.

Seawolf Detachments as of December 1967:

Det 1—Jennings County (LST* 846)
Det 2—Nha Be
Det 3—Vinh Long
Det 4—Garrett County (LST 786)
Det 5—Harnett County (LST 821)
Det 6—Dong Tam
Det 7—Binh Thuy

*Landing Ship, Tank

There were few other units that the Navy SEALs felt they owed as great a debt to as the men and machines of the Seawolves. On many operations, the Seawolves were on call to the SEALs, ready to come in at a moment's notice. More than one SEAL unit found itself in trouble until the Seawolves came in to get them out. In situations where no other helicopters would even fly, the Seawolves showed up.

The men of HAL-3 took pride in their exhausting work. As experience grew, they undertook more operations. Flying on night missions, the Seawolf pilots would land on floating platforms built onto Landing Ships stationed in rivers. The basic missions for the Seawolves included:

1. Reaction support of naval forces under attack
2. Reaction support of other friendly forces under attack
3. Armed reconnaissance
4. Overhead cover for naval and other friendly forces
5. Escort missions, including boats, convoys, and unarmed helicopters
6. Target acquisition and adjustment for gunfire support
7. Patrols, both day and night

To accomplish their missions, the Seawolves would operate from both land and water bases. Converted landing ships were bases for both the Seawolf detachments and PBR divisions. Unlike their Army counterparts, the Navy pilots were experienced with carrier-type landings, a difficult maneuver as the helicopter and deck were often moving in different directions.

The strength of the shipborne water bases was that they could be moved to new areas of operations as required. But the size of the landing areas on board ships gave the Seawolves some limitations. The recommended UH-1B combat load for a Seawolf operating off an LST was:

> M60C Flex guns (4)—800 to 1,000 rounds per tray per gun
> 2.75 inch rockets—14 rockets with six- or ten-pound HE warheads
> M60 door guns (2)—1,000 to 1,500 rounds per gun
> M16A1 rifles (2)—200 rounds 5.56mm (10 magazines) per gun, used primarily by the pilot, copilot if the aircraft had to be abandoned
> M79 grenade launcher (1)—50 rounds of 40mm HE grenades
> M18 smoke grenades—15 of different colors
> JP-5 fuel—800 pounds (about 142 gallons)

With this load, the UH-1B could take off easily from the limited area on board a converted LST. Seawolves stationed at land bases would try to carry a bit more in the way of ammunition, weapons, and fuel. Feed trays for the flexible guns might be filled to capacity and additional munitions, like hand grenades, may be brought on board. Often, the birds went out on operations carrying such a heavy load that they couldn't lift straight off. Instead, the gunner and crew chief would run alongside a laden Seawolf as it picked up some forward speed and then jump on. The bird would bounce down on its skids and then lumber into the air.

The men of the Seawolf squadron experimented with different weapon mounts on board their birds to see what would give them an additional edge. Increasing ground fire caused crews to try replacing one of the M60 door guns with a .50 caliber machine gun on a flexible mount or a pair of .30 caliber Browning M1919A4s. The .50s gave greater range to the door gunner, but the ammunition was bulky and ammunition cans were limited in size. The twin Brownings increased the amount of fire that could be put out from the door gunner, better saturating the ground target. But the Brownings didn't have any greater range than the M60. Even 40mm Mark 18 grenade launchers were mounted in the place of a door gun on some Seawolves. The Mark 18s would cover an area with 40mm grenades, looking like a "miniature B-52 strike," according to one Seawolf gunner. But the downwash of the helicopter blades took away any accuracy the grenade launcher would have had.

Everyone operated all out while on a call on board a Seawolf. On operations where a firefight was going on, the outboard M60s might jam, limiting the bird's firepower. It was the gunner's job to lean out from the bird, whether flying along at 3,000 feet or taking heavy enemy fire, and clear the jams.

In spite of the fact that, next to its flying ability, the Seawolf's greatest defense was its firepower, the pilots and crews would sacrifice that firepower if men on the ground were in danger. On a number of occasions a SEAL unit ran into far more than it could handle and needed emergency extraction. The Seawolves were sometimes the only helicopters available. By the time a troop-carrying slick came in to get the SEALs out, it would be all over.

On one SEAL snatch mission in 1970, a small unit of SEALs and PRUs were under assault by an overwhelming VC force. The VC didn't know exactly where the SEALs were in an area of rice paddies, and the SEALs were not shooting back so as not to draw attention. Their Seawolf air support were the only helicopters the unit had to get out, but there was no place for a helicopter to set down without coming under heavy enemy fire. It was not a matter of much question to one of the Seawolf pilots.

Calling in a Black Pony team to cover the SEALs, the

Seawolf pulled away from the area and returned to base. The Seawolf crew quickly refueled and stripped the bird of her weapons and ammunition in order to lighten it. With the other Seawolf in the fire team covering the extraction, the stripped bird went down to the level of the rice paddy, hovering just above the water and behind the paddy dike wall. The SEALs could only get on the helicopter one at a time, and even then it was a bit of extreme flying for the pilot. But the SEALs were extracted without a loss.

The Seawolves later received even more helicopters and additional gun packages to upgrade their capabilities. By 1969, the M21 weapons system was being seen on Seawolves. Similar to the earlier M16 weapons system, the main difference in the M21 was a single 7.62mm Minigun replacing the twin outboard M60s on each side.

The M134 Minigun had six rotating barrels and was powered with an electric motor. The control systems setting limited the Miniguns' rate of fire to 2,400 rounds per minute, over forty rounds every second. If the guns were aimed so that one side's weapon was cut out so as not to strike the helicopter, the remaining Minigun went up to a 4,000 rounds-per-minute rate of fire. Each Minigun was fed with 3,000 rounds of ammunition in the feed boxes inside the bird. Electric circuits limited each Minigun burst to three seconds.

With their new weapons and additional aircraft, the Seawolves continued their missions throughout Southeast Asia. Some of the last missions performed by the Seawolves before their decommissioning on 26 January 1972 were support operations with the last SEAL units in country.

BLACK PONIES

The most limiting factor for the Seawolf gunships was their small numbers. Stationed around the Mekong Delta, there were missions the Seawolves could not cover and calls they couldn't answer because they were already committed to an action. In addition, the Viet Cong were becoming increasingly able to strike helicopter gunships with small arms fire.

A larger number of heavy machine guns and better fire control in VC hands could reach the Seawolves at lower altitudes and rip the birds out of the sky. The new AH-1 Cobra gunship, which was designed to withstand such fire, would have countered the problem of the heavy guns being used by the Viet Cong. But the new Cobras were available in very limited numbers and the Army had first call on all production.

To aid the Seawolves, the SEALs needed a group of fixed-wing aircraft that could carry a large weapons load, were fast, and could remain on station for long periods of time. A specialized Navy squadron was commissioned, Light Attack Squadron 4 (VAL-4), on 3 January 1969 at NAS North Island, California. The men who would make up VAL-4 completed fifteen weeks of training to get ready for their mission. Fourteen aircraft and crews to man two eight-man sections arrived in Vietnam in March 1969. By April, the new squadron was in the air from their headquarters at Binh Thuy, where they covered the Mekong Delta, and from Vung Tau, where they operated over the Rung Sat.

VAL-4 was based on using the OV-10 Bronco aircraft in a close-support role. A two-seater, propeller-driven aircraft, the Bronco had a forty-foot wingspan and a very distinctive, high, twin-boom tail section. Operating at normal speeds of between 180 and 200 knots (207 to 230 mph), the OV-10 could stay on patrol for two to three hours at a time. Where the Bronco really stood out was in the number and types of ordnance it could carry under its wings.

Four M60 machine guns were internally mounted in the Bronco's wings, each gun with 500 rounds of ammunition. With the steady platform of the aircraft and the accuracy of the M60s, the bronco could fire as close as fifty yards from friendly positions and still have a margin of safety. In underwing pods, the Broncos could carry a mix of weapons that included:

- Up to thirty-eight 2.75-inch rockets in seven- or nineteen-round pods

- A 20mm cannon pod that fired at 400 rounds per minute and had 750 rounds of high-explosive shells available
- An SUU-11/A 7.62mm Minigun pod that carried 1,500 rounds of ammunition that its weapon would fire at 6,000 rounds per minute
- Eight to sixteen 5-inch Zuni high explosive rockets in either two- or four-round pods.

The five-inch Zuni rocket was the big punch of the little aircraft. The supersonic Zuni rocket carried a forty-eight-pound high explosive warhead that would hit with the power of a five-inch naval shell. The warhead could blast apart bunkers and tunnels, shred trees and hooches, and spread fragmentation over a wide area depending on the fuse it was fitted with and the type of detonation selected. In addition to the lethal ordnance, on night ops, the Bronco carried sixteen aircraft flares that would burn for over three minutes, illuminating a wide area.

Based on the Bronco name of their aircraft, VAL-4 picked up the nickname and call sign of Black Pony. Within a very short time of their arrival in Vietnam, the Black Ponies were flying escort missions over the waterways of the Mekong Delta. The heavy punch of the small aircraft made any VC force they faced pay a heavy price. SEALs called in Black Pony strikes on enemy troop concentrations, and they engaged those troops very effectively.

During their first year of operations in country, the eight aircraft of the Black Ponies flew over 7,500 sorties. Each plane had two crews, who would rotate twenty-four hours on and twenty-four hours off. But the aircraft would spend far less time on the ground than their crews. The rugged characteristics of the OV-10 allowed the craft to keep up this punishing schedule. And the overall design allowed for quick maintenance by the ground crews to keep the planes in the air.

The Broncos were not able to maneuver as easily or quickly as the UH-1B gunships of the Seawolves. Instead of being able to fine-aim their weapons with their movable mountings like the Seawolves, the Black Ponies had to aim the whole aircraft at the target. Unusual maneuvers soon became part of the skill package of a Black Pony pilot.

Operating in pairs, the Black Ponies hunted the areas of the Rung Sat and Mekong Delta when they were not on an active mission. Reconnaissance flights were also done with a single plane. When a Black Pony spotted a target, it could hold on station and engage the target itself until reinforcements arrived. One night operation the Black Pony pilots developed was called "chumming," as in fishing for sharks. One plane would fly low over an enemy area where they expected to draw fire. The low aircraft would have its standard flying lights on, as if it were a regular flight. The other Black Pony of the pair would be flying high cover with its lights out. The noise of the bait Bronco would cover the sounds made by the higher flying plane. If the low Bronco received fire, the upper plane would dive in with its weapons firing on the enemy positions.

Like the Seawolf crews, the air crews of the Black Ponies often slept in their flight gear, the planes ready for almost immediate takeoff. Within six minutes of receiving a mission call, a two-plane team of Black Ponies would be in the air. The speed of the Black Ponies could put them anywhere in the Delta within twenty minutes. The last Navy squadron in Vietnam to stand down and return to the States was the Black Ponies of VAL-4. On 10 April, 1972, after almost exactly three years of operations, VAL-4 was officially deactivated.

The SEALs, the Brown Water Navy, and the Seawolves/ Black Ponies formed the triad of Navy Special Warfare in Vietnam. Like the common symbol of the Navy, the three-pronged Trident, the three units each covered on point. The SEALs were the center tine of the trident and covered the Land operations. On one outside tine was the Brown Water Navy covering the water and the sea. On the opposite tine was the Seawolves and Black Ponies representing the air.

Mission Six, 13–14 March 1967:
"Into the Jaws of Hell"

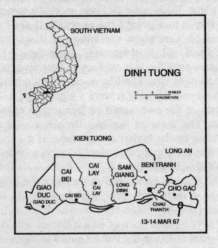

SOUTH VIETNAM

DINH TUONG

0   5   10 MILES
0   5   10 KILOMETERS

KIEN TUONG

LONG AN

CAI
BEI

CAI
LAY

SAM
GIANG

BEN TRANH

GIAO
DUC
GIAO DUC

CAI BEI

CAI
LAY

LONG
DINH

CHO GAO

CHAU
THANTH

13-14 MAR 67

In 1968, the major influence on SEAL operations, and the U.S. military as a whole, was the Tet Offensive. The Viet Cong acted throughout South Vietnam during Tet, attacking major towns and cities as regular military units. SEAL units fought house to house in some cities, moving as mobile infantry through the towns to hunt down and eliminate the VC. Though the Tet offensive was crushed and all VC-held areas recaptured, the image of the VC rising up against the U.S. military was one of the American public never recovered from.

After Tet, many SEAL operations centered on locating the remaining VC forces, preventing their resupply, and cutting their communications routes. But there were always other missions that took precedence over these operations. One of the foremost of these was the rescue of American POWs held by the Viet Cong. No American military unit would easily pass up the chance of rescuing their fellow soldiers being held by the VC. The idea of being captured and held interminably was a nightmare among many of the U.S. forces. As far as most SEALs were concerned, they had decided on their own that they would never be captured. The idea of a SEAL in VC hands, and what those captors would do to that SEAL, made most operators decide that the last grenade would be saved for personal use. It was a question to many of these men whether or not they could actually pull the pin on themselves, but the question was never answered. No SEAL was ever captured by the enemy—not in Vietnam, and not anywhere since.

But the draw of a rescue operation was tremendous. In the middle of March 1968, Seventh Platoon of SEAL Team Two was offered such a possible operation. Reports had come in that American POWs were being held by the VC in a certain area until they could be sent north. In spite of the draw of such a story, the SEALs were always careful about the intel they based their operations on.

The intelligence for this operation was cross-checked among a number of sources for confirmation. A report from the My Tho NILO would be compared to other information, including material gathered from the intelligence net the SEALs themselves developed. Any solid information on the location of American POWs was known to be time-sensitive. The Viet Cong moved prisoners constantly as a security measure. But the SEALs could react very quickly on good information.

With the information confirmed, the plan could be completed. The platoon would insert as a unit and patrol deeply into VC-held territory. The general location of the suspected POW camp was part of the intelligence package for the operation. But the camp could not be spotted from the air due to the heavy jungle canopy. The SEALs would have to search the area to locate the camp and then decide what action they could take. On the patrol, care would be taken to limit enemy contact. But given the value of a POW camp, a number of Viet Cong could be expected in the area.

The numbers of Viet Cong in general had declined. The failed Tet Offensive had devastated the Viet Cong ranks throughout the Mekong Delta and the whole of South Vietnam. Reinforcements in the form of whole units of North Vietnamese Army (NVA) regulars were moving into South Vietnam. But this information was not yet generally known, and it may not have mattered much if it was. The platoon wanted the chance to rescue American POWs, and they were willing to face heavy odds to do it.

Seventh Platoon was briefed in detail on what they were going to do. The platoon chief, a very experienced operator, gave the SEALs specific instructions on the weapons and amount of ammunition he wanted each man to carry. The operation would be a very deep patrol into VC-dominated territory. If the platoon ran into trouble, it would have to hold out until help could get to them, or fight their own way out.

The plan for the operation was a simple one, as the best plans generally are. The platoon would insert and patrol to the target area. After moving inland from the insertion point almost two miles, the platoon would break up into two squads. The squads would separate to better cover the search area. This op plan would give the platoon its greatest strength as it moved into the target area. Splitting the platoon would cover the target area faster and give the greatest chance of locating the POW camp.

The new assistant platoon leader was a young SEAL officer sent over from SEAL Team Two as a replacement for an injured man. The young officer would be on one of his first combat operations and, though he was fully qualified and trained, he still lacked practical experience. The very experienced platoon chief would go with the squad that had the young officer. This guaranteed experienced leadership for the operation.

It was going to be a long mission, possible a very important one, and certainly a very dangerous op. Everything that could be prepared ahead of time to help give the SEALs an edge had been accounted for. A Seawolf Light Helicopter Fire Team (LHFT) made up of two helicopter gunships, call-signed Seawolf 66 (Lieutenant Commander Myers) and Seawolf 69 (Lieutenant Commander Gyler), would be on thirty-minute alert for the SEALs. Within thirty minutes of receiving a call for support, the Seawolves would be on station over the SEALs. And the Seawolves would rarely need the whole thirty minutes to show up.

In addition to the Navy Seawolf gunships, Army helicopter support had also been arranged. UH-1B transport birds, slicks with only two M60s and the crew's own weapons for defense, were on call. The Army helicopters were call-signed Outlaw 66 and Outlaw 26. For the extraction, the SEALs would establish a landing zone and call on the slicks to pick them up. The plan was for the entire operation to be completed in one night, both the insertion and extraction done under the cover of darkness.

For the initial transportation on the river, the SEALs' Mobile Support Team (MST) would be crewing the Mike boat. The Mike boat would carry the SEALs to their target area with a STAB in tow. The SEALs would use the STAB for the actual insertion, and then return it to the Mike boat. Once the STAB had been secured, the Mike boat would withdraw a short distance and remain on-station in the area. The SEALs would receive fire support from the Mike boat with its 81mm M2 mortar and its 3,987-yard maximum range as needed.

Emergency arrangements had been made and established SOPs were already in place to cover most contingencies. If radio communications with any air support was lost, the SEALs could announce that with a certain colored flare. A different colored flare would tell any support just where the SEALs were on the ground. Procedures like this were standard and had been trained for back in the United States. The men of the Seventh Platoon had been operating together in combat for months. They knew all the procedures and, more importantly, knew and trusted each other completely. These SEALs knew how their platoon Teammates reacted, which way they would jump in what situation. They knew how each other smelled in the dark. Whole operations could be, and had been, conducted without any of the men uttering a single word. Hand signals and experience had proved to be enough. It was this closeness, the platoon or squad being of almost one mind, that was the SEALs' greatest strength. Even the addition of extra personnel for the operation, in the form of two South Vietnamese LDNNs (Vietnamese SEALs) and two members of the Army Ninth Division's Long Range Reconnaissance Patrol (LRRP) company didn't lessen the platoon's strength. The LRRPs were competent, and the Vietnamese LDNNs would be able to aid in interpreting the locals. This was a hard op, and the help would spread out the strain.

Preparations were made for what would be an all-night operation. The SEALs would be carrying a heavy load of ammunition. In some cases, individuals were carrying almost twice as much ammunition as they normally would.

Moving out from My Tho the afternoon of March 13, the SEALs traveled downriver some thirty-five miles to the target area. Changing to the STAB, the platoon inserted off the north branch of the Me Tho River, where it splits to go around Cu Lao Loi Quan Island near the South China Sea. The insertion took place at 2200 hours, early enough in the evening to give the platoon all night to conduct their operation. Establishing a perimeter in the brush at the insertion site, the SEALs waited to see if their arrival had received any unwanted attention. The insertion had attracted attention, but not exactly what the platoon expected.

The Mike boat had one major difficulty that couldn't be changed—it was slow. The long trip from My Tho gave the SEALs a great deal of time to think, though most of them were experienced enough that concern about the operation was not foremost in their minds. The platoon chief had done his job and was waiting for the real mission to begin. Combat didn't hold a lot of fear for the experienced chief, so he did what generations of fighting men had done before him. With a break in the action, the chief fell asleep.

In the darkness at the target location, no one noticed the

platoon chief asleep in the Mike boat. Little noise was made as the STAB left the Mike boat or when the men made the insertion itself. The SEALs had set up their perimeter and the platoon was waiting when the STAB made a second insertion. A seriously pissed-off, quietly fuming platoon chief arrived on the scene.

Now that the platoon was complete, they could move out on the mission. Following their plan of march, the SEALs moved north by northeast. Traveling as silently as they could, the platoon avoided all possible contact. The men suspected that Charlie (the Viet Cong) were all around them. And the march was uncomfortable, not only because of the heavy loads the men were carrying, but also because each step took the SEALs further and further away from the water.

SEALs and the Frogmen in general always felt safest in or near the water. What was an obstacle to other forces was a place to hide and a familiar environment to the men of the Teams. For this mission, the operational area was far from the water. Even the rice paddies were dry this time of year.

The platoon continued to patrol, avoiding hooches and moving slowly. Without incident, the platoon reached its separation point at coordinates XS 703 417, three thousand meters inland from where they had first left the river. They had now reached the treeline of the jungle, which was hiding the suspected POW camp. Alfa Squad moved off to the Northeast, Bravo Squad to the Northwest. It was about 0115 hours the morning of March 14.

Moving along the patrol line, the SEALs were covering only a few meters at a time. The strain of the patrol sapped even the SEALs' stamina and strength. It was their constant physical activity and workouts that allowed the men to continue on the grueling mission while remaining alert. Alfa Squad had covered less than a kilometer by 0200 hours. The three-quarters moon was well up and illuminated the jungle and rice paddies around them. The squad had been passing coconut groves, banana orchards, and other constant signs of the Vietnamese. The squad was almost to the objective area when they spotted two VC.

The platoon leader, Lieutenant Pete Peterson, took out both VC silently. One received a quick shot from the silenced 9mm Smith & Wesson Model 39, a SEAL "Hush Puppy," that Peterson carried. With no time for a second shot before the other VC could make a noise, the lieutenant struck the man down and silenced him in a fast hand-to-hand combat maneuver. In later reports, the SEALs would find that the two VC had been a doctor and a corpsman.

Alfa Squad continued, hoping no one in the jungle around them had heard the slight noise of the struggle with the two VC. As they approached an opening in the jungle made by a coconut grove, they began to hear sounds off to their right (east). To the left (west) of Alfa Squad was Bravo Squad and silence, but to their right, they could now hear voices.

It soon became clear that, between 500 meters and a kilometer away, Viet Cong were calling to each other. It was obvious to the men that the mission was compromised. The VC were searching for them, occasionally firing, hoping for a response from the SEALs. It was time to try and escape the trap.

The platoon leader decided to move north to try and reach an open area. Once they had an area secured, the squad would call in their extraction helicopters. It was no longer practical to continue searching for the POWs. It was now obvious that there were a lot more Viet Cong active in the target area than the SEALs had first thought.

The SEALs moved more quickly, but still maintained as much silence as possible. As the Viet Cong moved closer, Alfa Squad reached the edge of the jungle, where it opened out onto rice paddies. In the center of the group of rice paddies was a grove of trees that the squad could use for cover. The open rice paddies would give a clear landing zone for an incoming slick and expose any VC trying to approach the tree grove to the SEALs' fire. The rice paddies, however, were in the middle of an area of hooches and VC bunkers that the SEALs could see all around them. Movement told the SEALs that some of the hooches were occupied. When fire came out of some of the buildings, there was little question that those same people were VC.

The squad made it to the relative cover of the tree grove without taking any hits. Now the situation around them was heating up fast. About fifty VC had been pursuing the squad, though they hadn't known exactly where the SEALs were. But the men had been spotted crossing the open rice paddies, and their location was quickly becoming popular knowledge.

Once they reached the grove, the squad instantly set up a defensive perimeter to cover all avenues of approach. The time for silence was long past and the men began firing on any target that showed itself. The platoon leader was on the radio calling in the Seawolves and the Army slicks. While the Seawolves would make firing runs on the surrounding area, the slick could come in and pick up the squad, hopefully before they were overrun.

Until the Seawolves came in and suppressed the enemy fire, there was no way for a helicopter to land or otherwise pick the SEALs up without getting shot down. Surrounded the way they were, it would be next to impossible for the squad to break contact and make their way back to the river. Radio procedure had become short and messages from the platoon leader became blunt. "Get down here and get us the hell out of here!"

As twenty or more VC approached from the east, the SEALs kept up their steady firing. Targets weren't a problem, but the ammunition load that had felt heavy just a few hours earlier was getting uncomfortably light. The SEALs used the firepower they had to the maximum effect in suppressing the enemy. Even in this critical situation, they maintained their discipline. They directed their fire on targets and not in a "spray and pray" fan that wasted ammunition. The XM148 and M79 40mm grenade launchers in the squad were putting rounds directly into the surrounding hooches, many of which turned out to be barracks structures with a number of VC inside.

The call for extraction and helicopter gunship support had gone out from Alfa Squad at about 0300 hours. The Seawolves arrived quickly. As his ammunition ran low, the platoon leader directed the Seawolves in airstrikes against the surrounding VC. Finally, at 0300 hours, after a very tense half-hour of fighting, a slick was able to come in and get the SEALs out. With the Seawolves maintaining their curtain of fire, the SEALs were able to board the extraction bird without any losses.

The situation for Alfa Squad had been a bad one and could have been much worse. But the story from Bravo Squad was not such a good one.

The two squads had separated according to plan, moving diagonally away from each other. The distance separating them was slight, only three hundred meters or so. But in the dense jungle, that can be a very long way. Moving very slowly along the treeline, the squad kept finding small emplacements, individual firing position or "spider pits" in the underbrush. Positions like that were used by the Viet Cong to keep watch over an open area, like the rice paddies and groves behind the SEALs.

At about 0300, Bravo Squad heard gunfire coming from the direction of their fellow SEALs in Alfa. Speaking to the other squad over the radio, Bravo discovered that the unit had been compromised. The original mission was officially over. Bravo Squad was to move out to their planned extraction point and call in a slick.

The squad passed more dry rice paddies and then entered thickening brush. Crossing a small canal and going up the opposite bank, the SEALs spotted a large hooch. The building was larger than any of its type the SEALs had seen before (the size of a single-story U.S. military barracks). The bamboo structure was ten by fifteen meters in area. To the side of the large hooch was another building, this one much more the size of a normal Vietnamese rural structure. In the light of the moon, the SEALs could see trails and paths crossing each other all through the area and between the buildings.

Spreading out quickly into a skirmish line, the squad faced the buildings. Each SEAL on watch had a field of fire; all of them together overlapped and covered the area. Three of the men in the squad—the assistant platoon leader, platoon chief, and VN interpreter—decided to enter the main building. It was just possible they had found what they had been looking for—a small POW camp hidden under the triple canopy of the jungle trees. What they found inside was anything but the POW camp they were hoping to find.

Pushing the door to the hooch open carefully, the officer and chief saw beds lining the walls. With his rifle slung, his pistol in one hand and a red-lensed flashlight in the other, the young officer entered the hooch. Four beds were in the room, each covered with a mosquito netting bar to protect the occupants. The Viet Cong would never treat their prisoners so well, so this wasn't the POW camp the SEALs had been searching for. The AK-47 rifles leaning against the walls eliminated any lingering doubt. Bravo Squad had found a VC barracks, and the VC were still sleeping inside.

Each of the four beds had two VC in them, and the platoon chief spotted even more beds in the back portion of the barracks. What was in the second structure the squad never learned. The SEALs opened fire on the VC, hoping to take them all out before anyone woke up. With the officer firing his pistol, and the chief opening up with his M16, the SEALs eliminated most of the VC within the first few moments of fired—most, but not all.

The sound of their firing woke a woman sleeping in the smaller building. Showing great presence of mind for being wakened so suddenly, but little compassion for her fellow Viet Cong, the woman ran from her hooch to the larger barracks. Reaching the barracks, the woman threw an M26 fragmentation grenade into the structure.

The only warning the SEALs and interpreter in the building had was the flash of the explosion and the sound of the blast. All of the SEALs in the building were hit. The officer was peppered across his back left leg and foot with fragmentation. The worst wound was his left foot, where metal had penetrated his ankle. The platoon chief was also badly hit with fragmentation up and down his right side. The interpreter was hit the worst, blown under a bed by the force of the grenade's blast.

Some fragmentation easily passed through the thin hooch

walls and struck some of the SEALs outside the hooch. None of the outside SEALs were hit as badly as the men who had been inside the hooch. One of the injured SEALs on watch, hearing a call of warning from inside of the hooch and spotting the fleeing woman, cut her down with a single burst.

Of the six SEALs in the squad, four had been hit by the grenade, two seriously. The worst injured was the Vietnamese interpreter, who couldn't move at all. The SEAL officer was badly dazed. Staggering out of the building, the young officer passed out, slipped over the bank, and fell into the canal. The shock of the water woke the young man, who, momentarily confused by the blast thrashed around in the water.

In one of those odd jokes of fate, the injured SEAL who was nearest the young officer had been his instructor in Underwater Demolition Team Replacement Training. Besides being injured and dazed, the young officer was now faced with a snarling SEAL of whom he had been in awe not a long time earlier. Concerned for the noise, though later he couldn't explain why after an explosion and gunfire, the ex-instructor shouted for the officer to quit making noise.

Subdued and coming to himself, the officer told the SEAL that he was hit in the foot. The same instructor who had pushed the young officer into the water and the mud back at Little Creek, Virginia, now pulled his injured Teammate from the canal. Standing up, the officer promptly fell back down from the severe pain in his foot. Another of the less injured SEALs came over to assist the young officer. Using his weapon as a crutch, the officer found he could stand, but only barely.

Seeing that his officer was in good hands, the ex-instructor moved to the hooch, where the chief was calling his name. In the hooch, both the chief and the interpreter had been blown under beds by the explosion. Staggering up, the chief suddenly found himself in a hand-to-hand fight with one of the VC. Even badly injured, the SEAL chief made short work of the VC. Bodies of VC were lying about either stunned, wounded, or dead. What was certain was that after the ex-instructor had passed each VC, it was a body and not a wounded enemy lying behind him.

The chief told the SEAL to get the interpreter from where he was lying under the bed. Tossing the bed out of the way, the ex-instructor, who was large even for a SEAL, picked up the interpreter from where he lay on the floor in a puddle of blood. The squad was recovering quickly and getting organized. In spite of his wounds, the platoon chief led the men, making sure everyone was accounted for. The injured officer was able to move, but turned over command to the experienced chief. The situation was a very serious one. The squad was hurt and the Viet Cong had been alerted throughout the area. The SEALs had already been fighting about twenty VC from the barracks, but a lot more were moving about in the jungle around them, firing their weapons and searching for the SEALs.

They contacted Alfa Squad and told them that three men had been seriously wounded. The other two SEALs who had been hit didn't even consider their wounds worth noting, seeing how badly their Teammates were hit. It was then that the chief learned that the Seawolves had been called and the slick would soon be in the area. Now was the time to get out of the area as quickly as possible. The VN interpreter was so badly hurt, he couldn't move on his own. The SEAL who had picked him up just cradled the man in his arms. The interpreter had been hit all over so badly that the SEAL couldn't put him over one shoulder to free up an arm for his weapon.

Leaving over a dozen enemy bodies behind them, the squad moved out, heading south toward the river and looking for a landing zone. In spite of their wounds, the SEALs moved through the underbrush as quietly as possible. The Viet Cong were searching all around them and the men would be wiped out if caught in the open. A trail in the direction the squad wanted to travel made their speed a little better, but the men still had to keep a close eye out and avoid enemy contact. Throughout the area, the SEALs spotted hidden bunkers with cleared fields of fire covering approaches. The area was heavily saturated with VC, many more than the platoon ever expected.

The SEALs moved quickly over 1,200 meters toward the

river, the less injured men helping the more seriously hurt and every man who could keeping one arm free to handle a weapon. In spite of his own injuries, one SEAL continued to cradle the interpreter in his arms, there being no other way to carry the wounded man without his crying out in pain. The enemy was firing all around the squad, but the gunshots were sporadic and none seemed to be directed at the SEALs. Coming out of the jungle, the SEALs found themselves overlooking a collection of rice paddies and a single-family hooch sitting in the middle of the open fields.

One of the uninjured SEALs, who had been acting as the point man, went up and secured the hooch. As the rest of the SEALs came up to the modest building, the Vietnamese family inside it wondered if they were all about to be killed. Two children, frightened by the bloody, green-colored men who appeared out of the dark like a nightmare, ran out and slipped away before they could be stopped. The SEALs could have fired on the children, but could not bring themselves to do it. Besides, any gunfire would have told the VC where the squad was. Of course, it would be just a matter of time until the children ran into some VC in the jungle and the SEALs were found out anyway.

In the hooch, there was time for some of the less injured SEALs to see to the more injured ones. While the ex-instructor patched up the young officer and the interpreter, another problem arose. The radio had stopped working. One of the SEALs figured the radio had stopped a bullet and continued trying to aid the injured as best he could. With a fresh battery, along with some prayers and curses, the radio came back on line. Contact was made with the Mike boat and the location of the squad was relayed to the incoming helicopters. Unfortunately, it didn't look like the helicopters had a great deal of time.

In the moonlit night outside the hooch, between the stacks of rice straw, the SEALs saw movement in the tree lines—a lot of movement. To one SEAL's eye, dozens of VC were milling about. They hadn't started concentrating on the hooch at the center of the rice paddies, but they did appear to be circling the area. With the VC all around them, the SEALs would be cut off no matter which way they went. The helicopters were their only real hope for survival.

Now in contact with the Seawolf gunships directly, the platoon chief called the birds in to range. Not a shot was fired by the SEALs, since almost any kind of signal to the helicopters would have betrayed the squad's location to the VC. And the Viet Cong were getting closer. At a treeline only twenty meters away, one SEAL could see enemy movement clearly. The situation was getting more than a little tense.

The Seawolves were covering both squads. One of the extraction slicks was going to pick up Alfa Squad while the other would get Bravo. By this time, the VC were starting to fire their weapons more often, and in a much more organized fashion. As the slick neared the hooch, the landing zone started to see fire. To the SEALs' dismay, the Army bird refused to come down into the hot LZ.

The Seawolves told the Army slick that they would provide covering fire, suppressing the Viet Cong while it picked up the SEALs. The Army pilot said he was under orders not to risk his bird in a hot LZ. The situation was unbelievable to the SEALs on the ground. And the Seawolf pilots weren't too pleased with the situation themselves. Over the radio, one Seawolf called down that he would fire as much of his ordnance as possible to lighten his ship, land, and pick up the worst of the SEALs wounded. This would mean the balance of the squad would have to try and get to the river, over a mile away.

While this conversation was going on, the SEALs prepared for a firefight. At the windows and openings to the hooch, the men were laying out magazines of ammunition and grenades for a quick reload. Not a shot had been fired by the SEALs since the battle at the barracks. But it looked like they would soon be doing a lot of firing. The uninjured and least injured SEALs would put down a heavy covering fire while the more seriously wounded made their way to the pickup bird when it finally came down.

But now the Army slick agree to come in. The fact that

one of the Seawolves reportedly threatened to shoot the Army bird down itself may have helped the pilot decide to break his standing orders. At this point, the plan was very simple and quick. The Seawolves would make a count of fifteen at the end of the radio conversation. During the count, the gunships would begin their run down to the hooch, arriving as low as they felt they could safely get. At the end of the count, a SEAL would throw a burning Mark 13 flare from the hooch into the paddy to mark their position for the slick.

With the throwing of the flare, the SEALs' location would be immediately known to the Viet Cong. The red flare would be the signal for the Seawolves to open up on the surrounding treeline with everything they had available. There was nothing else to do; the count was running and the gunships were on their way in.

When the SEAL threw the flare out into the paddy, it was like the sky had suddenly caught fire above the hooch. The Seawolves were so low that the exhaust from the 2.75-inch rockets blew the thatch roof off the hooch. Rockets roared into the treelines as over half a dozen machine guns opened up in long ripping bursts. The SEALs were firing with everything available as the Army slick came down on the flare. Grabbing up the interpreter, the ex-instructor sprinted to the helicopter and literally threw the wounded man inside. Other wounded SEALs moved quickly to the extraction bird while their Teammates put out fire to cover them.

A big SEAL grabbed up the badly wounded chief and threw him into the bird. The SEAL was a little excited and so could be excused for throwing the man into the bird and right out the other side. Running to the other side of the helicopter, the SEAL quickly picked up the stunned chief and got him back inside the slick. Up between the pilots was the young officer, not in the best of shape but still holding his own. As more SEALs scrambled into the slick, the pilot started lifting off.

The VC were now firing full-bore at the helicopter and the SEALs they had been chasing. Two SEALs were still on the ground, firing at the VC with their Stoners. The helicopter didn't get a foot into the air before the officer and the large SEAL were both screaming at the pilot that there were still men on the ground. Settling back down, the helicopter picked up the remaining SEALs, who continued to fire at the enemy as they stood on the skids of the bird. Now the helicopter was seriously overloaded and the engine strained to lift the bird into the air. The young SEAL officer could see the maximum RPM light on the control panel of the helicopter flashing a warning as the engine whined to its limit. Finally, the slick beat its way into the air, gaining altitude as it started to move forward. Seventh Platoon had been extracted.

As the helicopter gained altitude, all of the VC on the ground opened up on their escaping quarry. The Seawolves had expended most of their ordnance in covering the two squads, but there was still some fire available to them. With Alfa and Bravo squads safely out of the way, one of the Seawolves acted as an artillery spotter and called in fire on the massed Viet Cong from the Mike boat still on station in the river. Fifteen rounds of 81mm high-explosive mortar shells came down on the Viet Cong. This was in addition to the over 10,000 rounds of 7.62mm machine gun ammunition the Seawolves had sent into the area.

The Army slick flew directly to the hospital facility at Dong Tam. Meanwhile, air strikes and artillery fire were called in on the coordinates the SEALs reported, devastating the VC still in the area. An Army company was later led into the area by the platoon Leader from Seventh. There were over two hundred bunkers found hidden throughout the area. No POWs were ever found, and no camp was located. But according to later intelligence reports, an estimated 550 to 600 Viet Cong, at least an entire battalion, had been routed from the area by the SEALs.

The actions of the men of Bravo Squad and Seventh Platoon did not go unnoticed. The Navy Cross, the second highest award in the service for valor, was awarded to the Seventh Platoon chief, Robert Gallagher. Michael Boynton, the SEAL who had carried the wounded interpreter over a kilometer in his arms, ignoring his own wounds, received the third highest award for valor, the Silver Star. Other members of the squad and platoon received the Bronze Star for their actions that night. The action from that night, March 13, was also specifically mentioned in the award of a Presidential Unit Citation received by SEAL Team Two in 1969.

All of the SEALs recovered from their wounds. The platoon chief, now Senior Chief Gallagher, returned to Vietnam for another tour of duty, even though the doctors had first thought he may never walk again. The Vietnamese interpreter also recovered to later continue operating with the SEALs.

```
BARDANCE #7-66 COORD: XS 692 388
DATES: 13-14 Mar 68   TIMES: 2200-0330
 1. UNITS INVOLVED: SEAL 7th Plt, Seawolf 66/69,
Outlaw 66/26, 2 USA 9th Div LRRP
 2. TASK: Recon area for POW camp
 3. METHOD OF INSERTION: Stab EXTRACTION: Helo
 4. TERRAIN: Rice field, jungle
 5. TIDE: Out WEATHER: Clear
 6. MOON: Three/quarters
 7. ENEMY ENCOUNTERED: At least 1, possibly 2 VC
Battalions
 8. CASUALTIES: Four USA WIA, 1 VN Interp WIA, 17
VC KIA (BC), 10 VC KIA (Prob)
 9. NAMES OF SEALS INVOLVED: (Sqd 7A) Lt Peter-
son, HMC Riojas, ADJ1 Jessie, SK1 Burbank, RM2
Rowell, EM3 Constance, FN Keener, 2 VN LDNN, 2 US
9th Div LRRPs (Sqd 7B) Lt (jg) Yeaw, ICC Gal-
lagher, AO2 Boynton, AE2 Ashton, PT2 Tuure, CS2
Matthews, Ming (Vn Interpreter)
10. RESULTS: Area heavily bunkered with fields of
fire on all avenues of approach. Many barracks
type structures in area.
11. REMARKS/RECOMMENDATIONS: Radios should be
checked with support boats periodically as dis-
tance from beach increases INCLUDE INTELLIGENCE
INFORMATION GATHERED, MATERIAL FOUND, DESTROYED,
CAPTURED, ETC.
```

COUNTER-GUERRILLA: OVERT AND COVERT OPS

Though the SEALs combat operations in the Delta and Rung Sat were conducted under a veil of secrecy during much of the Vietnam War, this was done for security considerations. It was open, overt warfare, but done in a low-visibility way.

The SEALs manner of operating in the field in small groups needed the element of surprise to be most effective. When ambushed themselves, the men of the Teams could be killed just as any other soldier in the field—it just usually took a lot more of the enemy to accomplish that feat.

But the SEALs did do a number of completely covert operations. Some missions were designed to give no provable sign of direct U.S. involvement, either from documentations, weapons, equipment, or captured and dead personnel. Most of these "black ops" remain secret to this day, and are likely to continue to be so for the foreseeable future.

But there was one major involvement of the SEALs in a covert operation that has become public knowledge. Though their involvement has not been fully described, and even parts of the major program are still not completely disclosed, almost one hundred SEALs served directly as part of the Phoenix Program during the Vietnam War.

Det Bravo and Det Alpha:
The Phoenix Program and the PRU Advisors

The SEALs manned a number of other detachments in Vietnam besides Det Golf with SEAL Team One and Det Alfa with SEAL Team Two, though those two commitments were the largest of the war for the Teams. Other detachments included Det Echo and Det Bravo. Det Echo was one of the oldest SEAL detachments in Vietnam, tracing its roots back to the first SEAL Mobile Training Teams (MTTs) sent to Vietnam in 1962. The SEALs of Det Echo were trainers and advisors for the LDNNs (Lien Doc Nguoi Nhia, or "soldiers who fight under the sea"), the South Vietnamese equivalent of the SEALs.

Det Bravo was probably one of the least known SEAL detachments, certainly one of the most secret of the Vietnam War. Few records were kept of Det Bravo in the standard yearly command histories for the SEAL Teams as the security classification of the unit was higher than that of the histories. What Det Bravo did was supply SEAL advisors to the PRU program, the action arm of the CIA-run Phoenix Program.

The Provincial Reconnaissance Units (PRUs) were paramilitary or militia-like organizations, each assigned to a particular province and Vietnamese province chief for operations. The PRUs could not operate in a province without the province chief's approval, but the chiefs did not direct operations as a whole. PRUs were made up largely of Vietnamese but also contained a good number of Humong (montagnards) from the mountains, Cambodian expatriates, and even some deserters from the South Vietnamese Army (ARVN). Probably the most unusual personnel in the PRUs were Viet Cong and even North Vietnamese deserters who had come in through the Chieu Hoi program.

The Chieu Hoi ("Open Arms") program had been instituted in 1963 at U.S. direction. In the program, Viet Cong (and later NVA) could turn themselves in and receive amnesty from the South Vietnamese government. Any enemy soldier who "Chieu Hoied" became a Hoi Chan (rallier) and would receive repatriation to his home and freedom as he gave up the fight. Between 1963 and 1973, almost 160,000 VC and NVA entered the Chieu Hoi program. Almost thirty thousand of that number were reported to be Viet Cong Infrastructure (VCI).

The PRUs' primary target were the members of the VCI. These were the higher level leaders in a province or other area who directed the guerrilla operations of the Viet Cong. The VC had proven themselves a resourceful enemy. The VC soldier would simply blend into the people of the countryside and city. He couldn't be told from the general population until involved in an operation and found with a weapon in his hand.

The average VC soldier was a Vietnamese male who followed the Communist ideology of the north. Many VC, however, weren't even Communists but simply South Vietnamese who had been press-ganged or otherwise forced to enlist in the VC ranks. These men might just be given a directive such as to plant a mine, dig a punji pit, or fire so many rounds at the U.S. and Vietnamese forces per night. Eliminating these rank-and-file men damaged the VC, but not to as great an extent as was desired.

The VCI, on the other hand, were the directors, suppliers, and planners of the Viet Cong. Their ranks included tax collectors, supply officers, political cadre, and local military officials. Eliminating these people had the same effect as cutting the head off a snake—the body might twist and turn, but it could take no action. Attacking the VCI was the most effective way of eliminating the VC as a cohesive force in South Vietnam. In addition, neutralization of the VCI was the best way of protecting the people of South Vietnam from the predations of the VC.

Protection of the general population of South Vietnam had been the priority of the U.S. ambassador to Vietnam, Henry Cabot Lodge, since at least 1966. Very knowledgeable of the situation in Vietnam, Ambassador Lodge had stated at that time: "Getting at the VCI is the heart of the matter." Lodge knew the intelligence community in Vietnam, both U.S. and Vietnamese, and he wanted action taken.

The intelligence community had been fractured into as many as seventeen services during the early part of the 1960s. A reorganization of the services was begun in 1966 with the establishment of the Intelligence Coordination and Exploitation program (ICEX). Officially established on 9 July 1967, the basic structure for the organization had been in place for a year. Run as a joint operation by the Military Assistance Command—Vietnam/Central Intelligence Agency (MAC-V/CIA)—ICEX was the direct forerunner of the Phoenix Program. Quarreling intelligence and police agencies now had to put aside their rivalries and cooperate under the new organization.

Groups of native Vietnamese conducted field actions for ICEX, operating in the same areas where they had been raised, worked, or lived. These men were very familiar with the countryside, people, language, and customs of their areas. U.S. Army Special Forces or the SEAL Teams gave these men military training. Once trained, the Vietnamese were assigned to a unit, and that unit became a PRU. The PRUs would operate along with the Vietnamese National Police and regular police field units against the Viet Cong. Payment, supplies, and support for the PRUs came from the CIA though ICEX.

The original men of the PRUs were fighting for their families and homes. Later, mercenaries were brought in to enlarge the PRUs. It was through these mercenaries, hired by the CIA, that the Humong, Cambodians, Chinese, and others came into the PRUs. Every PRU was under the direction of a U.S. advisor, usually a Special Forces soldier or SEAL, but the advisor could also be a Force Recon Marine or other competent individual assigned the task by MAC-V.

By mid-1966, SEAL Team One had assigned two officers and twelve enlisted men to Detachment Bravo. The SEALs were under the direction of MAC-V and were to operate as PRU advisors in the III and IV Corps areas. IV Corps, or Military Region IV, were the sixteen provinces south of Saigon that made up the Mekong Delta region of South Vietnam. III Corps were the eleven provinces that surrounded Saigon (the Saigon municipality) and extended to the north. The Rung Sat was part of Gia Dinh province, referred to separately as the Capital Special Zone.

A five-week program was set up back at SEAL Team One to give the Det Bravo SEALs specialized training. The SEALs learned how to set up an intelligence net, direct and instruct native troops, maintain the proper records (PRU advisors were also the unit's paymasters), and other details pertinent to running a PRU. Eventually, SEAL students ran simulated PRU ops in the secure Cuyamaca Mountains training area. The SEALs who entered the program from SEAL Team Two thought this particular part of the training was odd. Much of the mountainous training area was covered by snow for part of the year and snow was not the common weather situation in Southeast Asia.

The first SEALs in Det Bravo were quickly spread out among the IV Corps provinces. Soon after the program began, SEALs were leading PRUs in twelve of the sixteen delta provinces. Each PRU advisor pulled a six-month tour of duty and then rotated back to his original post. Some advisors emphasized a body count and the capture of weapons over other operational aspects of the PRUs. With the bounty that was paid to the PRUs by the CIA for weapons or dead VC, it was difficult for SEAL advisors to get the PRUs to concentrate more on intelligence gathering.

Since part of the PRU and ICEX mission was the gathering of intelligence, the SEAL advisors greatly preferred capturing VC and suspected VCI members rather than simply killing them. Once the SEALs had convinced their PRUs that they would get more information from a live prisoner than his corpse, and that they would still get paid, the direction of the operations changed.

With the change in emphasis came a rise in success. As their own intelligence nets developed, the SEAL/PRU teams could plan better operations against targeted VCI. Now the PRUs were capturing VCI members from their own huts and villages, pulling them out before their bodyguards could put up an effective defense. The ambush and the body snatch became two very common PRU operations, especially under their SEAL advisors.

In addition to ambushes and prisoner snatches that broke down the VCI command structure, the actions of the PRUs and SEALs also increased VC defections to the Hoi Chan program. As ex-VC began operating with the PRUs, they in turn were able to convince their ex-compatriots still in the Viet Cong to come over. The PRUs under their SEAL advisors were neutralizing eight hundred VCI members each month by 1968.

These numbers were good, but they shrank when compared to the size of the problem. When ICEX was initiated, one of the high-ranking individuals in MAC-V estimated that 60 percent of the South Vietnamese countryside was under the control of the Viet Cong. By 1968, it was estimated that there were between 65,000 and 85,000 VCI members or sympathizers in South Vietnam. These numbers did not include all of the rank-and-file members of the Viet Cong.

The hard-won intelligence gathered as part of these operations still wasn't getting fully processed and disseminated to the organizations that could best use it. The upper echelons of various U.S. and Vietnamese intelligence agencies were not sharing intelligence as they should. Information that was in bits and pieces was not being compared properly with other bits and pieces that might result in a more complete picture. Further coordination between intelligence agencies and the fact gatherers in the field were proposed by December 1967, but this idea was not acted on immediately.

In late January 1968, the lack of a complete intelligence picture of VC operations in South Vietnam became obvious. On January 31, 1968, the coordinated attacks of Viet Cong against the cities and town of South Vietnam began. The all-out VC attack quickly became known as the Tet Offensive as it began on Tet, the holiday of the lunar new year.

The fact that the Tet Offensive completely surprised the intelligence community was a mistake that could not be allowed to happen again. Even though the Tet Offensive turned out to be a disaster for the Viet Cong, it was a media and disinformation coup for the North Vietnamese government. The U.S. population sitting at home in front of their television sets saw Viet Cong attacking the U.S. Embassy in Saigon. Though the U.S. government had been making military inroads against the Viet Cong, and had told the public so, the appearance was that we were losing the war.

The president of South Vietnam, Nguyen Van Thieu, used the surprise of the Tet Offensive to push forward his new program. The program was to be an even more coordinated intelligence network, under the control of the South Vietnamese government. The new program was named after a mythical bird in Vietnamese legend, the Phuang Hoang, a Phoenix in Western mythology. The Phoenix Program was planned with the input of a number of U.S. officials, including the U.S. Ambassador Robert W. Komer and William Colby, who would later be the director of the CIA.

The Phoenix Program did not greatly change the way the earlier ICEX program had operated in the field. The PRUs were still operating with U.S. advisors and were paid and supplied by the CIA. But the intelligence gathered from the field operations of the PRUs in the rural areas and the National Police and the Police Field Force in the cities and towns could now be processed more efficiently.

Though the creation of a new bureaucracy—this one in the intelligence community—is not normally considered a path to greater efficiency, the Phoenix Program proved otherwise. Now intelligence gathered by the action arm was processed by joint U.S. and South Vietnamese teams. Each province now would have a Province Intelligence Coordination Center (PIOCC) that would initially analyze material and then move it on. Intelligence that could be used by the SEALs, PRUs, or other units would be sent to them as it became available. Otherwise, the findings of the PIOCC were sent on to the District Intelligence Operations Coordination Center (DIOCC). The DIOCC would gather intelligence from a number of provinces and further analyze the greater picture. Material would then be sent on to headquarters in Saigon.

For the SEAL advisors and the PRUs in the field, little had changed operationally. In the Mekong Delta, the PRUs continued to increase their effectiveness under the direction of the SEAL advisors. Hoi Chans joined the PRUs in greater numbers. Though in most cases not fully trusted for some time, the Hoi Chans came into the PRUs in part for the good pay and sometimes to get back at the VC or North Vietnamese government they felt had betrayed them. They were great assets as they knew the VC methods of operation and sometimes even the passwords and countersigns for a given area. For whatever reason they came over, Hoi Chans proved to be the single largest producer of intelligence for the Phoenix Program, and the material was often of high quality.

As the results of their operations increased in quality and volume, SEAL assignment to Det Bravo and the PRUs increased. The twelve original PRU advisors billets available had been filled by eight SEALs from SEAL Team One and four SEALs from SEAL Team Two. On 4 October 1968, the SEAL commitment to the PRU program was increased to three officers and twenty-one enlisted men. Again, about one third of the men assigned PRU billets came from SEAL Team Two. By the end of 1968, almost all of the IV Corps PRU advisors were SEALs. These SEALs were operators who did more than just advise their PRUs and make out the pay records. The average SEAL PRU advisor went out with his PRUs on operations fifteen times a month. Most of the time, the SEAL advisor would be the only American operating in the area.

It was the SEALs' dedication to their men, and their willingness to go into harm's way, that earned the PRUs' devotion. SEALs were always a top target for the VC and NVA; SEAL advisors to the PRUs even more so. Many SEAL advisors had prices on their head, payable by the Viet Cong, for their deaths. An even higher price would be paid for the capture of a SEAL advisor. Some SEALs saw their own wanted posters with bounties in the 35,000-piaster range (local currency). As they became an even greater danger to the VCI, SEAL PRU advisor bounties entered the multiple-thousand U.S. dollar range—the local equivalent of several years' wages.

Many times a SEAL advisor wearing civilian clothes would go into the local shops for a drink or a meal. The SEALs regularly did this with their PRU leaders and senior men to help build up camaraderie between them. And when these SEALs were moving through the general population, or were in exposed areas, PRU bodyguards would be nearby, without the SEAL ever knowing it. On one occasion, a VC assassination attempt was thwarted by the PRU bodyguards the SEAL never knew were there.

The quality of some of the PRUs made them among the most effective of the South Vietnamese military and paramilitary fighting forces. The PRUs cost the VC dearly for every PRU wounded or killed. This was especially so for the PRUs in the Delta. The quality of the PRUs was shown in the fact that by late 1969 the Viet Cong had been almost completely eliminated as a functional force in several parts of the Mekong Delta. Some of these areas had been controlled by the Viet Cong or their predecessors for up to ten years. The wholesale wipeout of VC bases by the PRU resulted in many units being forced to retreat to the relative safety of Cambodia.

The effect the SEALs, the Phoenix Program, and the PRUs had on the Viet Cong showed. For some operations where a PRU advisor thought he had too great a target for just his PRUs alone, he could call on a SEAL squad or platoon for a joint operation. A number of SEALs received decorations for their actions with Det Bravo and the PRUs, including the Silver Star. A number of SEALs were also killed on PRU ops.

The actions of the Phoenix Program and the PRUs was having an effect throughout South Vietnam. But Vietnamization and the cutting back of U.S. involvement in the war limited the SEALs' operations with the PRUs. In late 1969, orders were issued keeping the PRU advisors out of the field. U.S. personnel were ordered not to conduct combat operations with their PRUs. Some SEALs found creative ways around these orders. By March 1970, Detachment Bravo was disestablished and the SEALs were no longer part of the PRU program, though a large number of other U.S. military advisors and staff continued as part of the Phoenix Program through 1971. Most of these men left in the main U.S. withdrawal in 1972.

The official results of the Phoenix Program were brought forward in Congressional testimony after the Vietnam War was over. Rumors had grown that the program was simply one of assassination and terror. The testimony regarding the results of the Phoenix Program differed from the rumors. The testimony states that, of the approximately 67,282 people and VCI neutralized by the program, some 17,493 (26 percent) had sought amnesty, 28,981 (43 percent) were captured, and 20,857 (31 percent) killed. Most of the casualties were the result of direct military action. They were killed with a weapon in their hands, and the weapon was often turned in for a bounty.

The SEALs were in no way a part of an extramilitary or illegal program. They led their PRUs as military organizations, including the necessary discipline. They had a mission to perform and they did so. As one decorated SEAL PRU advisor said: "Nothing I did over there bothers me at night or any other time. . . . We had a job to do, and I'm not ashamed of the way I did it."

Mission Seven, Summer 1967: "Assassination"

One of the most lasting stories of the Vietnam War was how the Phoenix Program was one of assassination. With the deep secrecy covering the operation—which was the only way an intelligence-gathering operation could function—little information came back to the public about how the Phoenix Program conducted its operations, and what part the PRUs had in it. With the vacuum of information, any story, and the more outrageous the better, would quickly enter the public arena and be touted as fact. Disinformation from the Viet

Cong and the North Vietnamese Government would be added to these rumors to help the Communists' interests.

That people were killed in PRU operations is not in dispute. But the vast majority of those VC killed died with a weapon in their hands during a military operation. The silenced pistol shot to the head, a favored rumor about the Phoenix program, was not the way the PRU and their SEAL advisors operated. But there were occasions where the "civilized" rules of war took a backseat to the realities of the Vietnam War.

SEAL Team Two became involved with advisors to the PRUs early on in 1967. By the early summer, three SEALs from SEAL Team Two had volunteered as PRU advisors under the ICEX Program. Training was given to the SEALs at the MAC-V compound in Vung Tau. Detachment Bravo was relatively unknown to the SEALs from Team Two, but the idea of operating in the field and directing a group of men appealed to a number of operators.

Only three days and two nights were spent in Vung Tau by one of the new SEAL advisors. He was not very impressed with the speed of the training, though he found Vung Tau a very pretty place and would have liked to have spent more time there. Instead, the SEAL quickly graduated from the program and was sent on to Ben Tre in Kien Hoa province, where he soon found himself the advisor to a 130-man PRU.

Though not impressed with the handling he received at the hands of the CIA men, the SEAL did find the quality of the men in his PRU worthwhile. The 130 men of the PRU were divided into eighteen-man platoons. They were armed with an assortment of CIA-supplied weapons, mostly World War II—vintage hardware. The weapons included M1911A1 .45 automatic pistols, .45-caliber Thompson submachine guns, and M1 Garand rifles. These weapons were large for the relatively small-stature South Vietnamese, but the PRUs made good use of the hardware they had. M1918A2 BARs were also available to the PRU, but these twenty-pound automatic rifles were just too much to carry for the amount of firepower they provided. Early on, the SEAL advisor took to spending as much

time with the his PRU men as he could. The advisor knew
the best way to earn the PRUs' respect and to learn their real
capabilities was to live, eat, sleep, and operate with his men.
The CIA case office who was directing the Kien Hoa PRUs
did not want the SEAL going out on operations with the
PRU. What the CIA man feared was having an American
killed—or worse, captured—while working in a secret operation. The SEAL quickly found that the CIA man almost
never went into the field, so he simply ignored the orders
and operated with his men.

The PRUs were a motivated fighting organization, more so
than their regular South Vietnamese Army counterparts. But
the units were more of a group of men than a well-trained
fighting organization. The SEAL advisor spent months
training his men. Under the direction of the SEAL advisor,
and the further military training they received at the CIA-run
school in Vung Tau, the PRU became much more efficient in
operating against the Viet Cong. In the last few months of
his tour, the advisor was able to lead the PRU on missions
where they outfought the Viet Cong on their own ground.

One problem the advisor always encountered with his
PRUs was that their method of operating centered on simply
killing every VC they came across. The SEAL knew the
value of the intelligence they lost with each VC killed instead
of captured, but he was fighting an established procedure in
his PRU, and more than a little personal hatred as well.

Many of the men in the PRU had come from places that
had been devastated by the Viet Cong over the years. These
men didn't want to capture a VC, they wanted to see him
dead. It wasn't a war they were fighting sometimes as much
as personal retribution. But as the PRU came to know and
respect their new advisor, he managed to turn them more to
an intelligence-gathering form of operation. Prisoners could
talk, and that talk could lead to more and better prisoners.

The SEAL also learned some lessons about the realities of
the guerrilla war that the Viet Cong were fighting. The VC
also went through training, and attacking the South Vietnamese was often part of their training schedule. The gradu-

ation exercise for one Viet Cong platoon was the attack and destruction of a battery of 105mm artillery the South Vietnamese had located in an old soccer field near the PRU base. The soccer field was surrounded by a high, thick brick wall. Being over five feet thick at the base, tapering in on one side to a one-foot thickness, the walls appeared to be something that belonged near a medieval castle rather than a sports field. It was those walls that caused the local ARVN unit to establish their artillery battery within them.

About eighty VC attacked the soccer field one evening, blasting a hole through the massive wall. The province chief immediately called out the nearby PRUs to drive back the VC. Instead of acting like the cannon fodder the province chief thought they were, the trained and motivated PRU attacked the VC and eliminated them. Moving to the front gate of the soccer field, the PRU assaulted the VC on the field in a line. The firepower of the PRUs drove the VC, who were now trapped by the same walls that had originally kept them out, back though the breech they had made.

When the attack was over, a large number of VC dead were left behind in the field. Looking over the bodies the next day, the PRU advisor was astonished to see a body he knew. The body was that of a sixteen-year-old boy the advisor had seen regularly since he had come into the area. The young man worked as a barber at the shop the SEAL frequented. Many times, the SEAL had sat in the barber's chair while the young man shaved him. The boy had held a steel razor only inches from his throat, and the SEAL had never suspected him of being a VC sympathizer.

The advisor knew of other people in the population who were VC, and there seemed to be little he could do about it. The PRU had captured one young woman a number of times in their operations. A VC courier and liaison between VC cells, the woman carried messages and orders back and forth to different VC units near the little hamlet where she lived in the countryside. Being a very attractive woman, and thus someone an off-duty soldier would want to talk to, she also gathered information for the VC. She didn't cost very many American lives, but only because very few Americans were operating in that part of South Vietnam in 1967. The woman did cost a number of South Vietnamese soldiers their lives, however, and the situation wasn't one that could be changed easily.

The problem for the PRUs and their SEAL advisor was that the woman was well connected politically in the area. She was the sister-in-law of the province's police chief. When the PRU turned in the woman, having captured her in an area she wasn't supposed to have been in, she would be out the back door of the police station before the SEAL advisor had completed the paperwork and left by the front door. Over and over, the woman was captured and released. She was costing men their lives, but politics kept her out of official custody.

Finally, the advisor and his PRU had enough. There was one way of eliminating the woman, though they wouldn't be able to get any information from her afterward. This woman was a soldier for the other side and she killed men just as much with her actions as did a VC in the field with his rifle.

The advisor wasn't going to ask his men to do something he wasn't willing to do himself. Accompanied by his two bodyguards, the SEAL decided he would take one more trip to the hamlet where the woman lived. They would take the woman prisoner, as they had so many times before. This time, instead of taking her for a visit to the police station, the advisor would take her out into the jungle and put an end to the problem. The action would be fast and as painless as the SEAL could make it. But the situation was going to end.

On the day they had planned, the advisor, his PRU chief, and his two PRU bodyguards went out to the woman's hamlet. The SEAL's plan was to watch the woman's action and set up a pattern for her. Recognizing where she would be and when, they could choose their time and place to silently slip in and just take her away with a minimum of fuss. That was how the SEAL expected the day to go anyway.

Their two bodyguards leading the way, the SEAL advisor and his PRU chief approached the hamlet. As they came up, walking down the path toward them was the VC courier they had come to get. Very sure of herself, the woman approached the men. She had been though this before and had no reason to think anything would be different. The sudden approach of their target was not what the SEAL or the PRU men had planned for, but the situation was a simple one to adjust to. Stepping forward between the two bodyguards, the SEAL prepared to take the woman prisoner for the last time. Before a word could be said, the bodyguards drew their pistols and shot the woman where she stood.

Each bodyguard's pistol roared twice, the heavy .45-caliber slugs smashing into the woman, knocking her back and off of the path. The limp body collapsed and rolled to the side, settled in a ditch running along the small canal next to the path. As if nothing important had taken place, the bodyguards holstered their weapons and the group continued to walk into the village.

The SEAL was following the lead of his PRU bodyguards and chief, and they were making a point to the people of the little hamlet, and to the VC who would hear about the incident shortly. It seemed that every hamlet and village, no matter how small, had at least one hooch where a traveler could sit and drink a cup of tea and eat a meal. The advisor and his PRUs sat down calmly, ordered, and had a cup of tea while also eating a bowl of soup. Talking for a short while, the men drank a beer, got up, and left the hamlet behind them.

Not a word was said about the woman, not while the men were at the hamlet or afterward. Nothing came down from the police chief, and no furor was raised. It was as if nothing had happened. The people of Vietnam were used to the costs of war, after so many years of experiencing it. The death of the VC courier was just one more incident. She knew the risks and thought she had them beaten. She was wrong. But what the PRUs and the SEAL knew was that no more messages would pass by the woman. No more military outposts would be compromised and laid open to an attack.

When they were walking away from the hamlet, one of the bodyguards spoke to the PRU chief. If they had followed the original plan—tracked the woman, captured her, and taken her away somewhere to do the same thing he had just done—would it really have made any difference?

Mission Eight, 6 October 1968:
"POW"

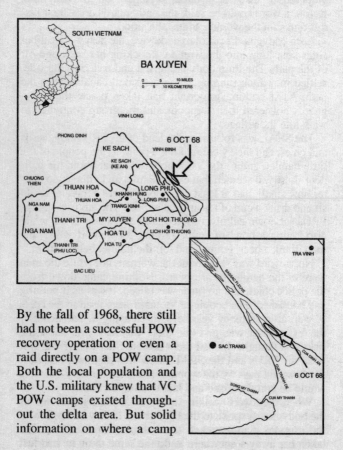

By the fall of 1968, there still had not been a successful POW recovery operation or even a raid directly on a POW camp. Both the local population and the U.S. military knew that VC POW camps existed throughout the delta area. But solid information on where a camp might be and when it would be occupied was very hard to come by.

The Viet Cong considered their American POWs a very high-value item. The VC took extreme care to keep the location of any American POWs secret. At the slightest hint of a compromised location, the VC would immediately move their most valuable POWs, and this always included any Americans, to another camp. A number of South Vietnamese servicemen and others were also prisoners of the Viet Cong, but their value was considered secondary to that of the American POWs.

The POW question was always in the mind of the military authorities and the American people back home. The POWs in both North and South Vietnam could be used by the North Vietnamese Government as political pawns to try and bargain with the U.S. forces and South Vietnam. The U.S. Services wanted to rescue any POWs they could for two reasons. First, any serviceman wanted to get his fellow American out of the hands of the enemy. Second, the rescue of any U.S. prisoners would be a tremendous morale booster both in Vietnam and with the people back home.

SEAL Team Two's Seventh Platoon had attempted a POW operation in March 1968. That op had turned up nothing more than hundreds of Viet Cong and had almost cost the SEALs an entire platoon. What had been confirmed in that operation was that if a POW camp was in an area, a large quantity of VC troops could also be expected in the immediate vicinity.

Warrant Officer Scott Lyon had been an enlisted man with SEAL Team Two when Seventh Platoon attempted their POW op. The action that followed contact with the enemy on that operation had resulted in the platoon chief receiving the Navy Cross, second only to the Medal of Honor as a symbol for valor. Such actions and awards do not go unnoticed.

When Lyon received his commission as a warrant officer, he was transferred to SEAL Team One on the West Coast to serve as a platoon officer there. This was a standard practice in the Teams to transfer a newly commissioned officer from the Team he had served in as an enlisted man to another Team for his first operations.

The experience he had learned during two combat tours in Vietnam with SEAL Team Two went with WO Lyon to his new post. On his second tour in Vietnam. Lyon had served as a PRU advisor in Chuong Thien province in the center of the Mekong Delta. Leading the 167-man PRU on operations had given Scott Lyon a great deal of experience and contacts with the PRUs and their intelligence nets.

Seal Team One's Alfa platoon deployed to Vietnam in August 1968 with Lieutenant Rip Bliss as Platoon Leader. Now Warrant Officer Scott Lyon returned in country for his third tour of duty, this time as Alfa Platoon's assistant platoon leader in charge of Second Squad.

It was during his tour as a PRU advisor the year before that Lyon had first begun hearing about VC POW camps in the Mekong Delta. None of the intelligence reports he had followed up on panned out enough to support a successful operation. During his tour with Alfa Platoon, Mr. Lyon maintained his watch for any POW intel that he and his SEALs would be able to react to. A SEAL PRU advisor knew of Mr. Lyon's interest in conducting a POW op and he brought him some interesting information.

On October 4, 1968, Lyon learned about two Vietnamese women who had walked into a PRU compound with information about the location of a POW camp. The women were both married to ARVN soldiers who had been captured during the Tet Offensive earlier that year. One of the women had eventually received a message from her husband about where he was being held. Contact with the VC had proved worthwhile for the women and they knew the location of the camp fairly well. The VC had even allowed the women to meet with their husbands at the camp, which was being run as a form of forced-labor camp. The women were willing to supply the military with the information they had for a price. They wanted the freedom of their husbands.

The women had been brought to the SEAL officer and Lyon had listened to their story. His enthusiasm for locating a POW camp was tempered with his concern for the men under his command. If the women were lying, the story was just the sort of thing that could bring a SEAL unit to a known location in VC territory. The VC could easily lay an ambush and wipe out the SEAL unit. Taking out even a small group of SEALs would be a coup for any VC. And the propaganda value of such an action would be obvious to the VC and their higher leadership in North Vietnam.

The women wanted their husbands back, and the SEAL officer wanted to put together the operation. But natural resistance to something that appeared so much like bait held up the warrant officer's decision. It was when the women agreed to lead the SEALs in themselves that he made his decision. A plan would be put together immediately and the necessary support units assembled and coordinated.

The reported location of the POW camp was in the Cu Lao Dung Island complex, commonly called Dung Island by the U.S. forces, near the mouth of the Bassac River. The Bassac was the northern boundary of Ba Xuyen Province. The camp itself was on Can Coc Island, a secondary island in the complex running parallel to the north shore of Cu Lao Dung Island itself. Can Coc Island was about twelve miles long and up to several miles wide, crisscrossed with a net-work of small canals and streams. The shore of Can Coc had been built up by river silt and tide actions for centuries and had banks ranging from three to ten feet high in places. A heavy line of brush and trees grew right to the water's edge, lining the high banks with a natural obstacle.

The SEALs were stationed aboard YRBM-18, a Repair, Berthing, and Messing barge, anchored at the fork of the Mekong and Ham Luong rivers near the western corner of Kien Hoa province where it met the northern edge of Vinh Long province. That put Alfa Platoon about forty-five miles northwest of their target.

Second squad quickly received a warning order to get ready for a quick move and a later operation. The SEALs moved to a compound at Tra Vinh in Vinh Binh province, only some twenty miles north of their target at Cu Lao Island. Now special considerations for the plan, support, intelligence, and guides for the operation had to be made.

The women had visited the camp and their descriptions had been noted and compared to each other. But the women had only been to the camp in daylight. They were willing to act as guides for the operation, but couldn't recognize the area in the dark. The heavy jungle covering much of the island, including the camp, would prevent the women from being able to guide from the air. Also, the noise of a helicopter insertion of the large unit of men that would be needed for the operation would make more than enough noise to warn the VC that someone was going in to their camp. The place could be emptied in minutes, or, in a worst-case scenario, the prisoners might be killed and the VC disappear into the jungle. It was going to have to be a waterborne operation done at daybreak to allow the women to recognize their surroundings and landmarks.

The Second Squad from Alfa Platoon would be the SEAL unit on the operation. A platoon of PRUs would back them up. This would give the operation a ground force of over forty men. Insertion would be from the PBRs of River Division 51. Det-3 of the Seawolves would supply a light helicopter fire team of two birds for air support. The Harnett County (LST 821), anchored in the Bassac River, would be the base of operations for the PBRs and the Seawolves.

The nine PBRs of the river division normally conducted patrols of the area around the Dung Island complex. To avoid suspicion, they would maintain this pattern until the SEALs and PRUs were ready to board the boats. Early in the morning on October 6, the nine PBRs traveled along their patrol routes, coordinating their movements to arrive at a selected site at the mouth of a small river. Waiting at the river's mouth for the PBRs were the SEALs and PRUs. The men and their two guides boarded the PBRs and the operation was underway at 0215 hours.

The PBRs moved off toward Con Coc island, cutting their engines and silently drifting with the river until they were within range of the target. Starting their engines and maintaining sequence, the PBRs moved closer to the island. In the lead boat was Scott Lyon, his SEALs, and the women guides. Still using the cover of darkness, the lead boat moved closer to the shore.

When within range of the shore, one of the women used a Starlight scope to see her landmarks in the darkness. As the lead boat moved along the shore, the woman pointed to a small indentation in the bank of the island where a canal emptied into the river. In the green screen within the starlight scope, this looked like where she had been taken in to visit her husband.

The SEALs made an underway insertion from the PBR, slipping off the boat as it continued down the river, maintaining its sound. The SEALs silently moved in to the island, slipping up the bank and establishing a perimeter. While the SEALs, with their two women guides alongside, waited to hear or see any sign of their insertion, the PBRs moved along slowly. Not finding any sign of the insertion being detected, the SEALs moved into the canal area, which turned to be little more than a ditch, and began moving inland. Without having moved fifty meters inland, the point man brought the SEAL patrol to a halt. The ditch had petered out and stopped. This was not the canal the women had said was the way in to the camp. The SEALs had inserted at the wrong site.

Calling the boats back for a pickup over the radio, the SEALs moved back to the shore of the island. The two women were now being watched even more carefully. The thought of a VC ambush wasn't far from anyone's mind. With the return of the PBRs, the unit climbed on board as silently as they could. Once everyone had been gathered up, the boats moved back out into the river.

The decisions that had to be made now were even more serious than when the op was being planned. The women had made a mistake, that was clear. But the women were very concerned about their mistake. They may have even thought the SEALs or PRUs would simply kill them out of hand. Lyon calmed them down and considered the situation.

The PBRs had lost a boat to a VC ambush in the vicinity of Can Coc Island on an earlier operation and were not happy about hanging around the area. The squad of SEALs were beginning to get a bad feeling about the whole operation since it was depending so much on the two women guides. SEALs do not like situations that are not in their control, especially in known enemy territory. The idea of a POW camp raid was a strong one. And the time was slipping past for the SEALs to be able to pull this one off. Dawn was fast approaching. If the SEALs had been detected at all, the operation would not only have to be scrubbed, the chances were that the VC would close down and move the camp. This was the time and the place. Lyon decided to continue the op.

Having moved another 800 meters down the water, the woman again pointed at a ditch in the riverbank wall. After another underway insertion, the SEALs prepared to patrol inland. There was no sign of VC activity where the SEALs had inserted, and the PRUs came in behind them while they examined the area. The area was muddy and wet with reeds growing up through the mud. The dense growth of two- to four-foot reeds were not a major problem for the SEALs, but the broken-off stubs of the reeds under the mud was another consideration. Many of the SEALs were barefoot to more easily travel through the island without leaving noticeably different tracks from the locals. Bare feet could also feel a tripwire or soft spot in the ground before a booby trap was tripped or a punji pit stepped in. The more sensitive feet also found the broken ends of the reeds sharp and not the most pleasant ground to travel over.

Silently slipping through the mud and reeds for almost 300 meters, the SEALs found no sign of enemy activity. Then the patrol found a well-worn trail. Can Coc Island, like most of the Dung Island Complex, had been investigated by the ARVNs some years before and then basically abandoned to the Viet Cong. Other SEAL units had performed operations in the area before, successfully engaging VC a number of times. There was at best a small civilian population on the island, and the trail had obviously been used recently by a much larger group.

The SEALs and PRUs followed the trail in the direction the women indicated. Tension was high as the men remained alert for booby traps and tripwires while also watching for the VC they now knew were on the island. The SEALs and even the PRUs had conducted this kind of patrol for some time, so the men acted carefully but professionally. Coming to a rise in the terrain that blocked any view of what was ahead, Lyon signaled the patrol to halt. With his SEALs behind him, Scott Lyon slowly crept up the rise until he could just see over it into the area beyond.

In front of the SEAL, with the trail leading up to it, was the POW camp. The arrangement of the various structures and general layout of the camp was just as the women had described it. The SEALs and the PRUs had been led right to the target they wanted most.

The camp buildings were the standard bamboo hooches found throughout Vietnam. Besides the three hooches, there was a raised thatch roof with open sides. Bamboo cages—the American public would later come to know them as "tiger cages"—were in the compound, one of which had two prisoners locked inside. Several sets of manacles and leg irons bound the inmates. Several of the inmates were secured to bamboo poles. All of the inmates looked drawn from poor food and abuse.

Watching closely, Scott saw the morning routine in the camp beginning to start. Several guards were up and about. Most looked like they were just waking up. One man was starting a fire, probably to cook breakfast. Including the prisoners and the guards, Mr. Lyon counted about thirty men. Only a few were obviously armed, eight or ten VC openly displaying weapons. Only three of the guns appeared to be automatic weapons, so the firepower of the guard force would be limited.

Getting back down to where his squad was waiting at the bottom of the rise, Lyon told the SEALs what he had seen. This was the jackpot, the target they hadn't expected to see, and the upcoming assault had to be carefully staged to limit danger to the POWs. Calling in to their support over the radio,

Lyon told the PBRs to move to the planned extraction point. Then Lyon called the Seawolves and told them to get into the air. The SEALs and PRUs would be able to handle the small number of guards that Mr. Lyon had seen, but there might be a number of other VC units in the area. The Seawolves would be able to give the SEALs and PRUs close air support if they ran into a force they couldn't handle. With the inland covered by the Seawolf gunships, the SEALs would be able to get additional fire support from the PBRs at the extraction site as the unit moved to the shore of the island.

Moving the PRU force to the left flank in order to cover the assault, Lyon told the men to come in after the SEALs had swept through the camp, eliminating the majority of any resistance. Experience told Lyon that the PRUs would probably take out their immediate anger on the VC once they saw the condition of the prisoners. Even prison guards could be important sources of information and Lyon wanted as many prisoners as possible. The strong fire discipline trained into the SEALs would also cut back on the chances of wounding any of the camp inmates; the PRUs would not be as careful.

With the sun up and daylight throughout the area, it was time for the assault. The SEALs slipped over the rise and were into the camp, past the outer perimeter, before the guards even noticed them. The squad had come heavily armed. Only Scott Lyon and the radio man did not have belt-fed weapons. Lyon had his CAR-15 and the radio man, Larry Hubbard, who was also the squad's corpsman, was carrying a 40mm XM148 grenade launcher mounted under another CAR-15. Four of the SEALs—John Ware, the point man; David Gardner; Leonard Horst; and Harlan Funkhouser—were all carrying Stoner 63A light machine guns. The last SEAL, Donald Crawford, was carrying an M60 machine gun.

With their overwhelming firepower, the SEALs moved into the center of the camp. Automatic fire in short, controlled bursts brought down the few guards who resisted. The first hooch in line received a 66mm M72 LAW (Light Antitank Weapon) through the front door before it was approached by two of the SEALs. The blast of the rocket's warhead, which could penetrate twelve inches of steel, shredded the interior of the building and set it on fire. A second hooch was on the receiving end of several 40mm grenades and also caught fire.

For the most part, the VC guards were stunned and put up very little resistance. Only a few of the VC even tried to fire back at the SEALs, receiving a burst of fire from several automatic weapons as a result. The balance of the guard force were running for their lives into the jungle and away from the camp.

As the rest of the squad assaulted the camp, one SEAL moved toward the prisoners along with the PRU interpreter. Yelling at the prisoners to lie on the ground and get their heads down, the SEAL waved at the milling POWs. The PRU interpreter had been carrying a bullhorn and called out to the prisoners, telling them to stay together and not panic. As the interpreter calmed the freed prisoners, the SEALs completed their sweep of the camp and now had some prisoners of their own. Most of the VC that were captured on the operation were guards. But one of the hooches that had been destroyed had not been just a sleeping structure for some officer.

As the hooch was burning, a VC lieutenant came out of the building, carrying with him his most important materials. The hooch had been a tax collector's station and the VC officer the area tax collector. The man had some 240,000 dong (about $68,000 U.S.) currency with him when he was captured by the SEALs. After months of looking for a POW camp, the assault to liberate the Can Coc Island camp was over in three minutes.

This was a situation the SEALs had never been in, though it wasn't a bad one. They had liberated twenty-six POWs and the ex-prisoners literally fell over to show their gratitude. Falling to their knees, the freed prisoners held their hands together, bowing and crying at the SEALs and PRUs. After just having dealt with a very lethal situation, the SEALs were at something of a loss as the Vietnamese cried in the dirt, kissing the feet and legs of the men who had freed them.

Finally, the SEALs had to literally start dragging some of the Vietnamese to the extraction site. Demonstrating that the SEALs had done a good job was well and good, but the men were still in hostile enemy territory and it was time to get out. Getting to the PBRs without any further contact with the VC, the SEALs, PRUs, and a very happy group of prisoners, including a husband and wife, pulled away from the island.

Returning to the Tra Vinh base, the SEALs turned the VC prisoners over to the intelligence people, who fed the freed prisoners. It was simple military C-rations, but the Vietnamese treated it like a banquet. It was an operation the men of Second Squad, Alfa Platoon would be proud of for a very long time.

Within a few days of the SEALs' operation on Can Coc, the South Vietnamese military staged a sweep of the entire island. Interrogation of the ex-prisoners and VC captured by the SEALs indicated that there was as many as two battalions of VC on Can Coc. There was also a communications station and a munitions factory with a VC security force guarding the sites. It was only the swift action and proper support preparation for the operation that kept the SEAL and PRU force from being engaged by a much greater enemy force.

Mission Nine, April 1969:
"K-Bar"

AN XUYEN

0   5   10   15 MILES
0   5   10   15 KILOMETERS

APRIL 69

KIEN GIANG   CHUONG THIEN

THOI BINH

THOI BINH

QUAN LONG   BAC LIEU

SONG ONG DOC   QUAN LONG
                    (CAU MAU)

SONG ONG DOC

DAM DOI   DAM DOI

CAI NUOC

• CAI NUOC   DONG CUNG

NAM CAN

The Provincial Reconnaissance Units performed the same
general-style operations as the SEALs and the general military. PRUs would go out on operations where they acted
much like an infantry company with small unit tactics and

company or platoon-sized movements. They also performed actions very familiar to the SEALs, especially the ambush and the snatch op. The military technology that was available through their advisors made new types of operations possible. One of these was very much like a helicopter-borne U.S. Army Airmobile raid. For the PRUs, this kind of operation was known as a K-Bar after the popular name of the Mark II knife issued to the SEALs and the fighting knife used by the U.S. Marines.

Many times, the intelligence gathered by a PRU was of a local nature and very time-sensitive. Not having the transportation services the U.S. military had at their disposal, the PRU often had to travel to a target area by whatever means they could obtain, such as truck, boat, or just their feet. The use of helicopter support, both for transportation and fire support, did allow the PRUs to act on some intel in a timely manner. In order to receive the air assets, K-Bar operation had to include an American. This was not a problem in many SEAL-advised PRUs since the operators wanted to get on the ground with their men anyway.

The advantage of the K-Bar operation was its speed and the potential size of the attacking force. For one province's K-Bars (Ba Xuyen) in early 1969, for example, the SEAL advisor took about sixty men from his PRU for the operations. The PRUs would be broken down into ten-man groups for transportation on Army UH-1 slick helicopters. In addition to the transportation helicopters, the K-Bar was supported by either a heavy or light helicopter fire team. At that time and place, a light fire team was two UH-1 helicopters gunships. A heavy fire team would be a pair of AH-1 Cobra gunships. A Command and Control (C&C) bird would contain the two commanding officers, one South Vietnamese, usually a major or lieutenant colonel, and the other a U.S. Army officer of equal rank who was assigned to MAC-V.

The number of PRUs that could be gotten into the target area on a K-Bar, along with the air support that was part of the operation, could effectively take on a much larger Viet Cong force than almost any other airborne raid. With the organization of the Phoenix Program and the PRUs, the request from an advisor for a K-Bar could be processed quickly and the op approved within hours.

SEAL advisors could also call on offshore gunfire support, air support from carriers or land-based planes, and artillery fire support. Most importantly to the PRUs, the advisor could also get them a fast medevac (dust-off) if some of the men were wounded. There was a great deal of animosity between the regular South Vietnamese Army and the PRUs, due in no small part to the success of the PRUs where the ARVNs had failed. Ethnic differences were also strong between the ARVNs and the various backgrounds of many PRU personnel. This resulted in long delays for medical assistance for a wounded PRU, if the ARVNs sent any at all. With an American advisor calling in support, the medevac came from U.S. assets and the PRUs usually went to U.S.-run hospitals.

These facts greatly increased the value of a good PRU advisor to the men of the unit. And the SEALs were considered some of the best advisors available. In addition the average SEAL advisor knew the value of cultivating unofficial contacts in the local military and intelligence units. These kind of meetings could yield very worthwhile information, such as the frequencies used to directly call in a fixed wing air strike from a carrier off the coast.

What had proven true for the SEALs while operating with their platoons—that the success of a mission can hinge on the quality of the intelligence—proved true for a K-Bar or any other PRU op. The numbers of Viet Cong taking advantage of the Chieu Hoi program gave the PRUs some of their best intelligence for ops.

On April 1, in Chuong Thien province, near the center of the Mekong Delta, a VCI member rallied in Kien Long, located in the southwestern area of the province. The VCI member, Tran, had been a guerrilla cell leader in Chi Phai village in neighboring An Xuyen Province. On 3 April, Tran was sent on to the Chuong Thien Chieu Hoi center. During his debriefing, Tran explained how he had been sent to a

work site (manufacturing center or jungle workshop) to get
supplies for his unit. Even though he was a member of the
VC in good standing, Tran had not been allowed to enter the
work site itself, only to pick up his materials near there.

But a number of Tran's friends had been working at the
site itself. Through conversations, Tran had a very good idea
of what was generally in the site location. The work site was
basically an armorer's station and a munitions factory for
ammunition bombs and mines. At any one time the site contained about 30 small arms, 100 mines of every type, 30
kilograms of TNT, and 200 recovered U.S. dud cluster bomb
submunitions that were used to make booby traps. In addition to the explosives and small arms, sometimes 60mm and
82mm mortars and 75mm recoilless rifles were brought in to
be worked on. There was also some kind of machine to
make ammunition, though Tran had few details of it.

Twelve men worked at the site: Sau Dien, who was in
charge of the site; Bay Chout, who was Dien's assistant; Ba
Thuong, who was in charge of the technics (technical workers); four workers named Nam Oai, Ba Hung, Tu Thanh, and
Bay Lo Ren; and five additional men that Tran didn't know
the names of.

Since he wasn't allowed on the site itself, Tran was not
able to tell exactly how the buildings, bunkers, and other
features were laid out. But he did have a location for the site
at the vicinity of map coordinates WR 167 413. The only
permanent enemy force at the work site were the twelve men
who operated it, but a network of cluster bomb booby traps
were all around the area, and the approaches were very dangerous. The work site also had radio communications with
other VC and NVA units in the area.

Another worthwhile target to come out of the Tran's
debriefing was the Viet Cong Western Region's headquarters. This was a location the Hoi Chan had been to himself.
Tran also had a cousin living on the Kinh Number 4 canal,
near the Kinh Dau Ngan canal where the headquarters was
located. That cousin had a grandmother in the area, living in
a house that had an X on the roof, visible from the air.

Tran had the opportunity to see the cousin's grandmother twice in late March. It was during these visits that Tran learned of two regional-level VCI cadre who came to the headquarters to conduct political courses in the Muoi Cu district. One of the cadre had the name Ong Nam and the other was unknown to the Hoi Chan. Tran was certain of the ranking of the two cadre since he had spoken to men from the cadre's support unit. These men openly said that the two men were important cadre from the regional level.

Because of the importance of the Western Region Headquarters to the Viet Cong, there was a company—about 100 men—who supported the activities of the cadres there. The men were armed with standard K2 and K3 small arms (SKS and AK-47s, respectively). There were two antiaircraft machine guns, one 60mm mortar, four B-40 (RPG-2) grenade launchers, and a few AR-15 and Garand rifles that had been battlefield pickups. Occasionally, the Second Battalion from the U-Minh came in to the area. Though not specifically fortified, there were a number of L-shaped bunkers around the headquarters area. Radio communications with other VC and NVA units was also set up at the headquarters.

The third probable target that the Hoi Chan had been able to describe was a hospital. The man did not know if the medical facility was regional or provincial level, only that it was well staffed. There were two medics and eight nurses working at the facility. The medics corresponded in ranking to South Vietnamese government doctors as they were in charge of running the surgery. In addition, the medics spoke French and English, indicating a high level of education. The Hoi Chan knew one of the doctor's names was Ut Vung.

Though the Hoi Chan knew where and what the hospital was, he could not tell the layout of the buildings as he hadn't been there personally. But a friend of his who was ill was at the Chuong Thien Chieu Hoi center and had been to the hospital. The friend could describe the layout of the hospital; Tran knew the location in the vicinity of map coordinates WR 168 436. The area was covered with fairly thick vegetation, but some of the structures might be visible from the air.

There was no specific combat support unit stationed at the hospital.

As a final proof of his sincerity, the Hoi Chan was willing to lead a military unit to the three operational areas. These were valuable targets and the intelligence seemed genuine. Interrogation of the ill Hoi Chan confirmed some of Tran's information. The collaboration was sufficient to go ahead with the planning of an operation. Due to the size of the possible enemy forces at the regional headquarters, the near vicinity of the two targets to each other, and possibility of radio communications, a joint K-Bar op would be done by the Chuong Thien and An Xuyen PRUs. The targets would be the work site (Target A) and the regional headquarters (Target B).

The mission was planned as a modern version of the old hammer-and-anvil military maneuver, where a mobile force would drive or sweep an enemy force against a blocking force they had already put into position. This operation would use a sweeping force and a blocking force on both targets simultaneously. Mission A would capture the work site and any VCI there. Mission B would attack and capture the region headquarters. The friendly forces would be two PRUs. The sweeping and blocking forces for Mission A would be from the Chuong Thien PRU based out of Vi Thanh, the Provincial capital. The forces for Mission B would be from the An Xuyen PRU.

The two forces would hit their targets and support each other as they operated. Force A would support the left flank of Force B. Force B would in turn cover the right flank of Force A. This would allow the two PRU groups to overwhelm a larger enemy force by outflanking them if necessary. The forces were the same in size and strength. Sweeping Force A consisted of forty-seven Chuong Thien PRUs, two American advisors, and one interpreter—fifty men total. Blocking Force A was thirty-one Chuong Thien PRUs.

Sweeping Force B was also forty-seven PRUs from the An Xuyen Province, two Americans, and one interpreter. In addition, the Hoi Chan who supplied the basic intelligence for the operation would accompany the PRUs as a guide.

The region headquarters was the more valuable, and dangerous, of the two targets. If the Hoi Chan was leading the PRU into a trap, he would be the first one to fall into it. Blocking Force B was also thirty-one An Xuyen PRUs.

The air assets of the operation were in two K-Bar "packets" and an additional unit. Packet A and B both consisted of five Huey UH-1 slicks as troop transports. Each slick would carry ten men, which is how the size of the fifty-man sweeping forces was determined. Each packet also had a helicopter fire team made up of three gunships to give fire support. One Command and Control helicopter was in each packet to direct the overall air effort. The blocking forces would both be transported on a single Chinook CH-47, which made up the additional air unit. Though crowded, the twin-rotor Chinook was capable of transporting the entire sixty-two-man blocking forces at one go to within striking range.

The Chinook would be too large and slow to insert the blocking forces at their two landing zones quickly enough to get both forces into position for the two sweeping forces. Instead, the Chinook would get the blocking forces to Kien Long, where they would be close enough for the two K-Bar packets to come back from dropping off the sweeping forces, pick up the blocking forces, and get them to their respective landing zones within a few minutes.

The time schedule for the operation was fairly tight. The attacks would take place on the morning of a single day, both missions over by 1130 hours. The schedule was as follows:

0730 Hours. The K-Bar transport slicks and gunships arrive at Vi Thanh for their full briefing on the operation. The pilots and crew would have already received a warning order on the op and so would be generally ready with the birds fueled and the gunships fully armed. The Chinook and its crew would also arrive at this time and be briefed.

0815 Hours. Both K-Bars lift off after loading their passengers. K-Bar A takes Sweeping Force A to their target area at the work site. K-Bar B takes Sweeping Force B to the region headquarters. With both blocking forces on board, the Chinook takes off for Kien Long.

0830 Hours. The Magpies are on station near the target area. The Magpies were a flight of Royal Australian Air Force B-57 Canberra bombers from the Second Squadron. The bombers carried loads of 750-pound bombs and were prepared to do a precise bombing mission on the target area. Even a nearby air strike of heavy bombs would be enough to disrupt and confuse any VC unit stationed in the area.

0845 Hours. K-Bar packets A and B arrive at the target area. The helicopters do not go into the targets at this point but wait some distance away with the PRUs on board. The Chinook arrives at Kien Long at this point and unloads the two blocking forces.

0850 Hours. The Magpies launch an air strike on both the target areas. The bombing runs are to be fast and furious with the K-Bars going in right behind them before the VC have a chance to recover.

0851 Hours. The K-Bars land. K-Bar A puts in Sweeping Force A at Landing Zone A1. K-Bar B puts its Sweeping Force in at Landing Zone B1.

0853 Hours. The K-Bar packets both lift off and head back to Kien Long to pick up the blocking forces.

0900 Hours. The K-Bars arrive at Kien Long. Blocking Force A puts out a red smoke grenade to signal its K-Bar where to land. Blocking Force B signals its K-Bar packet by putting out a green smoke grenade. Both forces are picked up and lift off as quickly as possible. Lining up for a rapid deployment on board helicopters is something both PRUs had practiced often.

0910 Hours. The K-Bar packets return to the target area and insert their blocking forces. Blocking Force A lands and sets up at Landing Zone A2. Blocking Force B puts up their positions at Landing Zone B2.

0912 Hours. The slick assets of the K-Bar Packets return to Kien Long to await the results of the operation. Limited refueling and full rearming facilities are available at Kien Long. The Chuong Thien PRU Command Post (CP) is also set up. The helicopter gunships and the C&C birds remain on station above their respective target areas.

Landing at the targets, the PRUs would conduct their primary operation as quickly as possible. While overrunning both the work site and the region headquarters, in spite of any fighting, the PRUs would strive to take as many VCI prisoner as possible. These prisoners and the intelligence they could deliver would be among the most valuable results that could come from the operation.

The sudden, intense use of the hammer-and-anvil technique would drive the VC into a retreat, slamming them up against the blocking force, where they would be stopped. The use of both the Magpie bombers and the shocking blast of their high-explosive bombs, combined with the sudden appearance of the PRUs dropping from the sky with their weapons blazing, could easily demoralize and confuse the VC forces, making them vulnerable and leaning toward surrender.

With Landing Zones A and B being in line with one another along a canal that would act as a landmark, the PRUs could go in to their respective targets in a straight line. The blocking forces insert between the targets with the tree line of the jungle some distance behind them. The two targets being only some 500 meters apart, both PRU forces could support one another. Much in the way of enemy movement to either side would also be prevented by the location of the PRU forces.

1100 Hours. Both K-Bar packets return to Landing Zone B2 and extract both of the B forces, extracting them to Kien Long.

1120 Hours. Both K-Bar packets return to Landing Zone A2 and pick up both elements of the A forces, extracting them to Kein Long.

1130 Hours. At Kien Long, the K-Bar packets return the A elements to Vi Thanh. The Chinook returns the B elements to Ca Mau in An Xuyen province.

Parakeet Ops:
Hiding in Plain Sight

The K-Bar was not the only airborne operation conducted by the PRUs. There was another operation done from helicopters that had all of the earmarks of being an airborne ambush. But the target of the ambush in this case was normally grabbed up alive. The operation was called a parakeet op and was conducted almost exclusively by SEAL PRU advisors in the Mekong Delta area.

The parakeet operation is reported to be mostly the creation of a SEAL Team Two operator, George E. "Fast Eddie" Leasure, with further development of the technique by Ronnie Rodgers, also of SEAL Team Two. The technique of the operation was a simple one and unique to the Vietnam War era. Helicopters were a common sight in the skies of South Vietnam. Single birds were often seen flying at altitudes of several thousand feet, out of the range of most VC ground-based antiaircraft weapons. The solitary helicopter was used to ferry people, carry mail and supplies, and generally be an airborne workhorse for the U.S. Military in South Vietnam.

Playing on this "hiding in plain sight" aspect of the single helicopter, the parakeet operation used a single unarmed slick to transport a squad of four or five PRUs and one PRU leader. Along with the PRU squad would be their SEAL advisor and at least one other SEAL, usually armed with a Stoner machine gun to give the most firepower in a compact package. Along with all of the PRUs and SEALs on the helicopter would be the agent who supplied the information for the operation.

Flying close to the target area, the agent would point out the specific building (hooch) that held the VC or VCI who was the objective of the snatch. With the target building lined up, the slick would swoop down, delivering the men aboard as close to the front door of the target as possible. Once the PRUs and SEAL had left the bird, the helicopter would climb out of the area to leave the field of fire clear.

A clear field of fire was important to the helicopter gunships that would be coming in very low to the ground behind the slick. Hidden at an altitude of only fifty to one hundred feet, the gunships would climb for altitude as soon as the slick went down to the target. Circling above the area, the gunships cold take on any reasonably sized VC unit that might respond to the sudden attack.

On the ground, the PRUs would establish a fast perimeter around the target. If there was more than one hooch to be searched, the PRU would take the secondary buildings, leaving the primary for the SEAL PRU advisor. The advisor and men would move as fast as was practical, sometimes running up and through the front door. The agent would identify the target, who was usually confused by the rapid way things had developed. Once identified, the target would be secured and a quick search made of the building and area.

The Team would call slick back down to recover and extract the PRUs, SEALs, and their captive. Lifting off under the covering guns of the surrounding gunships, the slick would return the Team back to their starting point. Parakeets were very fast and efficient operations, but they were also extremely dangerous. In a parakeet, the men on the ground were in a very exposed position. They could be quickly overrun and wiped out if even a medium-sized enemy unit was waiting for them. Some SEALs loved the parakeet for its speed; others hated it for the exposed position it put them in.

The key to the success of a parakeet operation was the quality and accuracy of the intelligence it was based on. Exactly who was going to be in what building at what time of the day had to be known, and confirmed if at all possible. Like many cultures in hot climates, the Vietnamese in the South took a rest, a siesta, during the hottest part of the day. The time of the siesta was roughly from eleven in the morning to one or two in the afternoon. This made noon a very popular target time for a parakeet.

More so than any other operation, SEALs who conducted parakeets made as sure as possible of their intelligence source. The intelligence agent would be shown aerial photographs of the area he said the target was in. Maps would be laid out and the agent would have to point out the target and any support or bodyguards that might be around.

Attempts would be made to trip up the agent. He would be shown other photographs, different maps, other locations, to try and see if he kept up the same story. If the agent's story couldn't be broken, he was often taken up in a helicopter for a quick identification flyover of the target area. Moving near the target, the agent would have to point out the proper buildings and identify whatever stood out to the SEAL advisor in the aircraft with him. With all the precautions taken, the parakeet was put on as quickly as possible, usually the first day after the flyover.

Mission Ten, 14 January 1969:
"Parakeet Snatch"

From December 1968 to June 1969, SEAL Team Two's Sixth Platoon operated out of Nha Be, north of the Rung Sat. This was the platoon's second tour of duty in Vietnam and almost all of the SEALs who made up the platoon had at least one combat tour behind them. The platoon chief was a hard-charging operator who had been with the first platoons deployed from SEAL Team Two for direct actions in Vietnam. The chief greatly preferred operating in the field to almost any other activity, and an unusual opportunity came up early in Sixth Platoons' tour.

The platoon was operating throughout the southeastern sector of III Corps, north of the Mekong Delta and to the east and south of Saigon, as well as the Rung Sat itself. Also working in this same general area was a PRU who were based just down the road from where the SEAL platoon was living. The PRU needed a new advisor and the agency man who was overseeing the area approached the SEAL platoon. The platoon chief jumped at the idea of both operating with Sixth Platoon as well as advising a PRU. Quickly volunteering for, and being accepted for the position, the platoon chief now found himself in charge of a 150-man PRU as well as a deployed SEAL platoon.

The SEAL chief loved every minute of his new position. When he wasn't out operating with his SEAL platoon, the chief was leading a PRU op. Since it was not considered a good idea for the advisor to accompany a PRU on every operation—setting a pattern was a good way to get killed—staggering his schedule between the two groups kept the chief in the field and turned out to be a great advantage to both units.

The PRUs had an established intelligence net that included the SEALs. The SEALs also inherited a net for gathering information in the area from the platoon they had relieved. Because the two units shared information, the SEALs could get involved on ops the PRUs discovered. The PRUs in turn had an active SEAL platoon that could be drawn on for operations when they needed more Americans on the ground.

It was during this tour with the PRUs that the Sixth Platoon chief learned about the parakeet operation. The technique appealed to the SEALs' style of action and he soon took to using it as a regular style of operating.

On a parakeet, the chief always had at least one SEAL with him, preferably a Stoner man he had operated with before. Personally, the chief either carried a shotgun or just a handgun on parakeets. The main "weapon" that the chief was armed with was the radio he carried on his back. Wearing a headset and the radio allowed the chief to maintain contact with not only the slick, but the orbiting helicopter gunships as well. Instead of having just the weapon in his hands, the chief had all the armament of the gunships at his immediate disposal. And contact with the slick was extremely important to the men on the ground during a parakeet. After all, that helicopter was their only ticket home.

In mid-January, information was brought to the chief in the form of an informant. Much of the material that the PRUs and the Sixth Platoon had operated on had come through the intel nets in the form of informants looking to sell what they had learned out in the countryside. Informants were also a very good way of leading a PRU, and especially their U.S. advisor, into a trap.

That was the risk of following up on any information that came in on the Viet Cong. And the SEAL chief had enough experience to tell when something looked like hot intel and when it would be best to just walk away from it. After going through their procedures with the informant, the chief was convinced he had the location of a VC platoon leader and his bodyguards. A VCI of this level could easily be expected to give information that would lead to others in his command chain.

The chief had already been out on a combined operation with a SEAL squad and a squad of PRUs the evening before. Outside of seeing some red and green flares, no other contact had been made on the op and the team extracted at 0110 hours. In the morning, the chief heard the new intel from the informant. He put a parakeet operation together quickly. He grabbed up the Stoner man from the operation the evening before and told him to get his gear together.

The chief had more than a reputation in the platoon as a hard charger, and the Stoner man would follow his platoon chief wherever he wanted to go. They had hit a dry hole as far as taking up any suspected VC in the area the evening before. Now another chance was waiting.

This was the SEALs' advantage; they could get up and

move on an operation within a moment's notice. On this operation, the chief would only have his Stoner man, three PRUs, and the informant on board the slick and then on the ground with him. A working relationship with the 117th Army Helicopter Company at Long Binh had already been established. Getting the needed air assets—a slick and a light helicopter fire team—was not difficult. By noon that same day, the parakeet operation was underway.

The target was a small group of hooches South of a curve in a tiny river, a stream really, called the R. Dap Huong, about twelve miles south-southeast of Nha Be. The target came into sight by 1245 hours, still within the normal siesta time for the locals. The informant pointed out the target hooch to the chief. The chief in turn crouched down between the two pilots and directed them at the specific building in a line of about three hooches.

As the slick went down to the target, the two following UH-1B gunships rose up from the treetops. The gunships began circling the area like hawks flying over a field. The sound of the gunship's engines had not traveled far since they had been down so low. What noise could be heard on the ground near the target was masked by the high-flying slick. The Vietnamese on the ground suspected nothing until the helicopter landed next to the small line of hooches.

The surrounding scenery was familiar for the delta area— several native hooches surrounded by rice paddies. Off to the north, by the side of the small stream, was a line of trees, maybe 100 to 150 meters away. The stream curved in a semicircle around the top two thirds of the fields, moving from the north west to the east.

When the slick landed, the SEALs immediately moved out to the target building. The PRUs moved on their assignment, covering the two buildings on either side of the target. With the Stoner man at the ready to the side, covering the building, the chief kicked in the front door. Within moments, the chief realized the target wasn't in the hooch. They had hit the wrong building. SEALs think fast and move quickly. Immediately, the chief and his Stoner man moved to the nearest hooch and repeated their assault. This time, they found their target.

Movement was so fast and the surprise from the parakeet so complete, the Viet Cong leader didn't even have time to pick up his weapon. With a fast punch, the chief knocked the VC almost unconscious. Grabbing up the VC, the burly chief quickly stripped him of his weapons and secured him. While this action was going on, the Stoner man saw activity in the treeline near them.

Running to the other hooch had put the Team away from the landing zone where their slick could pick them up. Now the SEALs and PRUs were seeing a lot more activity around them than the two or three bodyguards the VCI was supposed to have with him. Fire began coming into the small group of men from the tree line surrounding them on two sides.

Dealing with the incoming fire was the responsibility of the Stoner man, and he began returning fire as he acquired targets. The PRUs had dealt with the bodyguards they had found in another hooch and had come back up to the SEALs. The chief was on the radio, calling in the slick to extract the Team, when one of the PRUs was hit in the leg.

Diving down next to the injured man, the chief called up to the helicopters, telling them that the Team had a man down and to get the slick in fast. But the surrounding tree line where the VC were hidden was close to the team. The helicopter gunships had to maneuver carefully to be able to put out effective fire without hitting their own men. The incoming fire from two sides had the SEALs and PRUs pinned down in a crossfire.

The chief was down on the ground, trying to patch up the injured man and calling in the air support at the same time. The remaining two PRUs were controlling the prisoner and putting out their own fire as they could. The Stoner man could see what the chief was trying to do.

Standing directly over his chief, the Stoner man continued firing from his machine gun at the surrounding VC. As he straddled his chief and the injured PRU, the SEAL kept firing his weapon, reloading without conscious thought. The chief was lying on the ground, controlling the bleeding from the wounded PRU as the hot brass and links from the Stoner rained down all around him.

It was a long ten minutes on the ground for the SEALs and the PRU as the gunships helped put down the surrounding VC. The most effective fire came out of the barrel of the Stoner the SEAL was operating. Finally, the extraction bird was able to get back in and pull the unit out. Even as the team was leaving, the Stoner man was standing on the skid, firing at the enemy all around them. The last man on board, the Stoner man was going to help keep the enemy fire from coming in to the extraction bird as long as he was able. The door gunners of the slick also put out a heavy volume of fire from their two M60 machine guns as the loaded slick lifted off to safety. Now that the slick had gotten the men out of the area, the gunships could put in their heavy fire on the treeline with their rockets and machine guns.

The PRU recovered, and it was the actions of the SEAL chief with the injured man that stood him well with his PRU. Most of the SEAL PRU advisors had the same attitude toward the men under their command as they did their Teammates. You watched out for your own and you didn't leave a man behind. The Stoner man was later put in for a decoration for his actions that day, receiving the Bronze Star after the Sixth Platoon had returned home from their tour.

```
BARNDANCE # 6-27     SEAL TEAM 2; DET A; PLT. 6
DATE(S): 14 Jan 69
OTHER UNITS: USE Slick and USA LHFT-117th AHC, 3 PRU
MSG REF(S):-
NAMES OF PERS: Watson, Rowell, and 3 PRUs
MISSION TASK: Snatch

INTEL/INFO SOURCE(S): PRUs
INSERTION: TIME: 1245 METHOD: Slick AMS COORD: XS
865 645
```

EXTRACTION: TIME: 1259 METHOD: Slick AMS COORD:
XS 865 645
TERRAIN: Rice paddies
WEATHER: Clear TIDE:- MOON:-
BRIEF MISSION NARRATIVE: Inserted by slick to
abduct 3 VC. Abducted one VC Platoon Ldr with AK
50; [AK-47] and 45 cal pistol, 2 para grenades
and web gear. Was taken under fire from tree
line. One PRU WIA. Called in slick, suppressed
fire, and extracted.
RESULTS OF ENEMY ENCOUNTERED: 2 VC KIA, one VC
captured
FRIENDLY CASUALITIES: One PRU WIA
REMARKS (SIGNIFICANT EVENTS, OPEVAL RESULTS,
ETC.): Captured one AK 50 [AK-47] and one 45 cal.
pistol. Two para grenades [RKG-3 HEAT], web gear,
and documents.
RECOMMENDATIONS/LESSONS LEARNED:-
BD COPY DIST:-
BARNDANCE # 6-27
(Form Rev. 8/68)

Mission Eleven, Fall 1969: "The Big Hit"

SOUTH VIETNAM

BA XUYEN

0   5   10 MILES
0   5   10 KILOMETERS

VINH LONG

PHONG DINH

KE SACH

KE SACH
(KE AN)

VINH BINH

CHUONG
THIEN

THUAN HOA

THUAN HOA

KHANH HUNG

LONG PHU

LONG PHU

NGA NAM

TRANG KINH

THANH TRI

MY XUYEN

LICH HOI THUONG

LICH HOI THUONG

NGA NAM

HOA TU

THANH TRI
(PHU LOC)

HOA TU

BAC LIEU

PRU advisors had to keep ahead of the paperwork of the organization as well as oversee the operations of their men. SEALs, like many others, far preferred to man a weapon than man a pencil. But the organization of the Phoenix Program and the PRUs demanded a number of reports and additional paperwork be kept. Advisors were also the paymasters for a PRU, maintained a connection with the Phoenix intelligence people, and kept up supply. There were subordinate chiefs assigned to these duties to assist the PRU advisors, but it still helped a PRU advisor to be able to type as well.

One of the major forms that had to be filled out on a regular basis for a PRU was the Weekly PRU Report that was sent up to the region chief. The PRU report included such information as the total number of PRU ops conducted that week, with the numbers of covert paramilitary, paramilitary, and covert intelligence collection ops listed separately. Operational results such as men lost, wounded, or missing, as well as equipment losses, also had to be accounted for. Of particular importance was the results to the enemy, such as VC and VCI killed or captured. Separate listings of the names of all prisoners and the identified VCI who had been killed had to be listed. For the Ba Xuyen province, the report had to be sent up to the regional headquarters in Can Tho and then from there to Saigon.

It was while filling out one of these weekly reports the SEAL PRU advisor for Ba Xuyen province was interrupted by his PRU intelligence chief. The chief had an informer giving time-critical information on the passage of a COSVN-level VCI passing through the province. This statement received the immediate and undivided attention of the PRU advisor.

The VC, as any large organization, was built of layers. The largest layer was at the bottom and the number of people involved got smaller as you moved up through the layers of importance. The lowest VCI ranking involved people at the hamlet level. From there, the importance rose as the number of people under the control of the VCI increased. The level went up through village, district (of which there were eight in Ba Xuyen), province, and finally the Central Office of South Vietnam (COSVN). COSVN-level VCI were hard-core Communists who had been in the movement for a long time. These people were rare, and the opportunity to target one was not common.

The intelligence stated that VCI would be moving through the area—two COSVN level, one province level, and one district level. The VCI were moving along a communications/liaison route that connected hamlets throughout the area. Moving through the smaller hamlets allowed the VCI to have greater security. Not only would such high-ranking VCI not normally be found in such circumstances; any outsiders (and possible assassins) in the area would stand out. Also, a small hamlet was easily intimidated by the VC bodyguards who would undoubtedly be accompanying such a group.

The VC used the cell structure to organize their operation at a local level. A man in a three-man cell would only know his two companions. Only one man in the cell would know a man in another cell down the road. Messages, material, and people could move down this route. If a cell was broken, usually it only took out that one small group.

The compartmentalization of the Viet Cong gave it great strength in resisting infiltration. But it also limited the flexibility of the organization. General orders, passwords, and other such information could only be changed gradually. A Hoi Chan coming from the VC to the PRUs could easily know the proper codes and passwords to move through enemy territory for months after he Chieu Hoied. Another tremendous value of these Hoi Chans was that they could recognize the signs used by the VC to mark a booby trap or other hazard in the path ahead. These were valuable bits of information while on a patrol.

The normally tight security of the VC had failed in this case, and this Hoi Chan felt he could trade his information for a better life. The group of VCI had been on the road for at least several weeks. The VCI had already traveled through the Can Tho area, and they would be in the operational area of the Ba Xuyen PRU within about nine hours from the time the advisor received the report. It was about five o'clock in the afternoon when the information arrived at the PRU. The VCI group would be at a specific site pinpointed by the Hoi Chan at two A.M. This gave the PRU advisor enough time to put together an operation, but there was another question.

The ability of a good PRU to go out on an operation quickly given good intelligence was well known in some circles. It was one of the strength of the organization. But that same strength was one of the PRUs' worst weaknesses. To lead a PRU, and especially their Co Vahn or advisor, into a trap only took a good story. The best target was also the best bait. Part of the answer to this dilemma came from the quality of the PRU advisor, how well he had developed his relationship with his men, and how much mutual trust there was.

For this operation, the advisor asked his intelligence chief just how good the information was. The chief had checked the intel through his best sources and felt it was a straight story. The decision to go, however, was still the advisor's. Advisors, especially the SEAL advisors, were not known for being timid. Aggressive action could get you killed, but at the same time, the big bets won the biggest prizes. The op was a go.

About twenty PRUs would be going with the advisor on the operation. That would be enough men to ambush the five VCI and the six or seven bodyguards that traveled with them without getting too unwieldy in the darkness. The men would be hand-picked from the best in the local PRU camp. With his PRU chief's help, the advisor chose the men quickly. The advisor was still nervous to a certain degree as to just how far he could trust some of the PRUs. He didn't know who he could trust completely and who he couldn't. The men were were paid to fight. The question was, could someone else have paid them more?

But the question couldn't be properly answered. And it was this constant risk on a mission that kept some PRU advisors well out of the field when their units were operating. This SEAL was not one of those kinds of advisors. The list of supplies the advisor wanted on the operation was given to the men. Their transportation for the operation was also prepared. Nothing exotic, or even very fast. The men would move to the target area in a truck.

Other procedures still had to be followed for the PRU to put on an operation. But the advisor also was experienced enough to play things safe and not take unnecessary risks. Going into the CIA safe house to report the operation, the advisor did not speak to anyone in the outer offices. Instead, the SEAL went directly to the MAC-V officer and explained where the advisor would be going and why. Only the necessary people knew the right story about when and where the advisor would be. A number of South Vietnamese worked in the offices contained in the safe house, and it was well known that the VC and NVA targeted intelligence and military locations for penetration by agents. The advisor was not one to allow an information leak when he could control at least part of the situation.

Returning to his PRU, the advisor made sure that all the preparations he had asked for had been completed. A large quantity of ordnance was in the trucks, including several cases of M18A1 Claymore mines. The planned ambush was going to be an overwhelming one and a dozen or more Claymores would help to ensure that.

The PRU detachment and their advisor left on the operation soon after the final checks were made. The trucks drove to an ARVN outpost near the target area where they would be secure. The driver was told when the PRUs expected to be back and was then left behind to watch their transportation. The unit made contact with the commander of the ARVN post and exchanged radio frequencies, and that was about it. The unit shouldered their equipment and weapons and moved out to the target. The walk to the target zone was about a klick (kilometer) from the outpost. The Hoi Chan had come along to act as a guide. His situation was simple— if he led them into a trap, he was going to be the first person gone. On the plus side, if he identified the VCI the operation was targeting and they were captured or killed, he would get paid. There was still some time before the the target's scheduled passing and the unit still had to set the ambush.

The advisor laid out the Claymores in an overlapping pattern. The mines would send their hundreds of steel pellets through the kill zone of the ambush in a swarm. No portion of the kill zone would be missed. For backup, the PRUs were also laid out along the kill zone with their weapons at the ready. This was an operation they had done many times before and each man knew what was expected of him. The advisor was armed with a CAR-15 submachine gun, though he didn't often have the opportunity to use it. In his PRU's eyes, he was the paymaster. If the advisor was killed, the PRUs wouldn't get paid, at least not for some time.

The ambush itself was a standard linear one. The mines were laid out along the suspected line of march of the VCI unit. At the center of the mines was a short, six- to ten-foot no-kill area. The mines were set up with electrical command detonation. By not firing the mines that were aimed at the central no-kill zone, the VCI could be cut off from their guards and taken prisoner.

The path in front of the PRUs gave a good indication of just where the VCI unit would pass in front of them. The detonation of the mines would be the signal for the PRUs to open up with their weapons and cover the kill zone. Anyone still standing after the mines went off could be eliminated by the PRUs' fire. If they were not killed in the ambush the VCI would be taken prisoner if possible. The stunning aftereffects of a Claymore ambush would probably make the VCI a little easier to handle and more cooperative than they might be normally.

What might happen on the ambush was something for the future. Now the men were in place, the weapons set, and it was time to wait for the target. The wait was a short one.

Within about fifteen minutes of the PRU settling in at the ambush site, a group of VC came moving down the trail. This was the target the advisor had been hoping for, and he was very unhappy to see it. Instead of the six or seven VC he had been expecting, the PRU advisor saw some sixty men or more. A platoon of VC was taking point and moving ahead of the main body. Flanking guards were out to either side and a trailing platoon was covering rear security.

The twenty-man PRU element was outnumbered three to one or more. But the SEAL was going to take out the target. The Claymores were set up to cover a wide enough area and there were enough of them that the overkill he had originally planned for might just be enough for this sized unit. The Claymores might be enough if they were all set off together. But the PRU interpreter lying next to the advisor was reluctant to set off the Claymores.

To set off the Claymore electrically, an M57 firing device, kind of a fast electrical generator, would be squeezed. When the firing device was squeezed, it would make a loud *clack*,

so the device had the common name of clacker. The PRU
interpreter was holding all of the clackers for the Claymores,
and he wanted nothing to do with getting the attention of the
huge group of VC that was passing in front of him. After
whispering to the interpreter a number of times to give up
the clackers, the advisor finally took them over. Quickly giving some of the clackers to his PRU chief on the other side
of him, the advisor set to fire the mines.

On the advisor's count of three, just as the main body of
the VC column reached the center of the kill zone, the mines
were fired. A dozen Claymore mines would have some
eighteen pounds of C4 explosive. The mines were set out in
the open close in front of the PRU positions, and the shock
wave of the explosives blasted across the area. The sound
was a crashing wave of noise the advisor likened to a B-52
bomb strike. But the noise was nothing compared to what
the steel fragmentation from the mines did to the kill zone.

Immediately after the wave of steel from the mines had
gone out, the PRUs opened fire, adding their own touch to the
carnage in front of them. After an incredibly loud and violent
few moments, perhaps half a minute or less, the firing died
off and there was only dust and silence. The shock of the
mines going off followed by the fire from the PRUs had left
few VC in a position to moan or otherwise make any noise.

The advisor and his men got up from their positions and
ran to the killing zone. The PRUs were to grab up anything
that looked to be of intelligence value. They picked up papers,
maps, and other documents—those that weren't shredded,
anyway. The VCI that the Hoi Chan had identified had been
carrying a number of ammunition cans. This kind of high-
ranking VC official did not spend his time on patrols carrying
ammunition. The advisor made certain that his PRUs
grabbed up those cans.

As soon as the Hoi Chan had identified the VCI members,
the advisor had paid him the promised reward. Taking a roll
of money out of his pocket, the advisor put it in the hands of
the guide without any problems. The guide had been a good
one and the intel he had given had only turned out to be a
trap for the VC.

One VC was lying on his back with the AK-47 he had been carrying literally blown into his chest. Grabbing hold of the weapon, the advisor hadn't been able to simply pull it from the body. Calling over to one of the PRUs, the advisor told the man to recover the weapon as there was something odd about it. When the advisor returned to the PRU a few moments later, the man had cut the AK from the dead VC's chest. The reason the weapon had been so deeply embedded that it couldn't be withdrawn was that there was a crudely machined rifle grenade launcher attached to the muzzle of the rifle.

Time was getting short and the situation could turn critical at any moment. The ambush with the mines and small arms had wiped out about twenty VC, about a third of the enemy force. The reminder of the VC, who had either passed or not yet reached the kill zone area, were starting to recover from the shock of the ambush. The PRUs could hear the VC starting to get up from where they had taken cover. It was time for the PRUs to consider the mission over and unass the area.

The PRUs conducted a rapid tactical withdrawal. They ran for the ARVN outpost, firing at the pursuing VC over their shoulders as they moved. Getting the ARVNs on the radio, the advisor had his radio man call for fire support in the form of mortars from the outpost. After some argument in Vietnamese, the mortars from the outpost started firing.

The advisor hadn't wanted this kind of fire support. As the PRUs were running for their lives, masked only by the darkness from the VC behind them, the ARVNs put up illumination rounds from their mortars so they could better see the target. Now, the VC could better see the PRUs running across rice paddies.

In spite of the "assistance" of the ARVNs, the PRU came within small arms range of the outpost and the VC began breaking off pursuit. Only one of the PRUs was wounded, and that not a life-threatening hit in the calf. Getting in to their transportation without a word to the ARVNs, the PRUs headed back to their camp and the safe house back in town.

Arriving at the safe house, the advisor started opening up the ammunition cans they had grabbed. As suspected, some of the cans contained money, wads of it. Since the PRU had risked themselves for the capture, it was only right in the advisor's mind that they should directly receive some of the benefits. Handing the money over to his PRU chief, the advisor knew it would be properly spread out among the men who had gone on the op.

But it was what was in the other cans that caused the greatest commotion. As documents were pulled out, some of the local intelligence people began getting excited over what they found. By now, it was about six o'clock in the morning. The intel people's excitement suggested that the chief of the CIA station was going to have an early morning. Waking the chief up from his room in the safe house, the PRU advisor informed him of what had happened and what was being discovered in the office.

Pulling in his office people, the station chief ordered a full translation of the documents typed up. The SEAL PRU advisor had suspected that the operation might result in some good intelligence. But even he wasn't ready for what they had found.

The PRUs had captured a complete set of documentation outlining the 1970 Tet Offensive planned by the Viet Cong for the IV Corps area. This was the biggest intelligence capture the SEALs had ever been involved in. It showed what the VC were planning, how it would be done, and what units would be involved. The material was very time-sensitive, but only because of its importance. A special Air American flight was sent down from Can Tho to pick up the documents. From the Can Tho District Intelligence Operations Coordination Center, the papers were sent to Saigon.

Within thirty-six hours of being captured, the documents were on the other side of the world, being placed on the negotiation tables at the Paris Peace talks. The NVC and VC representatives could speak of how they were not the aggressors, but only wanted peace. The papers were solid proof of just how the VC and NVA wanted that peace brought about.

Mission Twelve, 6 May 1970:
"Listening on the Lake"

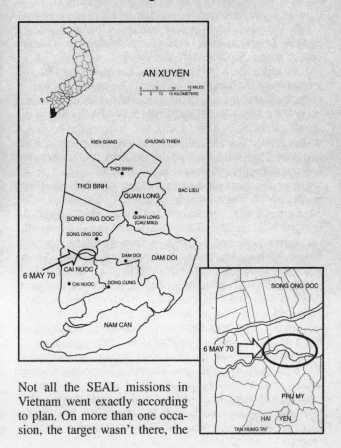

Not all the SEAL missions in Vietnam went exactly according to plan. On more than one occasion, the target wasn't there, the enemy was there in much greater force than expected, or nature took a hand.

The Song Ong Doc River is on the west shore of the Ca Mau peninsula, the southernmost point of South Vietnam, emptying into the Gulf of Thailand. Roughly at the center of the west side of the An Xuyen province, the Song Ong Doc travels up and to the north, into the center of the province. On the shores of the river, some ten miles inland, is the city of Song Ong Doc itself. This area is south of the U Minh Forest, an area infiltrated by Viet Cong.

Four miles south of the mouth of the Song Ong Doc is a second river, the Song Dong Cung. This river travels further to the east than the Song Ong Doc and passes the province capital, Ca Mau (Quan Long). Just six miles upriver of the mouth of the Song Dong Cung, the river opens up into a wide, shallow lake almost five miles long and one mile wide in places. This lake picked up the nickname VC Lake for the amount of enemy activity around its shores.

On its third tour of duty in country, SEAL Team Two's Sixth Platoon was stationed at Ca Mau to operate throughout the peninsula. The platoon had arrived in Vietnam early in April 1970 and had a very experienced cadre of both officers and enlisted men. The platoon chief was on his third tour of duty in Vietnam, having been with the Second Platoon when they were first deployed to Vietnam back in early 1967.

When a SEAL platoon arrived at their operating area, they did their first few missions in an easy manner to get a good feel for the enemy activity in their area. The SEALs performed all operations in the expectation of enemy contact. But a newly arriving platoon had to build up its intelligence network and establish the general movement and location of VC units in its area. To conduct one of these intelligence-gathering missions, the platoon chief took a fire team of four SEALs from Bravo Squad and himself down to VC lake to assess the situation there. The Naval Intelligence Liaison Officer in Ca Mau had stated that there was movement of VC forces across VC Lake.

Mobile Support Team Two's Detachment F was assigned

to work with the SEALs and other navy units in the Ca Mau area. Using Det F's Medium SEAL Support Craft (MSSC) under the command of ensign McChesney, the SEALs traveled down the Song Dong Cung river to the vicinity of VC Lake. Having towed a sixteen-foot Boston whaler with the MSSC to act as an insertion craft, the SEALs arrived at VC Lake at 2215 hours on April 6.

Running under power from its silenced outboard motor, the whaler moved into the shallow waters of VC lake as the MSSC remained on station in the deeper waters of the river. Some fish stakes, used by the Vietnamese fishermen to secure their fish traps, were located in the western portion of the lake and this was where the whaler tied up to await any VC movement. The SEALs were about ten kilometers southeast of the city of Song Ong Doc when they secured for their watch.

Much of the Ca Mau peninsula is very low to the water, in some places no more than a few feet above sea level. Marshy and full of canals, streams, and other bodies of water, the sea tides can have a greater effect inland than most sailors would expect. This was the situation for the SEALs on their guard post as the tide went out and the very shallow VC Lake became shallower still.

As a sampan started moving across the water some 600 meters from where the SEALs were waiting, they decided to approach the native boat and see who the occupants might be. It was at this point that the SEALs found themselves aground on a mud bank. The whaler drew too much water to move, there being only a few inches of water now over the muddy lake bottom. Even as far upriver as they were, the sea's tide had affected their situation, and not for the better. Unable to move, the unit spent a very interesting night waiting for any VC activity that might discover their predicament.

Even for the SEALs, trying to move through several miles of mud would be a bit hard. But the men were willing to consider that as the long night moved on. They were sitting ducks and they knew it. But discipline and training proved true and the SEALs silently spent the evening in enemy territory. This wasn't a situation the men had not been in before; not being able to extract had made a simple operation a possibly much more serious one.

After dawn, the tide rose again and the waters of VC Lake grew deeper. The whaler was freed and the SEALs spent little time extracting and moving back to the MSSC. The night had proven uneventful except for the unplanned grounding of the SEALs in the middle of a lake.

```
BARNDANCE # 6-9    SEAL TEAM Two; DET Alfa; 6th
PLT.
DATE(S): 062215H-070530H
OTHER UNITS: MST 2 Det F (Ens McChesney)
MSG REF(S): 070630Z May 70
NAMES OF PERS: CPO Watson (PL), Leonard, Hyde,
Barry, Tesci
MISSION TASK: Waterbourne guard post
INTEL/INFO SOURCE(S): NILO, SOD
INSERTION: TIME: 062215H METHOD: MSSC/Whaler AMS
COORD: VQ 91 96
EXTRACTION: TIME: 070530H METHOD: MSSC/Whaler
AMS COORD: VQ 91 96
BRIEF MISSION NARRATIVE: Set guard post at fish
stakes in center of lake. Sighted sampan at
approximately 600 meters. Unable to take under-
fire due to lack of water. Extracted by Whaler to
MSSC 07530H.
RESULTS OF ENEMY ENCOUNTERED: None
FRIENDLY CASUALTIES: None
REMARKS (SIGNIFICANT EVENTS, OPEVAL RESULTS,
ETC.): None
RECOMMENDATIONS/LESSONS LEARNED: Whaler will not
operate in VC lake at low tide due to lack of water.
BD COPY DIST: COMNAVFORV-CTF 116.6, OinC SEAL Det
Alfa, SEAL Team 2, SEAL Team 1
BARNDANCE # 6-9
```

Mission Thirteen, 22 August 1970:
"A Perfect Rescue"

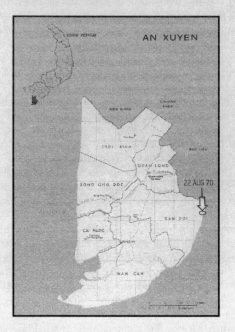

There was no greater target for the SEALs personally than rescuing Americans POWs from enemy hands. Every SEAL would do whatever it took to get a POW mission on line and operating if they felt they had the hot intel. And the SEALs' ability to conduct fast raids at a moment's notice gave them the chance to hit POW camps.

On August 21, 1970, a Vietnamese POW escaped from a

prison camp very near the eastern shore of An Xuyen province in the Dam Doi district, only a few kilometers south of the border with Bac Lieu province. The Sector S-2 intelligence office saw to it the information got to the SEAL platoon operating out of Ca Mau as quickly as possible.

SEAL Team Two's Sixth Platoon was more than halfway through their tour of duty in Vietnam and had already racked up an impressive number of successful operations and high-ranking targets. The platoon was competent, sharp, and had very high-quality leadership. The platoon leader received the information on the location of a POW camp in his operational area at about 1800 hours on 21 August.

The information for operations for Sixth Platoon had been coming in hard and fast. Lieutenant Louis H. Boink III, the platoon leader of Sixth, had been practically living in the Tactical Operations Center (TOC), he had been going in so often to arrange operations. When the intelligence came in on the POW camp, along with the escapee who could lead the SEALs back to the camp, all other operations were put on hold. The information was hot, the camp existed, and the SEALs had a guide who could take them in.

During the long night, Lieutenant Boink coordinated the effort to raid the POW camp with other support throughout the province. POW camp intelligence had the shortest life span of all according to the SEALs' past experience. The mission had to go ahead as quickly as possible to have a chance of success. Sixth Platoon didn't even have its full complement of SEALs on hand when the information on the camp came in. One of the squads was down at Hai Yen, over seventeen kilometers south of Ca Mau, operating in that area. The operation had to go ahead with the SEALs Lieutenant Boink had available—all four of them.

Even though he was limited in the number of SEALs, Lieutenant Boink was not short in the support department. For more local guidance, two Kit Carson Scouts (KCS) were attached to the operation. The Kit Carson Scout was an off-shoot of the Chieu Hoi program. VC ralliers to the Chieu Hoi program could volunteer to become Kit Carsons since the unit was formed in the summer of 1966. The KCS were sent out to various U.S. military units throughout South Vietnam and acted much like the old Indian Scouts from the days of the Wild West. The experience and abilities of a Kit Carson could add a great deal to the combat efficiency of a military unit, even one already as good as the SEALs.

To augment his manpower on the ground, Lieutenant Boink called on the 974th Regional Force, a paramilitary group of South Vietnamese national police who were under the direction of the province chief. An additional Vietnamese for the ground crew was an interpreter who had worked with the SEALs before. Additional U.S. support included a U.S. Marine lieutenant in a light plane to act as a naval gunfire spotter. The naval gunfire support would come from the U.S.S. *Southerland* (DD 743), a modernized U.S. "Gearing" class ship that mounted four five-inch guns.

A Seawolf Light Helicopter Fire Team was brought on board for air support. Additional helicopter gunships and transportation slicks would be coming from the Army's 175th Aviation Company. One of the more unusual forms of air support would be part of the operation in the form of six Royal Australian Air Force B-57 Canberra bombers carrying a load of 750-pound bombs. The B-57s were from the RAAF No. 2 Squadron (the Magpies) based at Phan Rang Air Base. Each could carry up to 7,000 pounds of ordnance (nine 750-pound bombs).

With the support arranged, the plan was finalized and the SEALs given their briefing. Operation STORY BOOK would begin early the next morning, when the Australian B-57s would start a bombing attack to the south of the suspected POW camp. This would block any escape from the camp to the south. The SEALs and the men from the 974th RF company would land by slick on the beaches of the South China Sea, to the east of the camp.

Helicopter gunship and naval gunfire would be directed as needed to block any escape of the VC and their prisoners. It was hoped that if enough pressure was put on the VC guards, they would break and run, abandoning their prison-

ers. If the operation went quickly enough, the VC guards
would not have the chance to harm their prisoners before the
SEALs and RF forces would be on them.

The mission began early the next morning, August 22. At
0815 hours, the Australian B-57s began their bombing runs.
The bomber's target was an 800-meter-long line following a
canal. Forty minutes later, at 0855 hours, the SEALs and the
RF troops inserted along the narrow beach facing the heavy
jungle to the west, some 600 meters to the northeast of the
suspected camp location.

The SEALs and the RFs made almost immediate contact
with a VC guard some fifty meters west of their insertion
position. As the frightened VC ran into a bunker, the men
quickly surrounded the emplacement. When the VC opened
fire on the approaching men, the bunker was immediately
taken under fire by one of the SEALs. As the SEAL kept the
bunker under fire, he covered the rest of the patrol as it was
maneuvering toward the emplacement. With complete disre-
gard for his own safety, the one SEAL kept firing at the position, eventually silencing the enemy fire.

The area was quickly swept for VC and three bodies were
discovered along with one weapon. The noise of firing had
alerted the camp as to the line of approach by the SEALs
and the RF troops. To prevent the escape of the POW guards
further inland, the helicopter gunships were directed to fire
to the west and north of the camp location.

Minigun fire and rockets tore into the jungle as the SEAL
moved further into the area. As they patrolled west, constantly alert for any VC contact, the SEALs were guided by
the escapee directly to the heavily camouflaged prison compound. The team arrived at the camp at 1015 hours. The
camp was deserted, but a large number of fresh footprints
led off to the south. The gunships were redirected to put
their fire in 500 meters to the south of the camp in hopes of
cutting off any further escape by the VC and their prisoners.

As the gunships moved to a new firing position, the
U.S.S. *Southerland* offshore began putting in five-inch
shells to the south of the camp. Moving as swiftly as they

could while remaining watchful, the SEALs led the units south, following the tracks through the jungle. After traveling some 1,400 meters southwest of the camp, the SEALs began finding bundles of clothes and other miscellaneous personal gear scattered along the trail. The VC and their prisoners were abandoning their possessions to speed up their travel. The guards were panicking and running. The SEALs knew the VC had to be only minutes ahead of them.

The air attacks were ordered increased. As the 2.75-inch rockets slammed into the jungle, the SEALs prepared to close in. Ordering the fire lifted, the patrol continued quickly after their quarry. The patrol had traveled only a short distance from where they had found the clothes and equipment when, at 1245 hours, after an almost two-hour chase, the SEALs came on a group of terrified prisoners.

There were no Americans with the twenty-eight South Vietnamese prisoners the SEALs discovered. Their VC guards had just abandoned them to their fate and fled into the jungle. In spite of the lack of Americans, the SEALs were overwhelmed with the gratitude shown them by the freed POWs when they were told who the patrol was by the interpreter. The Command and Control helicopter overhead directed the patrol to a clearing 200 meters west of their position for extraction. The patrol arrived at the indicated position at 1310 hours. Cutting back trees and brush, the landing zone was improved so the slicks could come in and pick the unit up. Maintaining a tight security perimeter around the small LZ, the slicks came in one at a time and pulled out the prisoners, RF troops, and SEALs.

By 1445 hours, the liberated prisoners and all the members of the patrol were back at Ca Mau. Investigation of the prisoners turned up some interesting facts. Among the twenty-eight POWs were several ex-VC. One man had been the commander of the 1109th VC Company. The commander, one of his platoon leaders, and a squad leader had been imprisoned when they were caught trying to Chieu Hoi to the South Vietnamese. Four additional VCI were among the liberated POWs, having been imprisoned for the same offense, trying to Chieu Hoi. Other POWs were South Vietnamese soldiers who had been captured when their outpost was overrun by the VC in 1968. The POWs had suffered at the hands of their VC captors for over two years.

Though no U.S. POWs were rescued in the operation, the SEALs had a hard time feeling bad about what they had done. Not one member of the patrol had been injured in the operation. The cooperation of the other services and units had been incredible. To the Platoon Leader of Sixth Platoon, the cooperation and interworking of all the different units had been something to read about in fiction books. Only the SEALs had actually done it.

```
BARNDANCE # 6-54    SEAL TEAM TWO: DET Alfa; 6th
PLT.
DATE(S): 220855H-211445H [22 August 1970]
OTHER UNITS: 975 RF co., Ca Mau, 175th Aviation
Co. Mini-Pac with heavy fire team (Maj Adams),
C&C ship (Capt Hernandez and NILO Ca Mau), 1 US
Destroyer (USS Sutherland), naval gunfire spot-
ter (LTJG Gerald), Shotgun 42 (WO Finch), Seawolf
69/68 (LTJG Blair), 6 Australian B-57 bombers.
MSG REF(S): 0 221700Z Aug 70
NAMES OF PERS: Lt. Boink (PL), Nelson, Lewis,
Sprenkle, Blackiston, 2 KCS, 1 interpreter, 974
Company
MISSION TASK: Liberate 58 Prisoners of war
INTEL/INFO SOURCE(S): Sector S-2, escapee from
POW camp
INSERTION: TIME: 220910H METHOD: Slick AMS COORD:
WQ 445 931
EXTRACTION: TIME: 221430H METHOD: Slick AMS
COORD: WQ 433 913
BRIEF MISSION NARRATIVE: Acting on intel supplied
by Sector S-2, the following sequence was fol-
lowed in targeting a fifty-eight man POW camp in
vic WQ 440 928. 220815H six Royal Australian B-57
bombers began placing 750-pound bombs along canal
```

from WQ 420 914 to WQ 435 908 to establish blocking force by fire to South of camp. At 220855
SEALs and 974 RF Co. inserted along narrow beachline and spotted armed male entering bunker 50m
east of our position. Surrounded bunker and took
under fire after VC attempted to shoot SEAL from
entrance. Searched area and discovered three VC
and one Chicom rifle. Directed heavy rocket and
mini-gun fire to North and West of POW camp to
establish further blocking forces being led by
out guide who had escaped from the camp three
days prior, patrolled 500m West and entered POW
camp at 221015H. Spotted many fresh footprints
leading South and directed US Army gunship and
Seawolves to fire 500m South of camp hoping to
cut off route of escape. At same time USS Sutherland began placing 5-inch rounds to South of
camp. Followed tracks South and in the vicinity
WQ 435 914 began finding miscellaneous personal
gear and called for intensified rocket runs by
gunships believing guards would abandon prisoners if enough pressure was applied. Continued
South and at 221245H linked up with 28 POWs who's
guards had just fled the area. C&C ship directed
patrol to area 200 m West, for possible pick up
point and arrived 221310H. Cleared trees in area
and were extracted by single slicks and returned
Ca Mau 221445H.
RESULTS OF ENEMY ENCOUNTERED: 3 VC KIA (BC),
other casualties by gunships unknown. One Chicom
carbine captured, 28 POWs liberated. FRIENDLY
CASUALTIES: Neg
REMARKS (SIGNIFICANT EVENTS, OPEVAL RESULTS,
ETC.): Preliminary readout indicates among POWs
was ex-VC Company Commander CD 1109 VC Company.
His platoon leader, squad leader, caught trying
to Chieu Hoi and four other VCI imprisoned for
same reason. Other POWs were members of outpost

which was overrun by VC two years ago.
RECOMMENDATIONS/LESSONS LEARNED: The cooperation
and professionalism shown by the various services
are like things one reads in story books. The
Sixth Platoon sends thanks and 28 liberated send
a great deal more.
BD COPY DIST: COMNAVFORV-CTF 116.6, OIC Det ALFA,
SEAL 2, SEAL 1 SIGNATURE OF PERSON MAKING OUT
REPORT: David D Hammer HMC (for) Louis H. Boink,
LT USNR
BARNDANCE # 6-54

The Silent Stalkers:
Submarines, Large and Small

Submarines had been used as a means of covertly transporting commando forces and raiders since World War II. Both
the Navy SEALs and the UDTs operated from submarines
as the mission required. The first submarine-borne mission
conducted by the UDTs was during World War II when the
U.S.S. *Burrfish* (SS 312), a 312-foot Balao class diesel/elec-
tric boat, moved out on a mission in the South Pacific.

The mission of the *Burrfish* was the reconnaissance of the
Japanese-held islands of Yap and Peleliu. On 9 July, 1944,
the *Burrfish* left Pearl Harbor, Hawaii, on her secret mission
with a detachment of two officers and six enlisted men from
UDT 10 on board. Launching the UDT operators in inflatable rubber boats, the investigation of Peleliu was accomplished without incident. During a later reconnaissance of
Yap island, the mission did not go well.

Chief Howard Roeder, John MacMahon, and Robert
Black of UDT 10 did not make their rendezvous with the
Burrfish, and the submarine had to leave the shallow waters
off Yap to avoid detection. Returning several times, the submarine was not able to recover the three UDT operators and
was forced to leave the area due to mission demands. Cap-

tured by the Japanese, the three operators from UDT 10 became the only men from the UDTs or the SEALs to ever be taken prisoner by the enemy. It is known that the three men did not break security under interrogation but they did not survive the war. All were posthumously awarded the Silver Star for their actions.

The loss of the three UDT men led to no more submarine-borne operations with the UDTs during World War II. After the war, the UDTs tested operational techniques that included locking in and out of submarines while underwater, while they were motionless and under way. The Balao-class submarines *Sealion* (SS 315) and *Perch* (SS 313) were converted after the war into submarine transport craft and designated Transport Submarines (SSP). The conversion of the *Sealion* was completed in 1948. Half of the craft's diesel propulsion systems and all of her torpedo tubes were removed to make room for an additional four officers and sixty-eight troops along with their equipment and support:

SEALION SSP 315—ORIGINALLY LAUNCHED AS SS 315 ON 8 MARCH 1944
Length—311 feet 9 inches
Beam—27 feet
Draft—17 feet
Displacement—2,145 tons (surface), 2,500 tons (submerged)
Guns—two 40mm AA
Main Engines—2 GM diesels (2,305 HP), 4 electric; 2 shafts
Batteries—Exide; 252 cells
Fuel—305 tons
Speed—13 knots (surface) 10 knots (submerged)
Complement—74 (6 officers, 68 men)

Both the *Sealion* and later *Perch* proved their worth in delivering commandos, Marines, or UT operators (frogmen) on covert operations. Men from UDT 11 were deployed aboard the U.S.S. *Perch* during some of the earliest Team actions in Vietnam. Gunners aboard the *Perch* used both the 40mm cannons and .50-caliber machine guns to support the fourteen-man UDT detachment performing beach reconnaissance and hydrographic surveys when the men came under fire from Viet Cong positions.

The *Perch* and her UDT detachment had been operating as part of Operation DECKHOUSE III in August 1966 off of Southeast Asia. Several recons had been completed without incident when, on the night of August 21, part of the UDT detachment became separated from the others. It was during a search for the missing men, who were later recovered, that the *Perch* used her .50-caliber machine guns to suppress enemy small arms fire coming out from the shore. In a later action, the *Perch* used both her machine guns and 40mm cannon to eliminate Viet Cong positions while also directing air strikes against the VC. This was the last time that a U.S. submarine conducted a surface action against enemy forces.

Additional operations off of South Vietnam that the *Perch* was involved in included Operation DAGGER THRUST in late 1965 with Detachment Charlie from UDT 12. Operation DOUBLE EAGLE in January 1966 also had the *Perch* off the coast of South Vietnam with a detachment from UDT 11 on board. In spite of her actions off of Vietnam, the *Perch* was a World War II boat that had a lot of mileage on her hull. Newer submarines were being converted to continue missions with the UDTs and the SEALs. The *Sealion*, which had been operating primarily in the Atlantic, still continued serving.

The *Perch* was declared unfit for further active naval operations in 1967 and was immobilized as a Naval Reserve training ship in San Diego in 1967. The year before, the U.S.S *Tunny* (SSG 282), originally a Regulus missile submarine, had been converted to a transport submarine. The large hanger behind the sail of the *Tunny*, designed for the winged Regulus missile, was converted to a transportation space that could hold men and their equipment. The *Tunny* was a Gato-class World War II submarine and, other than her large rear deck hangar, had much the same size and capabilities of the Balao-class subs.

Arriving at the U.S. naval base at Subic Bay in the Philippines in September, the *Tunny* was redesignated as a Transport Submarine (APSS) on 1 October 1966. The craft was immediately put to use training with detachments from both UDT 11 and 12 to prepare for operations off Vietnam. Several beach reconnaissance operations were conducted by the *Tunny* and her UDT detachments in Southeast Asia during 1967.

In January 1968, the U.S.S. *Pueblo*, an electronic surveillance ship, was taken by the North Korean government for spying in North Korean waters. A short-lived plan was put together to destroy the *Pueblo* and her secret electronic equipment through the use of the Navy SEALs and the *Tunny*. The *Tunny* was to transport a SEAL Team One detachment to within striking range of where the North Koreans had secured the *Pueblo*. The SEALs would move to the *Pueblo* and destroy the ship with explosive charges. Destruction was planned to be so complete as to eliminate any chance of salvaging and reconstructing any of the electronic equipment on board. Some training was done with the SEALs and the *Tunny* to establish the plan as feasible but it was not approved. Later political negotiations resulted in the release of the *Pueblo*'s crew.

Another SEAL operation against North Vietnam was planned in 1968 that was to include the use of the *Tunny*. A SEAL Team One detachment was going to be inserted into North Vietnam from the Tunny, after crossing the Gulf of Tonkin undetected. The SEALs would move inland and attack a target near Hanoi. Operation NIGHT BOLT as it was named was planned and practiced in the waters near the Subic Bay base. The SEALs could operate off the *Tunny* with ease, moving themselves and their equipment onto and off of the craft without ever breaking the surface. But like the *Pueblo* operation, NIGHT BOLT was canceled.

The conversion of the *Tunny* to the APSS configuration was considered a stopgap measure until a new craft could be made ready for operations. The U.S.S. *Grayback* was a unique submarine almost from the first day of her existence. Originally laid down as an attack submarine in 1954, the Darter-class *Grayback* and her sister ship, the *Growler*, were converted to a new type of missile launching submarine while still under construction. The hulls of the two submarines were cut in half and lengthened by about 50 feet. Two cylindrical hangers were built into the enlarged bulbous bow of the submarines, each hangar being eleven feet high and seventy feet long. To direct the new missiles, a very elaborate navigation system and electronics suite was installed.

The *Grayback* and *Growler* had been designed for high-speed underwater travel while using very quiet machinery to minimize detectable sound signatures. These capabilities would allow the craft to move undetected though the seas and maintain a nuclear deterrence against a possible first-strike or sneak attack against the United States.

The *Grayback* and *Growler* had their large hangars to hold the Regulus nuclear-tipped missile. By today's standards, the Regulus would be considered a cruise missile, the weapon resembling a jet aircraft without a pilot's compartment. The Regulus had to be moved from the hangar on a transport dolly while the submarine was on the surface and the wings attached for use. The large hangars were connected to the interior of the submarine to allow the missile crew to work on the Regulus while the craft was still submerged. Rendered obsolete in 1964 by more advanced nuclear armed submarines, it was the two large water-tight hangars built into the *Grayback* that appealed to Navy planners.

In November 1967, the conversion of the *Grayback* from a missile carrier to a troop transport sub was begun. The conversion was completed in 1969 and the *Grayback* was commissioned as an Amphibious Transport Submarine (LPSS) on 9 May 1969. The submarine had actually received the designation LPSS on 30 August 1968, but the completion of her conversion was delayed by other projects with a higher priority.

The new LPSS 574 *Grayback* could transport up to sixty-seven men and their equipment, both feeding and berthing the men without difficulty. But the really unique aspect of the *Grayback* centered on the two converted bow hangars. The hangars had been secured with internal bulkheads, changing the stern half of the hangar to a pressure lock. The rear half of the hangars could be entered while the submarine was still under water, sealed off and flooded, and the clamshell doors opened to the sea, releasing men and their equipment while the sub was either sitting on the bottom or under way.

The pressure locks of each hangar could hold two Swimmer Delivery Vehicles (SDVs), eight standard inflatable rubber boats, or a single high-speed surface craft. The SDVs would each be on a simple wheeled dolly that could be moved out onto the deck of the submarine for launching. A larger wheeled dolly would be used for the high-speed boat.

GRAYBACK LPSS 315—ORIGINALLY COMMISSIONED AS SSG 574 ON 7 MARCH 1958
Length—334 feet 4 inches
Beam—30 feet
Draft—19 feet
Displacement—2,670 tons (surface), 3,650 tons (submerged)
Torpedo Tubes—eight 21-inch, 6 forward, 2 aft
Main Engines—3 Fairbanks Morse diesels (4,500 SHP), 2 Elliot electric (5,600 SHP); 2 shafts
Batteries—Gould, 504 cells
Speed—20 knots (surface), 17 knots (submerged)
Complement—87 (9 officers, 78 men)
Troop Capacity—67 (7 officers, 60 enlisted)

The size of the *Grayback* made her the largest conventionally powered submarine in the world. To further support her mission as an amphibious transport sub, the *Grayback* had the largest decompression chamber in the navy installed as part of her standard equipment. Breathing equipment using boat air (supplied from the submarine) was in both of the pressure locks to allow work to be done under water, even on the sub's open deck, without depending on limited breathing systems. In addition, the boat kept stores of oxygen and other breathing gases for charging underwater breathing systems. A fully qualified doctor, well versed in diving medicine, was on board as part of the ship's normal complement. A large explosives magazine was also on board the *Grayback*.

The *Grayback* was also the only submarine in service at that time that could bottom on the sea floor for extended periods of time. All of the ship's seawater intakes were located ten feet above the keel rather than along the bottom of the ship as in other sub designs. The *Grayback* could sit on the bottom and run all of her important interior machinery without risk. Special silencing of the machinery also limited the detection rage of the *Grayback* so that she couldn't be easily heard on passive sonar systems searching for her.

To further support the *Grayback*'s primary mission of being able to launch large numbers of underwater swimmers from her forward hangars, twelve members of the ship's crew were qualified as divers. The *Grayback*'s diving gang could work on the outside of the submarine and in the flooded hangars, launching and recovering SDVs or combat swimmers while under water. This allowed the SEALs or UDT men involved to concentrate on their part of the mission rather than the technical aspects of working the submarine's gear.

Arriving at her home port at the Subic Bay Naval Station, the *Grayback* joined the U.S. Seventh Fleet for operations by February 1970. The LPSS *Tunny* had been retired and stricken from the Navy lists on 30 June 1969. The *Growler*, sister ship to the *Grayback*, had been scheduled to also undergo conversion into an amphibious troop transport and replace the *Sealion* but this conversion was canceled.

THE SDVs

The SEALs and the UDTs not only operated with the largest conventional submarine (the *Grayback*) in the U.S. Navy, they also worked with some of the smallest underwater craft in the service. The Swimmer Delivery Vehicles, or SDVs, are small underwater vehicles intended to increase the range and operational capabilities of underwater swimmers. The vehicles, small free-flooding or "wet" submarines, developed from ideas used by the Italian and British Navies during World War II. The Italians in particular had used small manned torpedoes to deliver swimmers and explosive charges to targets as early as World War I.

Normal fleet-type submarines are limited as far as secret close-in shore attacks go due to the depth of the water they need to operate in. The usual 1,500-ton displacement submarine cannot operate submerged in water less than sixty feet deep normally. Water depths of less than 150 feet are considered hazardous for standard submarine operations. The sixty-foot limit extends out for several miles from shore in many parts of the world. A covert, underwater approach would have to be made from a small submersible or even by combat swimmers equipped with breathing equipment. Even a very fit combat swimmer could reach near his exhaustion level trying to swim several miles in to shore while towing his mission equipment with him. Very few types of breathing equipment would carry enough breathing gas to even allow such an operation to be conducted.

A small submersible, rather than a true submarine, could be carried by a parent submarine or small boat to within striking range of a target and launched without detection. Even on extended missions, the underwater vehicle could be "parked" on the bottom, secured in place, while the men who traveled in it went in to shore to conduct their operation. Coming back several days later, the men could swim back down to the anchored submersible and return to their parent ship.

Since the underwater vehicles the Navy looked at were free-flooding—that is, they would fill with water while in use—the men who rode in them would have to wear breathing equipment and be exposed to the water. This meant that the men would be in for a long, cold ride in a cramped space, crowded with their mission equipment and diving gear.

The UDTs had been examining different types of underwater vehicles since the 1940s. By the mid 1960s, a design from the General Dynamics Corporation, their Convair Model 14 Swimmer Delivery Vehicle, was considered for adoption. By 1969, the Convair Model 14 had been accepted by the Navy as the Mark VII Mod 2 SDV. Operational testing and evaluations resulted in changes being adopted into the SDV and the modified vehicle being used as the Mark VII Mod 6. This SDV quickly became called the Six Boat by the men of the UDTs and SEAL Teams who operated in her.

MARK VII MOD 6 SDV
Length—18 feet 6 inches
Beam—35 inches
Draft—57 inches
Weight—2,200+ lbs
Main Engine—one 24-volt 1.83 (max) hp dc motor; 1 shaft w/18-inch, 5-blade propeller
Batteries—six parallel silver-zinc batteries; 16 cells each
Speed—0.5 to 4 knots (submerged)
Duration—8 hours at 4 knots
Complement 4 (2 crew, 2 passengers)
Life Support—Eight 90-cubic-foot 3,000-psi air tanks (720 cubic feet of air) w/4 Conshelf VI regulators

The hull of the SDV is made of 0.080-inch thick fiberglass with reinforcing plastic strips. Internal fittings and components are made of nonferrous metals where ever possible. These two construction methods help minimize the detectable magnetic signature of the Mk VII SDV. The operator sits on the floor in the front of the craft with another diver, the navigator, sitting behind him. The other two passengers are in the rear compartment, also sitting one in front of the other but facing backward.

A central buoyancy tank can be filled or emptied of water to control the buoyancy of the SDV. The tank system is sealed in that when the water is pumped in, the air in the tank is bled off into storage to keep any telltale bubbles from being released. The SDV is steered by bow and stern diving planes and a rudder controlled though a stick much like that in an old aircraft.

Travel in the SDV is at best cold and dark. Most SDV missions are conducted at night and any light bleeding off into the surrounding water could give the mission away. The sliding covers over the forward and stern compartments are solid fiberglass with no windows. The operator directs the craft with his instruments. Both the crew and especially the passengers cannot move about much and tend to lose a lot of heat to cold water on long missions.

The UDTs had run the majority of the SDV program during the 1960s. By 3 February 1969, SEAL Team One had established an SDV platoon consisting of two officers and fourteen enlisted men. The platoon trained with the Convair Model 14 prior to the Navy accepting it as the Mark VII Mod 2 SDV. The submarine U.S.S. *Rock* operated with the SEAL SDV platoon and their craft off the Los Coronados Islands in the Pacific in June 1969, establishing and proving out procedures and techniques for using the SDVs.

From 5 December 1969 to 7 January 1970, the *Grayback* in her new LPSS configuration arrived in San Diego to train with the SEAL and the UDT SDV units. In the month of training aboard the *Grayback*, the SEALs conducted over two hundred swimmer lockouts and eighteen SDV launches and recoveries. The operations were conducted both with the submarine underway and bottomed, during both daylight and at night.

The *Grayback* deployed to Subic Bay in January. The SEAL Team One SDV platoon had proven the capabilities of the SEALs to operate with both the submarine *Grayback* and the SDVs. Personnel from the SDV platoon rotated back through the rest of SEAL Team One, spreading their skills with the SDVs throughout the Team. This gave the SEALs a new method of operating and opened a new range of possible missions.

Mission Fourteen, 3 June 1972:
"Operation Thunderhead"

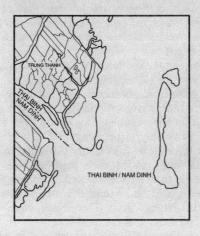

It was fitting that the last official SEAL operation of the Vietnam War was of the type the Teams held as most important, the rescue of American POWs from captivity. And it was during that operation that the last SEAL loss of the war took place.

In addition to the operations being conducted to rescue POWs in Vietnam, the POWs themselves were doing what they could to escape their captors. In North Vietnam, where the vast majority of prisoners were pilots and flight crews of U.S. aircraft, only a few actual escapes had been attempted from the POW camps during the war. The location of the various camps, usually hundreds of miles from friendly forces on land, was a major barrier. An additional problem was that the Caucasian prisoners stood out starkly in the Asian communities.

In spite of all that was operating against them, American POWs had attempted escapes on several occasions. The first known attempt was in 1967 when two POWs walked away from their captors when an American bombing attack sprang open the door to their cell. The men were seen and captured within hours of their walking away. A more planned break-out took place in 1969 when another pair of prisoners slipped away from their captors. Captured again some time later, the two Americans had remained at large for a longer time than the first pair.

In their rage at the insolence of the Americans to plan an escape attempt, the Communist captors punished the POWs severely. Torture and beatings were liberally dispensed among the prisoners in order to learn their covert methods of communication and planning. One of the 1969 POWs who had gotten away only to be recaptured. Edwin Atterberry, was beaten to death by his captors. After the interrogation sessions had finally ended, or at least had been cut back, orders went out from the highest-ranking POWs that no further escapes would be attempted without proven outside assistance in getting away. This requirement ended the POWs' escape attempts for several years.

A Prisoner Escape Committee remained in operation at most of the camps, though no Americans had escaped captivity in North Vietnam. The U.S. Military Code of Conduct stated that a soldier's duty was to escape, but the orders to prove outside assistance kept POWs from dying trying to follow that code. Through classified means, the Escape Committee at the Hanoi Hilton, an old French penitentiary called Hoa Lo by the North Vietnamese, managed to get information out to the U.S. Defense Intelligence Agency (DIA). The resourceful POWs would make another break, but they had to have help in getting out of North Vietnam itself.

The best escape plan the POWs had was a traditional one, to tunnel out of their location at the Hanoi Hilton and make their way to the Red River to the north of Hanoi. One of the prisoners on the Escape Committee had been one of the POWs to escape back in 1967. He knew it was possible to get to the Red River—that was where he had been caught before. Once at the river, the POWs would float in a stolen boat down the sixty miles or so to the Gulf of Tonkin. Once they reached the gulf they hoped to be picked up by U.S. forces.

It was the "being picked up" portion of the plan that the POWs had to prove to get permission to carry out their escape. Through difficult means, the POWs could get a message out of the camp and into DIA hands. It was the U.S. communication back to the POWs that was an even more difficult proposition. Finally, the escape plan and a very exotic and simple means of signaling the prisoners was put in the communications pipeline to the DIA.

By January 1972, the prisoners' plan and the request for aid had reached the desks of military commanders at the Pentagon. The prisoner's plan was code-named Operation DIAMOND. Proposed to Secretary of Defense Melvin Laird, the plan was eventually approved.

By 1972, the situation for U.S. Forces in South Vietnam had changed considerably. Very few U.S. combat troops of any type remained in the country. The defense of South Vietnam had been turned over to the government of South Vietnam and the ARVNs. Most of the SEALs had already left Vietnam by 1972. Tenth Platoon, the last SEAL Team Two deployed platoon, returned to Little Creek, Virginia on 12 June 1971. The last SEAL Team One platoon deployed to Det Golf was Mike Platoon, who left the country without relief on 7 December 1971. Operations for these last SEAL platoons had been few and far between, and the men finally left Vietnam gladly.

A small handful of SEALs remained in Vietnam, performing special duties as advisors to South Vietnamese units. These SEALs were also available for high-priority special operations. One of these operations took place in April 1972, when Lieutenant Thomas Norris of SEAL Team One rescued several American airmen who were downed behind enemy lines. Over several days of tight operations where the SEAL was constantly moving in VC territory without support, the men were found and brought out. The story was later fictionalized in part as BAT-21. Norris's part was intentionally left out of the tale. But the government recognized what had happened and later awarded Lieutenant Tom Norris the Congressional Medal of Honor.

Even as Norris was performing the actions that would later win him acclaim, other SEALs were preparing for another POW operation. On 10 January 1972, SEAL Team One had deployed Alfa Platoon to Okinawa to act as the Naval Special Warfare Western Pacific Detachment. The WESTPAC platoon was a normal deployment for the Teams as they were turning over their operational tempo from a wartime to peacetime footing. The platoon would be a contingency platoon for the Seventh Fleet, ready to act on any ops that might come up. Decisions had been made at a much higher level that the SEALs would have an operation coming up, but the platoon itself had no knowledge of what was a very secret operation.

The SEALs went into a training schedule in Okinawa, then traveled to Korea for cold-water training. A number of times, the platoon was called down to Subic Bay in the Philippines to work with the *Grayback* at the U.S. naval base. The *Grayback* was the only submarine of her kind in the Navy, intended to transport SEALs and UDT operators long distances under water without detection. From her large bow hangars, Swimmer Delivery Vehicles could be launched and recovered without the submarine ever breaking the surface.

Operations from the *Grayback* with SDVs were usually conducted by the UDTs who had the operational assignment of the small underwater craft. SEALs would usually work from the *Grayback* with rubber boats that could also be carried in the bow hangars. After several weeks of training with the SDVs, Alfa Platoon returned to Korea to attend the Marine mountain climbing school there.

Another unit working out of Okinawa became involved in the complex upcoming operation. A trio of SR-71s, the very high-altitude and super-secret spy planes, lifted off from their airfield on Okinawa, traveling over North Vietnam. The incredible SR-71 was a long, black, bat-winged aircraft that could fly at 80,000 feet, near the edge of space itself, at speeds of 2,000 miles per hour. The reconnaissance craft were well used to flying over North Vietnam, taking photographs of installations while moving well above the range of interceptor aircraft or missiles. But this time the SR-71s had been give a very specific and unusual set of orders.

Traveling at 75,000 feet, the pair of extremely valuable aircraft were moving at far below their normal speed. At exactly noon on May 2, directly over the North Vietnamese capital of Hanoi, the first SR-71 accelerated and broke the sound barrier ten seconds later, the second SR-71 did the same thing. The aircraft then continued on. The sonic booms of the two planes could be heard clearly through the streets and into the buildings of Hanoi. Some North Vietnamese were frightened by the sounds and took cover in the many small concrete foxholes lining the streets. Other individuals simply made note of the sounds and the times.

Two days later, two SR-71s committed the same strange actions. At exactly noon and then ten seconds later, sonic booms echoed through the skies over Hanoi. The pilots had done their jobs and their mission was finished. They were not to know why their mission was so critical, they only knew the timing had to be exact. In the Hanoi Hilton, over fourteen miles below the speeding aircraft, two POWs had their proof of outside help.

Now the POWs had four to six weeks to make their break for freedom. From one to five of the POWs would escape from the prison and move to the Red River. Once at the river, they would steal a small boat or sampan and travel downstream with all of the other river traffic. Hanoi was a major port on the Red River with ships coming up from the Gulf of Tonkin and many smaller craft coming in from the Red River Delta and upriver as well.

Once at the mouth of the Red River, the escaped POWs would signal either by flashing out to sea with a mirror or flying a red or yellow cloth from the mast of whatever craft they could steal. The POWs would be working on their own from leaving the prison to traveling downriver for pickup. The POWs and their Escape Committee had been working on different escape plans for years. Materials had been gathered by the prisoners to aid them in any escape. The POWs laid in supplies that included food, Vietnamese costumes, hats, a ladder, mirrors, even a key to the cell door.

The North Vietnamese were lax in their handling of materials around the prisoners. When something was lying about that the prisoners could use, it was quickly stolen and squirreled away. In the ceilings of some of the cells were supply stashes hidden in holes covered by cardboard the prisoners had made from toilet paper and lime. Charcoal coloring blended the covers with the rest of the walls and ceilings. The prisoners were caged, had suffered privations, and been tortured at the hands of their captors, but their spirits were still their own.

The prisoners had dropped the idea of a tunnel in their plan. Now the plan centered on waiting for the flooding season to begin in June. With the Red River at a high stage, the waters would be moving swiftly to the sea and the chances of avoiding detection that much better. The guards had stopped watching certain areas of the prison structure. At the right time, the prisoners would make their way through to the roof and slip over the wall with their ladder. Wearing their local costumes, the men would get to the river and float down it by whatever means they could locate. A boat theft would be noticed and something searchers would be alert for. The POWs planned to grab a boat only as a last resort. Logs, bamboo, mats, whatever would be floating in the river would do for their initial escape.

The higher command back in the United States thought the POWs had local help from Vietnamese resistance movements or sympathizers. That wrong assumption was a strong factor in the approval of Operation DIAMOND. DIAMOND was the code name for the prisoners' escape; now it was time for another operation to go ahead.

Operation THUNDERHEAD had been planned and finalized by the middle of May. The SEALs from the Westpac Det received a secret message while they were undergoing their mountain training in Korea. The orders were for the SEALs to immediately return to Subic Bay for further assignment. As Alfa Platoon arrived in the Philippines, they found the *Grayback* waiting for them. A detachment of fourteen frogmen from UDT 13 were already on board the submarine. The men of the UDT would operate the SDVs; the SEALs would be learning their part of the upcoming mission after the *Grayback* was under way. On 27 May 1972, the U.S.S. *Grayback* left Subic Bay, bound for the Gulf of Tonkin.

Lieutenant Melvin S. Dry was the platoon Leader of Alfa during their Westpac deployment. Lieutenant Dry; his senior petty officer from the platoon, Philip Martin; and two UDT operators, Lieutenant John Lutz and Tom Edwards, received briefings on the upcoming operation at the same time as the commanding officer, operations officer, and diving officer of the *Grayback* received theirs. Even on a sealed submarine, the information was compartmentalized for security. No one knew the entire operation, only the details of their part in it. What was known now was that the SEALs would be going into North Vietnamese waters to recover some POWs.

Even the final location of the operation wasn't known to the SEALs or UDT operators until they had to know. Only the officers in the Combat Information Center (CIC) of the *Grayback* knew the area of operations the submarine was bound for. With all of the secrecy surrounding the operation, the rest of the ships of the Seventh Fleet off the coast of Vietnam had no idea what was going on underneath them.

Because of her diesel/electric systems and large storage battery banks, the *Grayback* could move silently through the ocean. At night the ship would raise herself to periscope depth, run up a snorkle, and recharge her batteries as the diesels powered the boat. The electric systems were very close to absolutely silent; even the modern nuclear submarines were not as quiet as the *Grayback* could be when she wanted to. On June 3, 1972, after having traveled underneath most of the U.S. Seventh Fleet without detection, the *Grayback* arrived off the coast of North Vietnam.

There was no question to the men of the *Grayback* that

they were in the middle of a secret operation. They didn't know what the objective was, and they didn't have to. The routine of the ship continued as the UDTs and SEALs prepared for their part in the operation. Arriving on station, the *Grayback* settled to the bottom in over eighty feet of water, just three miles off the coast of North Vietnam.

Surveillance for the POWs was done over a wide strip of the North Vietnamese coast starting on May 29 and ending June 19. The section of coastline ran about fifty miles from north of the Red River to west of the "Hourglass" River. A small island blocked one of the prime sections of the surveillance area from the ship's view. In spite of the fact that the NVA had a small garrison on the island, the SEALs from the *Grayback* would set up an observation post on the island to try and pick up the POWs.

The nuclear-powered Guided Missile Cruiser *Long Beach* (CGN 9) would be the commanding vessel for the operation. Communications between the *Long Beach* and the *Grayback* would be by secure radio. If the POWs were spotted by one of the Search and Rescue (SAR) helicopters from HCC-7 Detachment 110 stationed aboard the *Kitty Hawk*, they would pick up the men and get them to the fleet. The U.S.S. *Harold E. Holt* would receive the POWs in their onboard hospital and then proceed at all speed to Subic Bay. The SAR helicopters would be the primary surveillance platform watching for the POWs. The SEALs on the island would cover one of the prime spots for the POWs coming out of the Red River, since the NVA garrison on the island would make it far too dangerous for the SAR helicopter to cover that portion of the coastline. The *Long Beach* would remain out in international water, fifty miles from North Vietnam. A SAR helicopter detachment on board the *Long Beach* were also prepared to take part in the operation.

The plan called for the SEALs to land on the island after approaching it under water from the *Grayback*. Because the SEALs may have to bring exhausted POWs, they could not be expected to swim from the island to the *Grayback*. If the SEALs recovered the POWs, the decision would then be made on how the men would get back to the submarine or be pulled out by air. Now, the SEALs would go to the island in SDVs operated by a pilot and navigator from UDT 13. At best, it would be a dangerous situation. The SEALs might have to remain on the island for up to twenty-two days, the length of the planned surveillance program.

The two SEALs and UDT operators who had received the briefing would go to the island by SDV on a scouting operation. The SDVs would check out the offshore waters, currents, and other factors. A lookout would watch for any red light showing as a night signal or any red or yellow cloth flags. If they saw no signal, the SEALs would exit the SDV and move in to the shore of the island, setting up their observation post (OP). The SEALs would man the OP for forty-eight hours and then a second team would come in by SDV and relieve them.

The leading petty office of Alfa Platoon, who had received official notice of his promotion to Warrant Officer only three days earlier, would be the man to approach the POWs if they were spotted. It wasn't known for certain if the POWs would be alone or in the company of a friendly agent, but the new SEAL warrant officer had a good deal of combat experience from Vietnam and expected to be able to handle whatever came along.

At 0200 hours on 4 June, the *Grayback* launched her first SDV of Operation Thunderhead. The UDT operators and the SEALs had plotted their course with care, trying to account for tides and currents from the river. With the water runoff from the river, and a heavy tide in the Gulf of Tonkin, the little SDV would be in trouble as soon as she moved into the target area, but no one on board the *Grayback* knew that.

With their swimming gear, breathing equipment, weapons, uniforms, gear, and radios, the heavily laden SEALs and UDT operators moved into the lockout chamber that was part of the bow hangars of the *Grayback*. The men climbed into the cramped cockpit and passenger area of the SDV and made ready for the operation. With the lockout chamber flooded, the huge clamshell door of the hanger opened into the dark waters of North Vietnam.

The SEALs and UDTs were using the very newest of the SDVs, the Mark VII Mod 6, which they called the Six boat. The nineteen-foot-long, fiberglass-hulled SDV had ballast tanks for buoyancy control, electric motors for propulsion, eight hours of its own bottled breathing air, and a communications system that could operate between the passengers and crew. What the SDV didn't have was much in the way of comfort. It would be a long, cold, and dark ride in to the island. No lights were shown in the SDV as she traveled along. And since the passengers and crew were just sitting, they couldn't warm up through exercise. While the pilot and navigator moved the craft along, the two SEALs sitting side by side in the isolated rear compartment could do nothing but sit in the dark and feel the cold.

The tides and river had combined to make a current that the SDV couldn't make much headway against. After hours of bucking the currents near the island, the men made a decision. The SDV just couldn't keep going much longer; it was time to call this portion of the op off and try again later. The *Grayback* would be sending out a special underwater signal at intervals. The SDV had the receiver necessary to follow those signals back to their source and rendezvous with the *Grayback* in the day without ever surfacing. The SDV turned around and started back for the *Grayback*, but it was too late for the little craft.

Bucking the heavy currents had been too heavy a drain on the SDV's power. The batteries ran flat halfway between the submarine and the island as dawn was coming up. Surfacing the SDV, the SEALs put out their call sign "Tom Boy" on the radio. It was time for the emergency pickup by a SAR bird from the fleet. At about 0800 hours, a helicopter from the *Long Beach* picked up the SEALs and UDT operators with what equipment they could salvage from the SDV. The little craft was full of water and far too heavy for the SAR bird to pick up. The UDT lieutenant told the door gunner to fire on the SDV with his Minigun and sink it.

As a final irony, the SDV had such a small target area in the buoyancy tanks, the helicopter gunner couldn't hit the proper place to sink the craft. Finally, the UDT lieutenant had to take the controls of the Minigun and sink his own boat. The helicopter flew the SEALs and UDT operators to the cruiser *Long Beach*. Secrecy still covered the operation, so the SEALs and UDT men were put up in the flag plot of the *Long Beach*. The men were allowed to rest, eat, and drink, but they were not allowed to mix with the crew of the *Long Beach* at all.

The men from the SDV discussed the operation and what had gone wrong with the insertion. They decided that the overall plan was operable, but the timing would have to be changed to meet the flow of the tides and currents. It was likely that the *Grayback* would have to move to a different position to release her next SDV in order for it to reach the island.

But on the *Grayback*, the decision had already been made to launch the rotation team out in an SDV the next night at the same time. Once the captain of the *Grayback* had been assured of the safety of the recovered SDV crew, he decided to put the operation on again, thinking it was just a mechanical or electrical failure that had prevented the SDV from reaching the target.

Communications with the *Grayback* from the *Long Beach* were limited. The submarine only put her snorkle up at night to charge her batteries. When the snorkle was up, the attached antenna allowed radio communications. The schedule for communications over the secure radio band with the *Grayback* was from 0500 to 0700 and 2000 to 2200 hours daily.

Communications were finally established with the *Grayback* that night and the message was sent that the first SDV crew would be coming back to the sub. To home in the SAR helicopter that would be bringing the SEALs and UDT operators to the submarine, the *Grayback* was going to "shine." That meant the submarine was going to put infrared equipment on the snorkle. With special vision equipment, the pilot of the helicopter would see the otherwise invisible infrared light and could come in right above the submarine. The SEALs and UDT men would jump from the helicopter into the sea and swim down to the submarine. This was not an operation for the faint of heart, but both the SEALs and the UDTs had practiced the techniques and knew what they were doing.

A heavy overcast blotted out the sun and removed any reference the helicopter pilot had to the horizon. The pilot had already been briefed on what the men were going to do. The bird was to be no higher than twenty feet from the water when the men jumped from the craft. It was also to be going no faster than 20 knots. It was a difficult airborne cast and recovery technique, but the SEALs and the Frogs had faith in their training. Warrant Officer Martin would be the jumpmaster for the insertion as he had the most experience with that technique.

The helicopter almost immediately had trouble locating the *Grayback*. The men on board the bird knew they had to get to the *Grayback* by 2300 hours, when the second SDV was due to be launched. After flying around and around, searching for his signal, the pilot finally called out that he had spotted the red light as he headed in to it. What the pilot had spotted was a red light on the beach, but it wasn't the POWs. Banking the bird hard, the pilot flew back out to sea and started searching again.

The pilot saw a red light again, and the warrant officer in the doorway could see they were about the right distance from shore, about three thousand yards. The wind was up, the water choppy, and the clouds made the whole scene very dark.

Experience told the SEAL that if the helicopter was very low, on the order of five or ten feet from the surface, the downwash from the blades would kick up a spray they would see straight below them. Up to about twenty feet up, they would be able to see a water spray just past the end of the tail rotor, behind the bird. The SEALs had monitored these signs in the past to determine if they were close enough to jump safely. Although the pilot now told the men to jump, the SEAL said they were too high.

Another pass over the light only the pilot could see, and again, the SEAL saw no spray. The pilot tried lowering the bird and coming in for another pass; again no spray, and the SEAL wouldn't call the jump. Finally, Lieutenant Dry told the SEAL they were running out of time. They had to get to the *Grayback* before the other SDV launched. The pilot took the bird down once more. On the last pass, the SEAL thought he could see the white spray from the water. The men started exiting the bird.

The jumpmaster was the third man out of the door. As he fell, he started to count off the seconds. At three seconds, he still hadn't hit the water and knew they were all in trouble. As that thought went through his mind, he slammed into the water, having jumped from close to one hundred feet and well over twenty knots in speed. The impact with the water twisted the SEAL's knee a bit, but otherwise he was okay. Turning about, he started calling out for his Teammates.

Lieutenant Dry didn't answer his call, but the UDT lieutenant was able to answer. The officer was hurt and could hardly swim. His knee had been injured as well as his back. Though in pain, there was nothing else to do but swim about looking for the other two men. Swimming in a twenty-five-yard search pattern, he could not find the other men. On his last pass, the SEAL raised his head up from the water and heard a quiet moan. The other UDT swimmer was not five feet from the SEAL, floating face down and barely moving.

Helping his stricken Teammate, the SEAL lifted the frogman's head. The man was so badly injured, he couldn't turn himself over on his back. Inflating the injured man's lifejacket, the SEAL towed him back to the other swimmer. Now the three men were looking for the lost lieutenant. As an hour went by, they continued searching and calling out. The SEAL still had much of his equipment and his weapon, a Swedish K submachine gun. He wouldn't abandon his gear or his weapon until he absolutely had to.

Finally the swimmers heard a return cry of "We're over here!" Moving along the water, they men found the two UDT operators and one of the SEALs from the second SDV's crew! The helicopter hadn't homed in on the signal from the *Grayback*; it was an emergency light from the second SDV crew. The men had launched their SDV from the *Grayback* and immediately got in trouble. The small craft sank to the bottom and couldn't be raised. Now the six swimmers had gathered together, still missing two SEALs.

It was late at night and the men in the water could hear enemy patrol boats starting their engines and moving around closer to shore. They were only a few thousand yards from shore and it was time to swim out to sea. The SEAL from the second SDV wasn't seen or heard from anywhere about the men. Thinking the man hadn't been able to get out of the sunken SDV, the men knew it was time to try and save those who were still alive.

It was 0100 hours. One of the operators pulled out his radio and tried to call the SAR bird. No response from the helicopter, which was not surprising since it hadn't been expected to be in the air until dawn. Lights were on along the shore and the swimmers continued on their way out to sea.

After an hour of swimming, one of the men bumped into someone in the water. It was the body of Lieutenant Dry. The SEAL had been floating face down for something close to two hours. There was blood on his face, and the man was cold and not breathing.

The men of the Teams do not leave a Teammate behind. As the men continued swimming out to sea, they towed the body along with them. As the sounds of patrol boats became louder, the SEAL felt the weight of his weapon in the water. For the men of the Teams, the water is home, a place to fight from and to hide in. If a patrol boat approached the men in the water, the SEAL would take out as many as he could with his weapon and then swim down and away into the darkness. Better to take his chances at sea than to be the only SEAL ever captured by the Communists.

After the men had been swimming for hours, the dawn came up and with it, the SAR helicopters. Calling in the birds on their radios, the exhausted men saw the helicopters five hundred yards away suddenly turn and go down to the water. The SAR birds had found the missing SEAL. He too had followed the procedure—if you get in trouble, swim out to sea. The men had been swimming side by side for hours with only a few hundred yards of ocean between them.

The injured Frogman was taken out of the water along with the limp form of Lieutenant Dry. The rest of the men were finally taken from the water and the helicopters made their way back to the Long Beach. The badly injured man and Lieutenant Dry's body were flown out to the carrier *Kitty Hawk*, where they could be better taken care of. The six SEALs and UDT operators remained aboard the *Long Beach* for five days while they were questioned about what happened.

The second SDV had been launched early to give the men additional time to get to the island. Miscommunication between the launch crew and the men piloting the SDV had caused the small craft to be overweighted. As the SDV left the deck of the *Grayback*, it sank almost immediately to the sea floor. Powering the boat to its maximum did no good. The SDV was on the bottom near the *Grayback*. For twenty minutes, the men of the SDV tried to get the ballast tanks blown and the boat lightened enough to continue with their mission. Some mechanical malfunction kept the SDV on the bottom. One of the men from the rear compartment got out of the SDV and moved forward to try and help. The situation was serious as the *Grayback* could move in the current and crush the fiberglass sub. The big submarine was bottomed but only slightly negatively buoyant to keep the bottom of the hull from taking damage from the sea floor. The men decided to abandon the SDV and make for the surface. It was at this point that they became separated from the SEAL who had remained in the rear compartment. As the men surfaced, the rough water drove them further apart.

Later examination showed that Lieutenant Melvin Spense Dry had crushed his throat against some flotsam in the water, breaking his neck and killing him instantly. The other man had suffered a broken rib. The SAR pilot who had dropped the men into the water had been low on fuel and immediately left the area to return to the *Long Beach*. The situation had deteriorated, but the command structure still held out hopes to rescue the POWs.

Four days later, the *Grayback* had raised her snorkle and was recharging her batteries. No further SDVs had been launched. The U.S.S. *Harold E. Holt* detected the *Grayback* from the noise her diesel engines made as the sub charged her batteries. That was the noisiest time for a diesel/electric boat.

Being new on station off North Vietnam, and knowing of no U.S. subs in the area, the *Holt* considered the contact hostile. The North Vietnamese Navy could have gotten diesel/electric subs from the Chinese or Soviets. Directing her five-inch gun at the target, the *Holt* opened fire on the *Grayback*. Orders from the *Long Beach* to cease fire immediately prevented any damage to the *Grayback*.

On the evening of June 11, the *Grayback* communicated with the *Long Beach* that they wanted their men returned. As had happened so much on the operation, things went wrong. As the *Long Beach* waited for a rubber boat to come in from the *Grayback* to pick up her men, the time for the rendezvous passed. At 2300 hours, the small boat was supposed to arrive. By 0330 hours, a rubber boat with a nonworking outboard motor, paddled by an unhappy crew, pulled up to the *Long Beach*. Instead of waiting longer on board the cruiser, the SEALs and UDT operators had climbed aboard their rubber boat and pushed off.

Within a mile of the big ship, the *Grayback* waited with her decks awash. As the rubber boat approached, one of the bow hangar doors slowly opened and the steel whale swallowed her missing children.

By June 15, the surveillance effort was called off. No POWs had been seen or heard from. Almost a year later, the first group of U.S. prisoners of war were released by North Vietnam as part of the U.S. peace settlement. As additional prisoners returned home, the story came out about the planned escape. Soon after the sonic boom signal, the POWs who had planned to escape expected to get permission to go.

Permission was denied. The cost to the rest of the prisoners would have been too high. Only three days after they had heard the second set of sonic booms, the POWs knew they would not be able to go.

Lieutenant Melvin Spence Dry was laid to rest with full military honors in Arlington Cemetery. He was the last SEAL to be killed in Vietnam. Within a year of his death, all SEALs had left Vietnam. Due to the very secret nature of Operation THUNDERHEAD, the original reason for Dry's death, killed in action (KIA) was crossed out. In its place was written "Death due to ops accident." The official explanation stated:

"The deceased officer, LT Melvin S. Dry, was killed in the Western Pacific on 6 June 1972 while his platoon was participating in a highly classified combat operation with units of the U.S. SEVENTH Fleet in the Gulf of Tonkin."

Sierra:
The Last Detachment

The Seals had begun their operations in Vietnam first as trainers and advisors to the South Vietnamese Navy in 1962. The Teams ended their time in Vietnam conducting much the same mission.

The new U.S. president, Richard Nixon, instituted a policy in Vietnam called Vietnamization, the turning over of the conduct of the war to the South Vietnamese. The policy was actually initiated in the late 1960s and increased considerably by the early 1970s. The SEALs now had a new detachment in country to help support the Vietnamization policy. Detachment Sierra was located at the Cam Rahn Bay naval base by early 1970 and was to supply U.S. Navy SEAL advisors to the South Vietnamese LDNN (Lien Doc Nguoi Nhai—"soldiers who fight under the sea"), the Vietnamese SEALs.

Det Sierra was under the direction of the U.S. Naval Special Warfare Group Vietnam (NAVSPECWARGRUVN) based in Saigon who assigned personnel and was part of SpecWar Task Force 214. The intent was to raise the training and manning levels of the LDNNs, increasing the number of VN students who attended LDNN school at Cam Rahn Bay. Each fielded LDNN platoon would be assigned one or two

U.S. Navy SEAL advisors to help in planning and to direct U.S. support elements while on operations.

The LDNN platoons were laid out in the same organization as the U.S. SEAL platoons at the time, two officers and twelve enlisted men per platoon, further divided into two squads. Some later LDNN platoons had fourteen enlisted men. By this point in the Vietnam War only five LDNN classes had graduated training and the available number of qualified men was limited. Deployments for the existing LDNN platoons and their SEAL advisors were planned for mid-July 1970. One LDNN platoon each would be stationed at Dong Tam, Sa Dec, Coastal Group 36, and Danang. A single LDNN platoon would be divided into two squads and one squad each sent to Ca Mau and Seafloat.

Each deployed LDNN unit was assigned a SEAL advisor taken from the seven enlisted men in Det Sierra. Of the four deployed full LDNN platoons, two were working directly with the SEAL platoons at My Tho and Dong Tam. The other two LDNN platoons operated independently except for the SEAL advisors.

LDNN operations were light during the latter half of 1970, but the LDNNs did conduct some operations with their SEAL advisors or SEAL platoons that showed they were capable of operating. Det Sierra varied in size during 1970 but averaged one officer and seven enlisted men with six of the enlisted operating in the filed with their LDNN units. The last year of full SEAL operations in Vietnam was 1970. The increased emphasis on Vietnamization caused major cutbacks in personnel and operations for all of the U.S. services. The rules of engagement with enemy forces had changed and the SEALs were not to actively participate in combat operations.

The remaining SEAL platoons in Vietnam did not follow the new rules to the letter, but in 1971, support was becoming harder to line up for operations. By February 1971, SEAL Team Two's Eight Platoon ended its tour of duty in Vietnam and returned to the States without a relief platoon taking its place. By the spring of 1971, the only active SEAL

Team Two detachment left in Vietnam was their four-man LDNN advisor group. Detachment Sierra was reorganized and by the spring was disestablished. Instead of SEAL advisors to the LDNN being part of Det Sierra, each advisor position was considered a det in itself. Advisors continued to be assigned from the NAVSPECWARGRUVN in Saigon.

Numbers of SEALs and UDTs in Vietnam continued to decline during 1971. Operations were being conducted but they were relatively few in number. By November 1971, only one or two SEAL operations were being conducted every week from the few detachments still operational in country. From a high of over three hundred men from the Teams in country a little over a year before, by 9 December 1971, only fifty-nine SEALs and UDT personnel remained in all of Vietnam.

But the men who remained in Vietnam continued to operate whenever possible. There were few slots available where a SEAL could expect to see any action at all and the competition for these available positions was stiff at times. But the missions the SEALs performed in Vietnam now were solely in advisory positions. And operating in the field was even more dangerous than it had been during the height of SEAL involvement in the war.

U.S. support had been heavily cut back in size and units deployed. What support was available was spread out among more units. Hard combat-experienced SEALs had been concerned when the response time for a medevac had gone from an average eight- to ten-minute wait to over twenty minutes. Now the few SEALs operating with their LDNNs often had no medevac units at all to call on. Gunfire support often wasn't available and the LDNNs and their advisors only had what they carried on their backs to fight with. Missions had changed and the LDNNs were primarily conducting reconnaissance ops behind enemy lines. VC and NVA base camps were charted out and targets identified for attack by naval gunfire or B-52 bomber strikes.

By 1973, the last operational SEAL and UDT men had

left Vietnam. But their time there had been well spent. Even during the last months of operations in 1972, SEAL operators demonstrated why the Teams had earned a reputation that was second to no other military unit in the world.

Mission Fifteen, 31 October 1972: "The Last Medal"

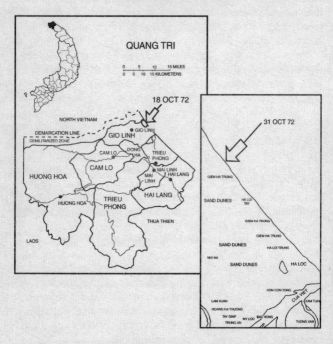

The Easter Invasion of 1972 changed the political landscape of South Vietnam considerably. On 30 March 1972, four divisions of North Vietnamese Army troops totaling some 40,000 men, including heavy armor support, poured across the demilitarized zone and into South Vietnam. ARVN units retreated in the face of the heaviest NVA action of the war. Firebases fell and the general idea of Vietnamization looked to be a complete failure. Within five days of the invasion beginning, the northern half of Quang Tri Province was securely in NVA hands.

On 5 April, the second stage of the invasion began with some 15,000 NVA troops, supported by artillery and armor, entered South Vietnam. The troops came across the Cambodian border over 600 kilometers to the south of the demilitarized zone between North and South Vietnam, to the west and south of Saigon.

President Nixon was not going to let the North Vietnamese action go unanswered. Though U.S. troops had been pulling out in large numbers, the president immediately authorized an increase in the amount of air support in Southeast Asia. When the weather cleared on 6 April, one of the largest bombing campaigns of the war was initiated against NVA positions along the border with Cambodia and especially the northern demilitarized zone. A third thrust was made into South Vietnam by NVA forces on 23 April from bases in northern Cambodia and southern Laos. The last action was targeted to the north of Saigon, in the central highlands of South Vietnam and was intended to cut the country in half.

By 1 May 1972, Quang Tri City, the provincial capital, had fallen to the NVA. But the flow of the invasion had slowed. By the second week of May, U.S. Cobra helicopter gunships, armed with TOW antitank missiles, attacked the NVA armor. An ARVN division in the central highlands resisted an NVA attack from two divisions due to the new U.S. support. Haiphong Harbor in North Vietnam was mined on 8 May 1972 on a U.S. presidential order.

For six months the fighting begun by the Easter Offensive continued in South Vietnam. North Vietnam committed fourteen divisions and twenty-six independent regiments to the fighting. But the tide had turned against the NVA. On 19 September, ARVN Marines raised the South Vietnamese flag once more over Quang Tri City, having taken it from the NVA. The northern part of Quang Tri Province remained in NVA hands, but massive U.S. bombing had severely limited the ability of the North Vietnamese Government to supply the army they had sent into the south. South Vietnamese troops had recaptured most of the land captured by the NVA by the fall of 1972, including the cities and major towns that had been overrun.

The LDNN and their SEAL advisors continued to operate throughout the Easter Offensive and through 1972. The objective of many of the LDNN operations, especially those in the northern sections of South Vietnam, was to recon and confirm enemy locations.

A number of SEALs from both SEAL Teams One and Two were operating as LDNN advisors in the same area, both officers and enlisted men. The SEALs would switch off with each other on operations, giving everyone a chance to get some operational time in. On operations in the field, the LDNNs liked to have two American advisors, an officer and an enlisted man, with them. It was a simple matter of support for the LDNNs. If the situation got hot on an op and something happened to the advisor, the U.S. air or gunfire support wouldn't respond as quickly to a VN voice on the radio as another American advisor. The VC and NVA had been known to use the same radio frequencies more than once to confuse an operation and mislead support.

By October 1972, there had been a number of LDNN scouting missions conducted along the shore of Quang Tri Province to determine the numbers of NVA and VC in the area. Tanks had been discovered dug into beach emplacements on one op. After emplacing a time-delay marking device near the dug-in armor, the SEALs and LDNN called in an air strike to destroy the otherwise undetected heavy vehicles.

One operation in mid-October involved a deception of enemy forces in Quang Tri Province. The LDNNs and their SEAL advisors would conduct a hydrographic recon of the offshore waters, just as would be done prior to an amphibious landing. The operation was a dangerous balancing act for the SEALs and LDNNs; they allowed themselves to be seen, but maintained their distance to avoid enemy fire. As in World War II during the Pacific Island Hopping campaign, the enemy did not want to expose their heavy weapons emplacements to return fire in the chance of getting some Frogmen in the water. The deception worked, and a number of NVA assets were turned to the beaches for an invasion that never came while ARVN ground forces moved on the attack further inland.

In late October, a SEAL/LDNN mission came up again in the Quang Tri Province area. The mission was to gather intelligence on the Cua Viet Base on the Cua Viet River. The base had been captured by the NVA early during the Easter Offensive and higher command needed to know the extent of NVA forces at the base. One of the questions that needed to be answered was if the NVA had taken any prisoners of the RVN personnel at the base or if the men defending the base had been simply killed or scattered throughout the area. To answer this question, a prisoner would have to be snatched from the area of the Cua Viet River.

Normal rotation had the same officer who had been on the earlier deception operation, Lieutenant (jg) Ryan McCombie of SEAL Team Two, up for the Cua Viet recon op. Lieutenant Tom Norris was scheduled to return to the States within a relatively short time and knew he would not be seeing any action for some time to come after he finally left Vietnam. Norris was the senior officer of the SEAL detachment at the Cat Lai LDNN base and simply pulled rank a bit and took command of the upcoming operation.

As his SEAL assistant for the operation, Lieutenant Norris chose Mike Thorton, a SEAL Team One Engineman Second Class with extensive combat experience in Southeast Asia. Norris was trying to break in a new LDNN officer, to build up his confidence and raise his level of enthusiasm for their job. The LDNN officer would be one of the three LDNNs taken on the mission. Norris left the choice of the other two enlisted LDNNs for the op up to Thorton. Thornton's choice was two experienced LDNNs he had operated with on a previous tour. The five-man SEAL/LDNN unit would conduct their operation late during the night of October 31, Halloween.

The five-man unit moved out aboard a Vietnamese Navy junk, the same kind of craft that had cruised the waters of the South China Sea for generations. In addition the Vietnamese Navy crew on board the junk was another SEAL enlisted advisor, William L. "Woody" Woodruff. Woodruff was going to operate the radio on board the junk, maintaining communications between the detachment and the boat. The junk's Vietnamese captain assured the SEALs that he could insert them at the desired location on the beach, about eight kilometers south of the mouth of the Cua Viet River.

Arriving near their insertion point, the SEALs and LDNN transferred from the junk to a rubber, boat for the insertion itself. At 0400 hours, the team landed on the shore, and two Vietnamese sailors paddled the rubber boat back to the junk. There was no sign that the SEALs and the LDNNs had been detected. After a short wait to confirm they had not been spotted, the patrol moved inland, into an area of sand dunes.

Lieutenant Norris was on point for the patrol. Norris was relatively slight of stature and could be mistaken for a Vietnamese in the dark. To increase his chances for deceiving the enemy, Norris was carrying an AK-47. With the AK's distinctive outline Norris might be mistaken for an NVA even close up. At least the deception might give Norris that short edge in time and surprise that could mean everything during a combat op. And if he did have to fire, the sound of the AK-47 would blend in with the enemy's weapons, cutting back on their ability to locate the SEALs and LDNNs.

Mike Thornton's was a different situation. He was a very large man, even for a SEAL. Tall with a powerful build, Thornton could not be mistaken for a normal Vietnamese even on the darkest night. Also armed with an AK-47, instead of the M60 machine gun that he could handle so well, Thornton pulled rear security for the patrol. Also carrying an AN/PVS-2 Starlight scope, Thornton was able to carefully observe the surrounding area even in the dark and make sure the small band of SEALs and LDNNs hadn't been detected.

As the unit continued patrolling to the north, Norris began

looking for the Cua Viet River. It wasn't long before the SEAL lieutenant realized that the unit had been inserted into the wrong area. They weren't south of the Cua Viet River, they were north of it, moving into the demilitarized zone and North Vietnam itself. During a security halt, Thornton moved up to where Norris was leading the patrol and told him that he couldn't spot the river though the Starlight scope either.

As it turned out, the junk captain had inserted the SEALs and LDNNs about eight kilometers north of the Cua Viet River rather than south of it. The new LDNN officer was showing some initiative and wanted to continue the operation. Norris thought it would be a good training op for him to continue, and besides, the unit could always come back on another night and grab a prisoner. Selecting to continue the operation, Norris again moved out on point. His decision may have been a different one if Lieutenant Ryan McCombie had been along on the op as was originally planned. McCombie would have been able to recognize the area as being the same one he had brought the LDNN crew in for their deception operation only a week or so earlier.

The patrol had passed numerous enemy installations. Bunkers, enemy encampments, even dug-in armor had been spotted during the patrol. Whatever the others might have missed in the dark was noted by Thornton with his Starlight scope. Dawn was quickly approaching and the unit had been pressing its luck. Norris decided to turn back, return to their insertion point, and call for pickup. Chances were they had already crossed over into North Vietnam and they did not want to become the only SEALs ever captured during the Vietnam War.

The lack of recognizable landmarks among the sand dunes made it very hard for Lieutenant Norris to pinpoint the unit's location on the map. Without knowing their location, the SEALs would have a hard time calling in the gunfire support available to them from offshore Navy ships. The unit had continued moving back among the dunes toward their insertion point. Nearing the end of the sand dunes, Norris could now better locate their position on the map. As the SEALs and LDNNs came close to the open beach, the luck that had been with them on the operation finally ran out.

The NVA ran small two-man security patrols along the beaches in their secured areas. North Vietnamese supply craft off shore would sometimes toss packages of supplies into the water to drift in to shore, rather than risk a landing. The U.S. air and other forces had been cutting deep into the supply lines from North Vietnam to their units in the south. The two-man security patrols could find the packages of much-needed supplies as they also kept an eye out along the beaches for signs of landings. The SEALs and LDNNs were exactly the kind of intrusion the security patrols were intended to spot.

Freezing in place among the sand dunes, the SEALs held their breaths and waited for the security patrol to pass. Perhaps the LDNN office had been thinking about the objective of the mission being to capture an enemy for information. Or maybe he thought he had been spotted and was trying to bluff his way out of the situation. For whatever reason, the new LDNN officer stood up from where he was hidden in the sand dunes and called out to one of the NVA soldiers.

No matter what, the SEALs and the LDNNs would be discovered now. Surprisingly fast for such a large man, Thornton quickly moved around the sand dune he was hiding behind and silently struck down one of the NVA security men with the butt of his rifle. The other NVA soldier opened fire on Thornton, but then suddenly threw his weapon down and ran away. Quickly taking off after the fleeing enemy soldier, Thornton was the first to see the NVA squad coming in over the sand dunes.

Returning to the others, the SEALs and the LDNNs made quick work of the NVA squad, killing or wounding all of them. Looking into the distance, Norris spotted a large number of NVA troops, forty to sixty of them, coming in to back up the eliminated NVA squad. Getting on the radio, Norris started calling in gunfire support from the offshore Navy ships.

It seemed that every time Norris called out for gunfire support, a different Navy ship answered him. As five-inch shells from the offshore destroyers rained on the beach, the SEALs and LDNNs staged a heavy firefight with the NVA troops over a period of some forty minutes. The NVA tried to close with the encircle the SEALs and LDNNs. Experience in fighting the Americans over the years had taught the NVA that the safest place to be when the Americans were calling in fire support was as close to them as you could get. The Americans, the NVA knew, never called in fire too close to their own positions.

The South Vietnamese junk that had brought the SEALs and LDNNs in on their mission was close to the area. Woodruff could hear the radio calls going back and forth between Norris and the ships offshore. The junk wanted to come in and support the SEALs with the mortars and weapons they had on board, but the Navy ships told them to stay out of the area for the time being and give the heavier guns a clear field of fire. All the SEAL aboard the junk could do was sit and listen to his Teammates on shore in the firefight of their lives.

The NVA troops had closed to within twenty-five meters of the SEALs' and LDNNs' position. A fragmentation grenade came sailing over a sand dune to land near Mike Thornton. Thornton immediately snatched up the grenade and threw it back. The same grenade again came sailing in over a dune and once more Thornton threw it back even harder the second time. On its third trip over the sand dunes, the grenade finally exploded behind Thornton, peppering his back and legs with hot bits of fragmentation. One of the LDNNs was also wounded in the hip during the exchange. With a sudden curse, Thornton absorbed the fragmentation, then immediately flopped down on his back behind the sand dune where the grenade had come from.

It wasn't long before Thornton saw what he expected. The NVA grenadier came running over the dune to follow up on his grenade and finish off the wounded SEAL. What the NVA found was a slightly wounded SEAL with a very functional weapon in his hands. That was the last thing that particular NVA soldier ever found.

Now Norris was receiving gunfire support from the *Newport News* off shore. The *Newport News* was a Salem-class heavy cruiser mounting eight- and five-inch guns. As the heavy rounds landed around the SEALs' position, even the large Mike Thornton was tossed into the air from the blast of the exploding shells.

The situation had gotten too close, the SEALs and the LDNNs were running very low on ammunition, and it was time for some extreme measures to get the men off the beach. Calling out to the *Newport News*, Norris instructed the ship to hold its fire for five minutes, and then drop in all it had on the SEALs' own position. Either the SEALs and LDNNs would be out of the area when the shells hit, or they wouldn't care anymore.

Norris ordered all of his men back to the last sand dune that offered any kind of cover before the open beach. The SEALs and the LDNNs did a leapfrog maneuver, part of the unit moving while the other covered for them and vice versa. Within a few minutes, the dunes where the SEALs were taking cover would be the last place on earth they wanted to be when the 260-pound, eight-inch and fifty-five pound, five-inch shells started to land.

The SEALs had been carrying some M72A2 LAW rockets with them on their operations. Instead of being used for their antitank capability, the rockets could be fired directly into enemy positions, making them take cover as if an artillery barrage had begun. Extending the collapsible tube of the last launcher he had with him, Norris raised up to his knees. As Norris took aim with his M72A2 LAW rocket, an enemy round struck him in the left side of his forehead, just above his eye.

The bullet tore into Norris's skull and exited the left side of his head. The terrible wound knocked the SEAL back. Norris felt himself slip into a long dark tunnel of unconsciousness. The LDNN who saw Norris hit continued to pull back to where the rest of the unit was waiting.

When the last LDNN got to Thornton, he told him, "Mr. Norris shot in head. Dead now."

Throughout training in the Teams, from World War Two and up to today, it is drilled into every SEAL and UDT operator that you never leave your buddy behind. In an underwater operation, a swim buddy could be a man's only chance for life in the unforgiving sea. You never, ever, leave your swim buddy. No Teammate, alive or dead, was ever left behind.

Mike Thornton did the only thing that a SEAL could do under the circumstances. With time slipping away before the sand dunes were blown out of existence by the heavy cruiser, Thornton exploded, "Bullshit!" Through 125 meters of enemy fire, Thornton ran to where his Norris lay in the sand. As far as Thornton knew, he was going to recover a body. But that fact didn't matter, or even register.

As two NVA soldiers crept up to where Norris lay, Thornton quickly blew them away with a burst of fire from his AK. Seeing the terrible wound, Thornton was sure that Norris was dead. But then the SEAL officer's eyes flickered open for a moment and he said, "Mike, buddy . . ." before falling back down that long, dark tunnel.

His Teammate was alive! Grabbing up the wounded man, Thornton ran back though the heavy enemy fire, back to where the LDNNs waited. Reaching the men unscathed, the LDNNs turned to Thornton for leadership. When they asked what they should do next, Thornton turned and fired into the radio. Now the radio wouldn't fall into enemy hands, and the incoming fire couldn't be stopped. As the LDNNs stared at the huge SEAL; he told them what they would do next. "We swim."

Two hundred and fifty meters away lay the ocean, across a beach with no cover in sight. In spite of his own wounds and condition, Thornton picked Norris up, tucked him under his arm, and moved for the sea. As the LDNNs put out what fire they could to cover the two SEALs, Thornton reached the water. Turning, Thornton fired his own weapon back at the NVA as his LDNNs now made their dash for safety.

The SEALs, like the UDTs before them, always look to the water as the safest place they can be. If a soldier is discovered, the water can hide him. When he is fired upon, the water can protect him. When giving chase, most enemy troops will stop at the water's edge, the same water the SEALs call home.

Of course, the water can cause trouble as well. Standing in the four-foot surf, firing back at the NVA, Thornton felt his burden struggle weakly under his arm. Pulling Norris up, Thornton took his Teammate, the man he had been trying so hard to save, and raised the wounded SEAL's head above the water before he drowned.

Inflating the lieutenant's UDT life jacket before filling his own, Thornton started swimming out to sea. As he moved forward with a powerful breast stroke, pushing Norris ahead of him, Thornton felt one of his LDNNs pulling at his side. It was the LDNN who had been wounded when Thornton was struck by the grenade fragments. The Vietnamese was struggling in the water and had barely made it through the surf. Holding on to the man until the rest of the LDNNs caught up to them, Thornton again turned and moved out to sea.

The NVA troops rushed up to the water's edge when they saw their quarry getting away. As they fired at the swimming men, the last moments of the five-minute wait ticked away. The *Newport News* opened fire and a large chunk of the beach disappeared forever.

Once a distance from the shore, Thornton performed what inadequate first aid he could do for Norris and his terrible wound. Then the powerful SEAL continued to swim out to sea, pushing his Teammate in front of him. Thornton towed the wounded LDNN along behind him. Norris slipped in and out of consciousness during the swim. At one point, the SEAL officer came around long enough to ask his Teammate, "Did we get everyone out?"

"Yeah," answered Thornton, "We got 'em all."

For hours, the small band of men swam through the water. There was no question of whether they would make it. There wasn't any thought of quitting. There was just the sea and the next stroke of the arms and kick of the feet. Even the tireless strength of Mike Thornton was beginning to flag badly after so much exertion. But there was no thought of surrender. If the ocean wanted them, it would have to wait.

On the junk that had brought the team in, Woody Woodruff had heard the last call Norris had made over the radio. Hearing the fire off in the distance, the men on the junk saw the glow over the horizon and heard the distant explosions of the salvos fired in from the *Newport News*. Not one man in the Vietnamese crew thought any of the SEALs or the LDNNs had survived such a fire storm. The captain of the boat and the crew wanted to give up the search and return to their base. But, like Thornton, Woodruff was a SEAL and a Teammate. He convinced the others in the boat to continue the search. The Vietnamese were not pleased with the SEAL's demands, but neither did they want to refuse him—not that Woodruff would have accepted any other answer.

At 1130 hours, the men in the junk spotted the swimming SEALs and LDNNs. As they pulled alongside the men in the water, Mike Thornton's immense strength and will drained away from him. The herculean effort had spent any reserves the big SEAL had. As the men of the junk tried to carefully pull Tom Norris out of the water, Mike Thornton was too exhausted even to pull himself over the side of the junk. Hanging on to a rope on the side of the boat, Thornton himself had to be pulled aboard.

The junk immediately moved out to sea to rendezvous with the *Newport News*, the nearest ship certain to have a doctor on board. The faith of Woody Woodruff had been proven, and Thornton had carried through the tradition that no one is ever left behind in the Teams.

It was when the doctors aboard the *Newport News* took Norris away that Thornton finally reacted to the situation. The fate of his Teammate, his buddy, was out of his hands and there was nothing the big SEAL could do. Even while he recovered from his own ordeal, Thornton's thoughts were with his Teammate.

When Norris was taken to the medical facility at Hue, the other available SEAL advisors were there. Lieutenant

McCombie was told that Norris had to be kept awake until he could be evacuated to the Philippines. The concern was that if Norris slipped into unconsciousness, he might become comatose. McCombie sat at his Teammate's side all night, talking, telling good jokes, telling bad jokes, making up stories as he went along—anything to get Norris through the night.

On October 15, 1973, the cease-fire between the United States and the North and South Vietnamese had been signed. All SEALs had returned to the States. For the U.S. forces, the war in Vietnam was over. Operation Homecoming brought the POWs released by North Vietnam back to the United States and freedom.

On that day, Michael Thornton was in Washington, D.C. He slipped away to the medical center, where his Teammate Tom Norris was recovering. Kidnapping his Teammate, Thornton returned to the important engagement he had to keep.

In the years since its creation, the Congressional Medal of Honor has stood as the utmost sign of valor for a U.S. soldier. Since the first award during the Civil War, the Medal of Honor had been awarded 3,394 times, eighteen men have received the Medal twice. In this century, most of the men who were awarded the Medal of Honor received it posthumously. Two hundred thirty-eight men received the Medal of Honor during the Vietnam War; 150 of them died performing the acts for which it was awarded. Fourteen of those Medals went to men of the U.S. Navy, three of them to SEALs.

When he received his Medal of Honor for his actions that Halloween night, Mike Thornton had his Teammate Tom Norris standing at his shoulder. Norris had also received the Congressional Medal of Honor for actions that had resulted in the rescue of Iceal Hambleton in April 1972.

But on the October day in Washington, for the first time in the history of the award, a Medal of Honor recipient received the Medal for saving a Medal of Honor recipient.

As far as Michael Thornton is concerned, his Medal is for all men in the Teams, past and present.

Epilogue:
Vietnam—The Cost

Vietnam was over. The SEALs' legend had been built in the swamps, rivers, deltas, and mud of Southeast Asia. Forty-nine men from the Teams gave the ultimate sacrifice.

- Thirty-four SEALs were lost from SEAL Team One.
- Nine SEALs were lost from SEAL Team Two.
- Three UDT Operators were lost from UDT Thirteen.
- One UDT Operator was lost from UDT Twelve.
- Additional losses included one UDT officer assigned to SOG and one man from the naval Special Warfare Group-Pacific, assigned to Detachment Golf.

By only the most conservative numbers, the men of the Teams accounted for fifty of the enemy for each Teammate lost. By a more realistic accounting, there were over 200 enemy losses for each SEAL or UDT operator killed. Over one thousand VC and VCI were captured by the SEALs. Hundreds of weapons were confiscated along with tons of munitions and supplies.

Nuy-nai—the most feared of all predators in the Southeast Asian jungle, the mythical Tiger-man—part human, part tiger, all demon. Slipping through the darkness, he took his prey without warning.

Nuy-nai—a name that could also be applied to the U.S. Navy SEALs.

Appendix A:
SEAL Team Platoons

The basic organizational and operating unit of the SEAL
Team is the platoon. SEAL Team One platoons are identified
alphabetically by the phonetical name of the letter except for
I (India), as it could be mistaken for the number 1. Originally called Assault Units on the East Coast, the term *platoon* was adopted by SEAL Team Two in 1966. The standard
SEAL platoon is made up of two officers, a platoon leader
and assistant platoon leader, and two squads of enlisted men.
In 1966, A SEAL Team Two platoon consisted of two officers and ten enlisted men making up two six-man squads,
identified as A and B, which could be divided down into four
three-man fire teams. SEAL Team Two platoons were identified numerically from the Second through the Tenth.

Soon after the first Direct Action platoons from SEAL
Team Two arrived in Vietnam, the number of enlisted men in
a platoon was increased to twelve. Occasionally a platoon
had an odd number of enlisted men or officers. The additional man would normally be to supply an advisor or officer
for a detachment or other unit that might not be operating
with the parent platoon.

SEAL Team One operating platoons originally consisted
of two officers and ten enlisted men during 1966, their first

year of deployments of direct action platoons to Vietnam. In March 1967, the SEAL Team One platoons in Vietnam were increased to two officers and twelve enlisted men each, a size they retained until the end of the war.

The first SEAL Team One deployments for direct actions in Vietnam were not platoons but a sufficient number of men to make up the detachment. The operating detachment (in this case Det Golf) had squads numbered from 1 to 10 instead of platoons. As the size of the detachment increased, the number of squads grew as well. Starting with Charlie Platoon in October 1966, SEAL Team One changed Det Golf from squads to platoons. The platoons from SEAL Team One were identified alphabetically from Alfa to Echo platoon. By mid-1967, each SEAL Team One platoon had two squads identified as 1 and 2.

During 1967, SEAL Team One consisted of ten operating platoons, designated Alfa to Kilo. An eleventh platoon, Lima, was added to SEAL Team One in March 1967 to meet additional commitments to the Mekong Delta.

Primary operational areas for the two SEAL Team detachments in Vietnam were the Rung Sat Special Zone (RSSZ) and Mekong Delta. In February 1966, SEAL Team One sent a pilot group of three officers and fifteen enlisted men (three squads) to Vietnam to act as an operational detachment. This group was under the operational control of the Commander Naval Forces Vietnam. From 26 March to 7 April 1966, during Operation Jackstay, these SEALs were part of the first amphibious landing in the Rung Sat Special Zone. They became the first SEALs assigned to Detachment Golf, which had the primary responsibility for operations in the RSSZ.

Direct Action platoons from SEAL Team Two started arriving in Vietnam in late January 1967. The first two platoons, Second and Third, were assigned to the new Detachment Alfa, which would initially operate in the Mekong Delta along the Bassac River. After initial operations to gain field experience with SEAL Team One platoons in the RSSZ, Second and Third platoons began operating in the Mekong Delta in February 1967.

SEAL Team Platoon In Country Dates

Det Golf—SEAL Team One

PLATOON/SQDS		TOUR DATES	RELIEVED	LOCATION(S)
Alfa	1/2	Feb 66–		
Charlie	5/6	Oct 66–14 Apr 67		
Delta†	7/8	Jan 67–18 Mar 67		
Echo†	9/10	Jan 67–17 Mar 67		
Hotel†	5/6	12 Feb 67–Apr 67		
Juliett†	9/10	Mar 67–20 Aug 67		
Kilo	1/2	4 Apr 67–Aug 67		
Lima	3/4	7 Apr 67–30 Jun 67		
Echo	1/2	16 Jun 67–9 Dec 67		
Foxtrot	1/2	Aug 67–20 Jan 68		
Alfa	1/2	–21 Feb 68		
Bravo	1/2	9 Dec 67–6 Jun 68	E	Nha Be/Binh Thuy
Delta	1/2	20 Jan 68–6 Jul 68	F	Nha Be/Binh Thuy
Mike	1/2	21 Feb 68–9 Aug 68	A	APL-55
Juliett	1/2	1 May 68–1 Nov 68	B	Nha Be/Vinh Long

†Unconfirmed data and/or dates

PLATOON/SQDS		TOUR DATES	RELIEVED	LOCATION(S)
Hotel	1/2	20 Jul 68–20 Jan 69	D	Nha Be
Charlie	1/2	1 Nov 68–20 May 69	J	My Tho
Delta	1/2	20 Jan 69–20 Jul 69	H	Cam Rahn Bay
Echo	1/2	9 Feb 69–20 Aug 69	H	Nha Be
Golf	1/2	20 May 69–28 Nov 69	C	Ben Luc
Kilo	1/2	20 Jul 69–Dec 69	D	Cam Rahn Bay
Mike	1/2	20 Aug 69–Feb 70	E	Seafloat
Alfa	1/2	6 Oct 69–Mar 70		Sa Dec
Bravo	1/2	28 Nov 69–Apr 70	G	Ben Luc
Charlie	1/2	27 Dec 69–20 Jun 70		Dung Island
Delta	1/2	13 Jan 70–13 Jul 70		Rach Gia
Echo	1/2	28 Feb 70–28 Aug 70		Nam Can
Foxtrot	1/2	28 Mar 70–28 Sep 70		Nam Can
Hotel	1/2	12 Apr 70–12 Oct 70		Sa Dec/My Tho
Golf	1/2	10 May 70–10 Nov 70		Nam Can
Juliett	1/2	20 Jun 70–20 Dec 70	C	Long Phu

Name		Dates	Code	Location
Kilo	1/2	13 Jul 70–9 Jan 71	D	Rach Gia
Zulu	1/2	28 Aug 70–Feb 71	E	Nam Can
Yankee	1/2	28 Sep 70–Mar 71	F	
Xray	1/2	12 Oct 70–Apr 71	H	Kien Hoa
Whiskey	1/2	10 Nov 70–May 71	G	Nam Can
Victor	1/2	20 Dec 70–Jun 71	J/8	Dong Tam
Romeo	1/2	9 Jan 71–9 Jul 71	K	Rach Soi
Papa	1/2	Feb 71–Aug 71	9	Ca Mau
Quebec	1/2	Mar 71–Sep 71		Bac Lieu/Ben Luc
November†	1/2	Apr 71–Oct 71		Dong Tam
Oscar†	1/2	May 71–Nov 71		Nam Can/Ben Luc
Mike	1/2	Jun 71–7 Dec 71	Q	Ben Luc
Alfa	1/2	10 Jan 72–Jul 72		Westpac Plt (Lt Dry)
Delta	1/2	3 Mar 75–11 Oct 75		Westpac Plt (Mayaguez)

Det Alfa—SEAL Team Two

PLANTOON/MEN		TOUR DATES	RELIEVED	LOCATION(S)	OPS*
2nd	2/10	31 Jan 67–30 May 67	—	Binh Thuy/My Tho	30
3rd	3/10	31 Jan 67–26 Jun 67	—	Binh Thuy	42
4th	2/11	30 May 67–24 Oct 67	2nd	My Tho	68
5th	2/12	26 Jun 67–17 Dec 67	3rd	Binh Thuy/Vinh Long	60
6th	2/11	28 Aug 67–12 Feb 68	—	Vinh Long	38
7th	2/11	24 Oct 67–22 Apr 68	4th	My Tho	80
8th	2/12	17 Dec 67–15 Jun 68	5th	Binh Thuy/Chau Doc?	82
9th	3/12	12 Feb 68–25 Aug 68	6th	Vinh Long/Binh Thuy	61
10th	2/11	22 Apr 68–22 Oct 68	7th	My Tho	79
3rd	2/12	15 Jun 68–11 Dec 68	8th	Nha Be	94
4th	2/11	12 Aug 68–12 Feb 69	9th	Vinh Long	76
5th	2/13	12 Oct 68–12 Apr 69	10th	My Tho	122
6th	2/12	12 Dec 68–12 Jun 69	3rd	Nha Be	104
7th	2/11	12 Feb 69–2 Aug 69	4th	Vinh Long	89

8th	2/12	12 Apr 69–12 Oct 69	5th	My Tho	96
9th	2/11	12 Jun 69–12 Dec 69	6th	Nha Be	150
10th	2/12	12 Aug 69–12 Feb 70	7th	Vinh Long?	109
3rd	2/13	12 Oct 69–12 Feb 70	8th	Ca Mau—Song Ong Doc	132
4th	2/13	12 Dec 69–12 Jun 70	9th	Binh Thuy/Nha Be	103
5th	2/12	12 Feb 70–12 Aug 70	10th	Nha Be/Dong Tam	89
6th	2/13	12 Apr 70–12 Oct 70	3rd	Ca Mau	60
7th	2/12	12 Jun 70–12 Dec 70	4th	Nha Be/Frogsville/Quang Tri	38
8th	2/12	12 Aug 70–12 Feb 71	5th	Dong Tam	48
9th		12 Oct 70–12 Apr 71	6th	Ca Mau/Hai Yen	54
10th		12 Dec 70–12 Jun 71	7th	Vi Thanh	?

Estimated minimum number of operations based on available Barndance cards and Spotreps

Appendix B:
Barndance Cards

The SEALs kept a unique set of records for each deployed platoon during the Vietnam War. These were the Barndance cards, a form that was filled out by each SEAL unit after they returned from an operation. The unit could be the entire platoon, a squad, fire team, or even just a pair of SEALs working on a simple op.

The forms changed several times over the years the SEALs were operating in Vietnam. But they all contained the same basic information. The primary idea behind the Barndance cards was to prevent the repetition of mistakes, to maintain the "lessons learned," as the Teams called them.

Identification numbers for the Barndance cards usually consisted of the SEAL platoon's identifier, either a number for SEAL Team Two or a phonetic letter for SEAL Team One. The identifier was followed by the number in sequence of the operation. Sometimes when a single unit went on a split operation, the cards would be identified by the same Barndance number with a final letter, A or B, to identify the squad. Some cards from SEAL Team One were identified simply by a sequential number over a period of a year. For the very earliest operations of SEAL Team Two, the Barndance cards system had not yet been established, and the unit maintained a standard Navy log book.

The mission briefs that appear throughout this book are verbatim transcripts of the Barndance cards created after that particular mission. In other words, they are the actual reports written by the SEALs who performed the actions.

Unfortunately, many of the Barndance cards unique to SEAL operations of the Vietnam era have not survived. The physical cards and later page-sized forms were copied on "flimsies," a thin tan or pink tissue paper, that did not age well. The SEALs, being mission-oriented, considered the old mission records a waste of space after the Vietnam War had ended. With the declassification of the records often came their destruction. Only through the actions of some far-seeing individuals who recognized the historical significance were some of these records saved.

The following are reproductions of some of the surviving mission reports. They appear here exactly as the SEALs and their commanding officers completed them decades ago.

This is the first ever public replication of these original records.

BARNDANCE # 6-54 _____ SEAL TEAM TWO; DET ALFA ___; ___ 6th ___ PLT.

DATE(S) 220855H-221145H ___ OTHER UNITS: SEE REVERSE SIDE ___

MSG REF (S) O 221700Z AUG 70 ___

NAMES OF PERS PARTICIPATING LT. BOINK (21.), NELSON, KRUG, SPRENKLE, EMACHISTN, 2 KCS, 1 INTERPRETER, 27L COMPANY ___

MISSION TASK: LIBERATE 68 PRISONERS OF WAR ___

INTEL/INFO SOURCES: SECTOR S-2, ESCAPEE FROM POW CAMP ___

INSERTION: TIME 220810H METHOD: SLICK COORD WD 446593I

EXTRACTION: TIME 221130H METHOD: SLICK COORD: WD 433713

BRIEF MISSION NARRATIVE: ACTING ON INTEL SUPPLIED BY SECTOR S-2 THE FOLLOWING SEQUENCE WAS FOLLOWED IN TARGETING A FIFTY EIGHT MAN PRISONER CAMP IN YTC WD 440928. 220810H SIX ROYAL AUSTRALIAN B-57 BOMBERS BEGAN PLACING 750 LB BOMBS ALONG CANAL FROM WD 420574 TO WD 445706 TO ESTABLISH BLOCKING FORCE BY FIRE TO S. OF CAMP. AT 220855H SEALS ___ AND 27L RF CO. INSERTED ALONG NARROW BEACHLINE AND ___

RESULTS OF ENEMY ENCOUNTERED: 3 VC KIA (BC), OTHER CASUALTIES IN GUNSHIPS UNKNOWN, ONE CHICOM CARBINE CAPTURED, 28 POWS LIBERATED. ___

FRIENDLY CASUALTIES: NEG ___

REMARKS (SIGNIFICANT EVENTS, OPNVAL RESULTS, ETC) PRELIMINARY HEADCOUNT INDICATES AMONG POWS WAS RF VC COMPANY CDR 271C. VC COMPANY, HIS PLATOON LEADER, SQUAD LEADER. CADRES TRYING TO CATCH HOT AND RAIN OTHERWISE IM PRISONERS FOR SAME REASON. OTHER POWS WERE MEMBERS OF OUTPOST WHICH WAS OVERRUN BY VC TWO YEARS AGO. ___

RECOMMENDATIONS/LESSONS LEARNED: THE COOPERATION AND PROFESSIONALISM SHOWN BY THE VARIOUS SERVICES ARE LIKE THINGS ONE READS IN STORY BOOKS. THE SIXTH PLATOON SENDS THANKS AND 28 LIBERATED SEND A GREAT BIG REAL WELL.

BD COPY DIST: COMNAVFORV, CTF 116.6, OIC DET ALFA, SEAL 2, SEAL 1

SIGNATURE OF PERSON MAKING OUT REPORT: David D. Hamman HMC (for) DENNIS W. BOINK, LT. USNR

BARNDANCE # 6-54

OTHER UNITS: 974 RF CO., -OA NAU, 175th AVIATION CO. MINI-PAC WITH
HEAVY FIRE TEAM (MAJ. ADAMS), CLAND C SHIP (CAPT HERNANDEZ AND HILO-CA NAU),
I US DESTROYER (USS SUTHERLAND), NAVAL GUNFIRE SPOTTER (LNJG OSWALD),
SHOTGUN 42 (WO FINCH), SEAWOLF 69/68 (LTJG BLAIR), 6 AUSTRALIAN B-57 BOMBERS.

(CON'T NARRATIVE)
SPOTTED ARMED MALE ENTERING BUNKER 50m W. OUR POSIT. SURROUNDED BUNKER
AND TOOK U/F AFTER VC ATTEMPTED TO SHOOT SEAL FROM ENTRANCE. SEARCHED
AREA AND DISCOVERED THREE VC AND ONE CHICOM RIFLE. DIRECTED HEAVY ROCKET
AND MINI-GUN FIRE TO N. AND W. OF POW CAMP TO ESTABLISH FURTHER BLOCKING
FORCES. BEING LED BY GUIDE WHO ESCAPED FROM CAMP THREE DAYS PRIOR,
PATROLLED 500m W. AND ENTERED POW CAMP AT 2210ISH. SPOTTED MANY FRESH
FOOTPRINTS LEADING S. AND DIRECTED US ARMY GUNSHIP AND SEAWOLVES FIRE
500m S. OF CAMP HOPING TO CUT OFF ROUTE OF ESCAPE. AT SAME TIME USS
SUTHERLAND BEGAN PLACING 5 INCH ROUNDS TO S. OF CAMP. FOLLOWED TRACKS S.
AND IN VIC WQ 45914 FROM FINDING MISC PERSONAL GEAR AND CALLED FOR
INTENSIFIED ROCKET RUNS BY GUNSHIPS BELIEVING GUARDS WOULD ABANDON
PRISONERS IF ENOUGH PRESSURE WAS APPLIED. CONTINUED S. AND AT 221245 H
LINKED UP WITH 28 POWS WHO'S GUARDS HAD JUST FLED THE AREA. C & C SHIP
DIRECTED PATROL TO AREA 200m W. FOR POSSIBLE PICKUP POINT AND ARRIVED
221311SH. CLEARED THREES IN AREA AND WERE EXTRACTED BY SINGLE SLICKS
AND RETURNED CA NAU 221445H.

6-27   SEAL TEAM   2   PLT   A

14 JAN 69   OTHER UNIT: USA SLICK AND USA LFT-117
                          5 PRU

WATSON, ROWELL AND 5 PRUS

SNATCH

PRUS

INSERTION   TIME   1245   METHOD   SLICK   XS 865645
EXTRACTION   TIME   1259   METHOD   SLICK   XS 865645

TERRAIN: RICE PADDIES

WEATHER: CLEAR   TIDE:

MISSION NARRATIVE: INSERTED BY SLICK TO ABDUCT 5 VC. ABDUCTED ONE VC
PLATOON LCDR WITH AK 50 AND 45 CAL PISTOL. 2 PA RA GRENADES AND
WEB GEAR WAS TAKEN UNDER FIRE FROM TREE LINE. ONE PRU WIA . CALL-
ED IN SLICK SUPPRESSED FIRE AND EXTRACTED.

ENEMY LOSS ACCOUNTED: 2 VC KIA. ONE VC CAPTURED

FRIENDLY CASUALTIES: ONE PRU WIA

EQUIPMENT CAPTURED (UNITS, GEAR, WEAPONS, ETC.):
CAPTURED ONE AK 50 AND ONE 45 CAL POSTOL. TWO PARA GRENADES
WEB GEAR AND DOCUMENTS

REMARKS/RECOMMENDATIONS:

6-27

BARNDANCE # 6-9   SEAL TEAM TWO   : DET ALFA , 6th PLT

DATE(S): 062215H-070530H   OTHER UNITS: 1ST 2 DET F (ENS. McCHESNEY)

MSG REF(S): 070630Z MAY 70

NAMES OF PERS: CPO WATSON (PL), LEONARD, HYDE, BARRY, TESCI

MISSION TASK: WATERBORN GUARD POST

INTEL/INFO SOURCE(S): MILO, S/D

INSERTION: TIME 062215H METHOD: MSSC/WHALER ANS COORD: VG 9196

EXTRACTION: TIME 070530H METHOD: MSSC/WHALER ANS COORD: VG 9196

BRIEF MISSION NARRATIVE: SET GUARD POST AT FISH STAKES IN CENTER OF LAKE.
SIGHTED SAMPAN APPROX. 600m., UNABLE TO TAKE UNDER FIRE DUE TO LACK OF
WATER. EXTRACTED BY WHALER TO MSSC 070530H.

FRIENDLY PERS/MATERIAL CASUALTIES: NONE

ENEMY PERS/MATERIAL CASUALTIES: NONE

REMARKS (SIGNIFICANT EVENTS, OPEVAL RESULTS, ETC.): NONE

RECOMMENDATIONS/LESSONS LEARNED: WHALER WILL NOT OPERATE IN VC LAKE AREA FOR
TLONDUE TO LACK OF WATER.

2D COPY DIST: COMNAVFORV-CTF 116.6, OINC SEAL DET ALFA, SEAL TM 2, SEAL TM I

(FORM REV. 4/69)   BARNDANCE # 6-9

X 001

17 MAY 67 - 0001 - PREPARE TO GET UNDERWAY ON
(WED)   LCM-6. STARTER ON PORT ENG. NOT
               WORKING. 0230K CANCELLED OPS
               FOR 24HRS. 0300K SENT OUT REQ.
               FOR 24HRS. EXTENSION AND NOTIFIED
               SEAWOLF OF CHANGE. IN HOPES THEY'LL
               COMPLETE REPAIRS IN TIME TO MEET
               CHARLIE #3. STARTER PULLED & REPAIRED.
               LCM-6, RANDY FOR OPS. TONIGHT. SLEEP +
               CONVOY TO SAIGON - NO SEALS ON IT.

18 MAY 67 - QUARTERS, 0001K. UNDERWAY FOR OP. AREA.
(THURS)   INSERT ON ILLO ILLO 0500K. STBD. RUN
             AGROUND + FRAZZLED. N.C. END OF ISLAND 0600K.
             PATROLLED FROM 0600 - 1500. WIDTH + LENGTH OF
             ISLAND. FOUND WELL TRAVELLED FOOT PATHS ON
             SOUTH WESTERN TIP OF ISLAND. FOUND AID
             STATION AT C.P.X. DESTROYED STATION, CAPTURED
             MEDICAL SUPPLIES + DOCUMENTS. WENT SW ON C. PHONE
             FOUND 6X OF 34HTS. 2BUNKERS 2 SAMPANS 5 VC
             BLD, IVR AND 50TH RICE DESTROYED, BOOBY TRAPS
             DESTROYED. CAPTURED 4 CHICOM RIFLES + DOCUMENTS.
             EXTRACTED BY STABS 1730K. RETURN RDV TWO
             2130K. B.A., BOUNDARY FOX. CLEANED, INVENTORIED
             + STOWED EQUIP. IN QUONSET HUT. MAIL FROM
             SKIPPER. HOA BINH SUB SECTOR COMPROMISED. SEAL OPS
             AGAIN IN CLEAR.

motors 2 banana caches destroyed. Seawolf 1 VC KIA while
covering our extraction. Received S/A fire upon extraction.
ROLDER received frag corner of left eye - released to duty.
LCM-6 returned from Can Tho 0600H. Spent day at CAS translating
documents from 14 May raid.

16 May 1967 - Brief for tomorrow ops. UNODIR sent. Work on turnover reports.
(Tue)

17 May 1967 - Prepared get underway 0001H for OPAREA. LCM-6 port starter out
(Wed)   of commission. Ops delayed 24 hrs. Need another boat as back
             up.

18 May 1967 - Underway 0001H for OPARREA. Insert 0600H. Extract 1730H.
(Thurs)   Combat patrol whole island, all mangrove around VC Aid Station,
             destroyed same, confiscated medical supplies and documents.
             Found 3 huts, 2 bunkers, 6 VC in command. Detonated booby
             trap area. 5 VC KIA, 1 WIA, documents, 4 CHICOM rifles,
             booby traps captured. 2 sampans, 2 bunkers destroyed. 2B
             plus Mr. Kochey. 2A at My Tho cleaning and inventorying gear.
             Hoa Binh Sub Sector compromised, Seal ops again in clear.

19 May 1967 - Plan Ops. Mr. Kochey to Hoa Binh to check on next Op and
(Fri)   continued compromises. Porter RM2 delivered 3 VN UDT to My Tho.
             Discussed VN awards for platoon with RAG Cmdr. Ops altered
             due to DIV/SECTOR Ops.

20 May 1967 - Underway (2B) 0600H to blow bunkers in area while PBR's have
(Sat)   continued harassment. Destroyed 8 bunkers, 7 sampans, 14
             covered foxholes, 6 huts. Used MK137 Kits. Took 3 VN UDT
             on ops., all aggressive. One to be sent to Vinh Long, one
             to Can Tho and one to remain at My Tho. Transfer to be effected
             this weekend. Return My Tho 1130H. Clean gear and pack for
             transfer to Can Tho. Gallagher to take E-8 exam at Saigon.
             Work on turnover data and award recommendations. End of
             ops. Second Platoon.

                                        Very respectfully,

                                        RICHARD MARCINKO
                                        RM3, USN

        *And a most interesting & successful
         finish!*

```
RBNWZCYLA698
OTTCZYUW RUHGCHU#126 8763804-CCCC--RUCILAA.
ZNY CCCCC
OZ RUHFAA 3828 8760450
ZNY CCCCC
RUGFAA 2012 VLAG
RBMSTN T NAM THREE DET SIX
P O 960736 MAY 60
FM CTU ONE ONE SIX PT THREE PT ZERO
TO ZENCTF ONE ONE SIX
INFO ZENCOMNAVFORV
RUHFAA/CTF ONE ONE SEVEN
ZEN/VCTG ONE ONE SIX PT THREE
ZEN/VCTR ONE ONE SIX PT SIX
ZEN/USA 1V CORPS
ZEN/USA SEVENTH ARVN DIV
ZEN/USA DING TONG
ZEN/CATD MY TMO
ZEN/VCTU ONE ONE SIX PT ONE PT ZERO
ZEN/VCTU ONE ONE SIX PT TWO PT ZERO
ZEN/VCTU ONE ONE SIX PT FOUR PT ZERO
ZEN/VCTU ONE ONE SIX PT SIX PT ONE
RUHGCHU/CTU ONE ONE SIX PT THREE PT NINE
ZEN/VCTU ONE ONE SIX PT FOUR PT ZERO PT ONE
RUMMEA/NAVFAC
RUCILAA/HCMSOLANT ----- 2GV- UDT-22 ---PHOTO--
BT
                              LAA
                              MC
```

INFO: UDT-21
GNOSUA
BJR-2
BSC-2
SEAL-1

action (A)
Info (I)

CO	OR+	Action	
XO			
ADMIN			
OPS			
AIR			
SUR			
COMM			
INTEL			
TNS			
DET			

```
CONFIDENTIAL
GAME WARDEN SPOTREP 3/10/1 916.3.2/110
1. DEN, DET ALFA SEVENTH PLATOON MST LCM, SVNB, SEABDLE 66/19
LCDR MYERS, LCDR CULER, CWO LAR 26/26, 2 LINKS, VN INTERPRETOR,
2 US 9TH DIV LARP, LT PETERSON.
2. 160290H MIN PLATOON INSERTED AT XS 692380 BY SLAG, ESTABLISHED
NORTH TO XS 703417, 590 TO CONDUCTED AREA RECON IN NO DET
TTD ME., 160230H 7A EXTRACED END VC, AT XS 705423, PATRO MANY TIMES
TO EAST EVADED NORTH BEING STRIKE CLOSE ACROSS 56 ..., SET PERIMITER
AT XS 706406, CALLED SOP SEABDLE COVER AND SLICK EXTRACTION.
160360H ENEMEN APPROX CLOSE APPROACHING FROM EAST, 160330H 7A EXTRACT-
ED BY SLICK FOLLOWING SEABDLE STRIKE, 160230H 7B ENCOUNTERED
APPROX 20 VC IN BARRACKS TYPE STRUCTURES AT XS 702422, EVADED
SOUTH, SET PERIMETER AT 7S 703416, CALLED FOR SEABDLE STRIKE
AND SLICK EXTRACTION, 160385H 7B EXTRACTED BY SLICK FOLLOWING
SEABDLE STRIKE.
3. 160290H-760330H
4. SAME AS PARA 2
5. A USN WIA BY ENEMIE FRAGMENEN GRND 703 VN INTERPRETOR WIA
ENEMIE FRAGMENT, 07 VC KIA (CONF) 06 VC KIA (PROB), ALL VC
ARMED UNABLE CARRY OUT VC WPNS DUE WIA, AREA HEAVILY BUNKERED
WITH FIELDS OF FIRE ON ALL AVENUES OF APPROACH, MANY BARRACKS
TYPE STRUCTURES IN AREA, BARRAMOX T-66 SEABDLE EXPENDED 18,761
RDS 7.62, MST LCM EXPENDED 15 RDS 81MM MORTAR, SEABDLE SPOTTING.
6. CLOSED,
GP-4
BT
```

Handwritten annotations: Silent Kill · YERXA'S OP · 16 KIA · 10 WIA · 7-3 63

7A Flynn Hewitt · 7A Gallagher Yerxa (corr?) · Baynham V · Tuw · Ashbaugh · Matthews